# HolyAnger
## Jacob, Job, Jesus

# HolyAnger
## Jacob, Job, Jesus

**Lytta Basset**

NOVALIS

© 2007 Novalis, Saint Paul University, Ottawa, Canada

Cover design and layout: Pascale Turmel
Cover image: Lynne McIlvride Evans (www.mcilvride-evans.com)
Translators: Bruce Henry, Monica Sandor

Originally published in French under the title *Sainte Colère: Jacob, Job, Jésus*
© Bayard Presse S.A./LABOR ET FIDES, 2003.

Published in English in Canada by Novalis
Business Offices:

Novalis Publishing Inc.
10 Lower Spadina Avenue, Suite 400
Toronto, Ontario, Canada
M5V 2Z2

Novalis Publishing Inc.
4475 Frontenac Street
Montréal, Québec, Canada
H2H 2S2

Phone: 1-800-387-7164
Fax: 1-800-204-4140
E-mail: books@novalis.ca
www.novalis.ca

Library and Archives Canada Cataloguing in Publication

Basset, Lytta
    Holy anger : Jacob, Job, Jesus / Lytta Basset.

Translation of Sainte colère.
Includes bibliographical references.
ISBN 978-2-89507-719-0

    1. Anger in the Bible. 2. Anger–Religious aspects–Christianity.
I. Title.

BS680.A49B3813 2007        220.8'15247        C2007-903240-0

Printed in Canada.

We acknowledge the financial support of the Government of Canada through
the Book Publishing Industry Development Program (BPIDP) for our publishing
activities.

5    4    3    2    1            11    10    09    08    07

# Contents

# Hebrew and Greek Transliterations

| Hebrew | | | | Greek | |
|---|---|---|---|---|---|
| | | | | *Aspirations at the beginnings of words are indicated by an "h"* | |
| א | ' | | | α | a |
| בּ ב | b v | | | β | b |
| ג | g | | | γ | g |
| ד | d | | | δ | d |
| ה | h | | | ε | e |
| ו | = | w | = | וֹ ō | ζ | z |
| | | | | וּ u | η | ē |
| | | | | ֻ ou | θ | th |
| ז | z | | | ι | i |
| ח | *h* (italic) | | | κ | k |
| ט | *t* (italic) | | | λ | l |
| י | y | | | μ | m |
| כ | k | | | ν | n |
| ל | l | | | ξ | x |
| מ | m | | | ο | o |
| נ | n | | | π | p |
| ס | s | | | ρ | r |
| ע | ' | | | σς | s |
| פּ פ | pff | | | τ | t |
| צ | *s* (italic) | | | υ | u |
| ק | q | | | φ | ph |
| ר | r | | | χ | ch |
| שׂ | s | | | | |
| שׁ | sh | | | ψ | ps |
| ת | t | | | ω | ō |

## To Marc Faessler,

who succeeded in leading me
to greater freedom in theological reflection.

# Introduction

"Resist": this word was carved in stone by Marie Durand, a Protestant from the Ardèche region of France who, out of fidelity to her Reformed faith, spent thirty-eight years locked up with a group of fellow prisoners in the Constance Tower at Aigues-Mortes. Like so many others in different times and places, she refused to meet aggression with the logic of an eye for an eye. Instead, she opened up a third way: a rock-solid resistance, an unshakeable will to remain true to herself, regardless of the consequences. For this was more important to her than life itself. We can see plainly that her sights were set on something else. Rather than looking for ways to counter *the other*, to dominate or even to eliminate him or her, it is a matter of focusing entirely on who we are: what is there in me that must be saved at all costs in order for my life to be conceivable? What can I never, for any reason, be willing to renounce? How can I come to know better the "I am" that is within me, and that will never allow itself to be silenced?

"The sufferings of Job" is an expression that has entered our everyday language, and we evoke his social demise when we refer to someone as being "as poor as Job." Why don't we also speak of "the anger of Job"? For most of his words have a tone of

vehement complaint, reproach, aggression. Even his name, ['iov],
is an agenda in itself. It may in fact derive from the root ['aiav] and
have a double meaning: "to be the object of hostility" and "to be
hostile."[1] Job would thus represent suffering humanity, who, seeing
itself constantly forced to choose between being the attacker and
the attacked, gradually discovers a third way – the ability to *face*
the OTHER, the resolve to remain true to oneself, the willingness to
confront the other whatever the cost.

The rich palette of anger offers us a broad spectrum of expressions:
from refusal to confrontation, through challenge, resistance, protest,
and more or less violent accusation, contradiction and reproach, we
are dealing with one and the same family of existential attitudes.
Some might wish to replace the terms "anger" or "violence" with
another, more appropriate one. Experience shows that our vocabulary needs to have a certain fluidity: what one person may regard
as unbearable violence, another may perceive as "resistance"; what
we experienced at one time as confrontation may seem to us later
a challenge. It is well known that the more fragile we are, the less
we are able to accept criticism.

Hence it is helpful to name as precisely as possible which member
of this family of words corresponds best to what we are capable of *at
this time*: it is a long way from a timid challenge to the most explicit
confrontation, but from the very first step we are asserting the human ability to affirm oneself in the face of the OTHER. By OTHER I
mean all that happens to us, all that befalls us and does violence to
us, without anyone asking for our consent and without our agreeing to accept it. This OTHER may come from people, from God, or
from the circumstances of life. It arouses, awakens and reawakens
our ability to stand up for ourselves. It pushes us to take a stand,
to defend ourselves even if this means accusing and rejecting the
OTHER that sought to colonize us. The battle we wage against it
is perhaps the most fundamental challenge of human existence: in
the process we come face to face with the OTHER that was there all
along, or at least that is how it appears.

This book tries to show how anger can give structure to faith. We
will never cease to oscillate between the life instinct and the death

instinct, to borrow Freud's notion of life as an endless struggle between Eros and Thanatos. "The efforts of Eros to unite and bring people together come up against the persistent offshoots of the death wish that constitute aggression and violence," L. Beirnaert observes. It is a desperate oscillation "that makes our steps falter on the way, as though afflicted by an incurable limp."[2] It is in light of this that we can fix our gaze, without any illusions, upon Jacob as he limps along the road from Jabbok.

We could, of course, just as easily remain hostage to the "sufferings of Job" all our lives, without ever deciding to acknowledge the injustice that is at the root of this endless suffering. The violence imposed by the OTHER is thus never recognized as such, and neither anger nor struggle ever surfaces. But the infection festers within. It manifests itself in the form of a chronic bitterness: "Who put this will into me?" asks St. Augustine. "Who sowed this seed of bitterness in me, when all that I am was made by my God, who is Sweetness itself?"[3]

Finally, we could take refuge behind the notion that some things are unforgivable, or that we are prey to a tragic force that can never be overcome. Our own life story is thus cast as a drama whose outcome we refuse to call into question. We shield ourselves permanently from any confrontation, including with God. Yet anger could open up the way towards the "anti-tragedy." We could be angry with God, rather than bow our heads beneath the blows of fortune as if they were the result of God's anger. Paul Ricœur says that the theme of God's anger is invincible, "for there is no rational justification for the innocence of God": no one can prove that God is not responsible, or that God is pure benevolence. "Only a conscience that has fully assumed suffering," adds Ricœur, "could begin to reintegrate the wrath of God into the love of God."[4] Yet to assume our suffering fully ultimately leads us to stand up straight and come face to face with the OTHER that has knocked us down. Without this growing awareness of our own capacities, without this confirmation of our own power through confronting the OTHER, we will never shake off the doubt in our own ability to face up to the tragic in our lives.

It is very likely, therefore, that "anger," in all its many shades, is part of a living faith; it is through such an experience, constantly renewed, that our faith life takes shape as it matures. Anger – a healthy reaction to unjust violence coming from an incomprehensible OTHER – leads us to push against God's defences because we are unable to retreat any farther into our own: the more lucid our view of the violence we have endured, the more determined our challenge against the OTHER. Our need to face what threatens us is thus all the greater, so that we do not allow the tragic to have the last word.

The anger of Jesus is an invaluable help to us as we move in this direction. Some of the words he addressed to his listeners, and some of the actions described by the evangelists, show us the anger that was at work in the fully human Jesus of Nazareth. If certain of these passages do not use the word "anger," others are absolutely explicit. Thus, when he healed a leper for the first time, in the gospel of Mark, Jesus was "moved by compassion" or, according to some manuscripts, "moved by anger." For the leper had begged him, saying, "If you will, you can *purify* me" (Mk. 1:40).[5] It seems clear that in the original text, Jesus had compassion. The variant reading that speaks of anger is interesting, however, because it indicates a particular kind of anger: one that insists upon difference and refuses to be dragged into confusion. For, in fact, the impurity that kills the leper physically and socially refers to our fear of contagion by that which is not us and which threatens our integrity. We can therefore guess that Jesus is vehemently opposed to what leprosy symbolizes: the prohibition against being independent, clearly different, "untainted" by any compromise with death.

Accepting Jesus' anger encourages us to accept our own anger, especially if we understand what is at stake: for Jesus, in each case it is a matter of finding his own way, discovering his own difference, refusing any confusion with what he is not. The second passage tells the story of the healing of a man with a withered hand. Before healing him, Jesus "looked around at [the Pharisees] with anger, grieved[6] at their hardness of heart" (Mk. 3:5).

Here again it seems that anger and compassion go hand in hand, because a particular type of anger is involved. True compassion never leads to confusion; this anger speaks of distance from the dysfunctional other, without which differentiation would be impossible (you are you, I am me, free to obey "the breath of the Lord that rests upon" me) – a distance without which compassion would be impossible. This essential and mysterious link between compassion and anger in the broad sense gives us a hint of the distinctive conception of anger that the Bible proposes.

The anger of Jesus is mentioned again in Mark 10:14, when his disciples rebuke the people who have brought children to him for a blessing: he "loses his temper," "boils with rage," is "indignant" or "irate," and once again thwarts the constraints of social and religious custom. This time it is his disciples whom he resists and opposes: you are you and I am me, there is in me a little child whom I welcomed as one welcomes the kingdom of God itself, and I will not allow myself to be co-opted by the world of pious, right-thinking adults. An anger of differentiation, once again. Mark is the only one to speak of this anger – and his Gospel is considered the earliest. The parallel passages in the other Gospels do not speak of it: as we can see, the censure of anger in Christian circles is nothing new. It remains to be seen what this anger means in the life of the "Prince of Peace": this is the central question of this book.

Greek civilization generally considered anger a disaster: one had to undergo a *katharsis* or purification from one's emotions, for they would only impede rational thought, detract from good conduct, and even cause physical illness. Anger, like all passions, placed human beings at the mercy of the first manipulator willing to harness these energies to his or her exclusive benefit. Anger meant losing touch with the real, and thus it was to be nipped in the bud: "For as the shapes of persons seen through a fog, so things seen through the mist of rage appear greater than they are," remarked Plutarch in the first century of our era.[7] However, along with Seneca and many other moralists of antiquity, he argued against expressing emotion but provided no help in avoiding doing so. He ignored the possibility that anger might be a vital energy that needs to be properly channelled, satisfied simply with repeating that one must struggle against anger ... by not getting angry!

> For the first way, my friend, to suppress anger, as you would a tyrant, is not to obey or yield to it when it commands us to speak loudly, to look fiercely, and to lash out; but to be quiet, and not increase the passion, as we do a disease, by impatient tossing and crying out ... So the weeping and lamentation which we permit in mourning doubtless carry forth much of the grief together with the tears. But anger, quite on the contrary, is more inflamed by what the angry persons say or do.[8]

It would be better to regard anger as an engine capable of transforming a potentially devastating energy into the violent life force that accompanies every birthing process. We must be attentive to the true anger that lies hidden beneath the false words of a feigned peace. Underlying the outburst of anger, we will discern the desperate quest for justice. We shall evaluate the fearsome countervailing force of anger in the broadest sense, when it confronts ideologies of all kinds, as well as the potential for social transformation that lies within the simple fact of thinking differently and saying so. Anger will be seen to be a real force for personal change, capable of mobilizing unsuspected powers on behalf of a new life that is different from what is expected: something intolerable, which we previously accepted as normal, is suddenly no longer tolerated. We find ourselves speaking a new language, and realize that it is a universal one, one that brings divine blessings, as did the tongues of fire with which the Spirit came to rest on the heads and the lips of the witnesses to Pentecost.

C. Vigée notes that, according to the Jewish Kabbalah, the universe was created from the twenty-two original letters of the alphabet. The first of these is [aleph], which is not pronounced and which symbolizes God – "the silent letter," "the first being of silence"; the second is [beth], "sign of duality, of conflict, that is also the first letter of blessing, [berakah]."[9] We humans can say nothing about [aleph]: it is in duality that we begin our earthly pilgrimage, marked by conflict already in our mother's womb, according to the biblical teaching of Jacob and Esau. This duality is a necessary element of all relationships, but it also brings with it the inevitable risk of the other's hostility. It is, however, a duality enfolded in blessings, one that is prior to the emergence of any conflict, for it is preceded by the divine [aleph], the indestructible One whom every human being is invited to resemble by means of a more or less violent affirmation of his or her difference. Could there be any clearer sign that we should do so in full confidence?

# I   Fear of confrontation

# 1 Anger censured

> I would like to think that Cain did not rise up against his brother
> but against God, whose ways he found incomprehensible, intol-
> erable ... Had God treated him unfairly? He should have told
> Him so ... But he chose to remain silent, to swallow his grudge
> and transform it into poisonous hate.[1]

When, for the first time in his life, and for the first time in the Bible,
Cain brings an offering to God, and his brother Abel immediately
follows suit, the author of Genesis 4:1-16 tells us that "the Lord
had regard for Abel and for his offering," but "for Cain and his
offering he had no regard." The text continues, making God apparently the sole witness of the first human fit of rage – and of the
first attempt to repress anger:

> It burned Cain badly, and his countenance fell.
> The Lord said to Cain:
> "Why did this burn you and why has your countenance
> fallen?"[2]

In Hebrew, anger is named in very concrete, even physiological
terms: most often, it is expressed as "the nose is burning."[3] It is as
if God were asking Cain: "Why did this burn you up? Why are
you red with rage?"

And yet, the incident is so stinging precisely because it causes Cain to lose face. The word ['af] shows clearly the link between anger and the falling countenance: it signifies anger as well as the nose, the nostrils and the region around the nose – that is to say, the face. We can see in this episode the first hints of the self-censuring of anger in the Bible. In fact, God was asking two different questions: "Why did this burn you up?" and "Why did your countenance fall?" In other words, try to name the object of your anger and stop censuring it; let it come out and be *written on your face* rather than losing face and destroying yourself!

God's concern for Cain is all the more understandable since God knows what it is to be angry. Anger is one of the most frequently mentioned divine emotions in the Hebrew Bible, making it much more a feature of God than of human beings: ['af] is used 170 times with reference to God, and only 40 times with reference to a human.[4] We have not always understood what makes God angry, but the more we have become aware of a relationship with God, a relationship of covenant, of partnership that implies some common code of ethics (especially in Deuteronomy and in the Prophets), the more it has become clear that God shows his angry side when human beings are no longer in relationship with him – when they have "sinned," as the Bible says. If we can say that God's anger is first and foremost action, and always provisional action, it is because we have had the experience of a Partner who *faces us*, very concretely, until his human partners show their face to him.

The prophet Isaiah spoke especially eloquently of God's passion for humanity, consisting of both tenderness and outbursts of anger, of unshakeable fidelity and profound disappointments:

> In overflowing wrath for a moment I hid my face from you, but with everlasting love I will have compassion on you, says the Lord, your Redeemer. For this is like the days of Noah to me: as I swore that the waters of Noah should no more go over the earth, so I have sworn that I will not be angry with you and will not rebuke you. (Is. 54:8ff.)

Yet, the original meaning of the word translated here as "love" [*hesed*] is apparently "consistency," as in Isaiah 40:6b-7b, which reads:

> All flesh is grass,
> and all its consistency is like the flower
> of the field.
> The grass withers, the flower fades,
> when the breath of the Lord blows upon it.

Speaking anthropomorphically, we could say that God shows us how to deal with anger: to let it out and even allow it to "overflow," though this means temporarily withdrawing oneself from the face-to-face relationship (by "hiding one's face"), but returning again and again to the relationship with the "consistency of everlasting friendship." To be someone's friend should mean to be unfailingly consistent in our relation to him or her, even if this may be eclipsed at times because of anger. If, then, in the Bible God loses his temper much more often than human beings do, it is because of God's infinite constancy towards us. It is no accident that Genesis speaks of humanity as "made in [his] image, after [his] likeness," (1:26)[5] and says that our natural tendency is to "hide from the face of God" (3:8).[6] According to Isaiah, God can also "hide his face," giving free rein to feelings of anger. Yet God remains God in his inexhaustible capacity to confront us. His constant friendship can be summed up as follows: whatever happens, there is someone there in front of you!

A censured anger feeds off the relationship to self, to others and to God. Yet how can we speak of anger without taking into consideration its psychological aspect? It is worth noting that in psychology, aggression is linked to the search for identity. When excessive suffering crushes our personal identity, the aggression that once helped us find our interior structure is aroused and helps us to recover it. If the identity is always repressed, then we will need first of all to build up our backbone by discovering, through confrontation, who we are and what makes up our unique identity. A hatred for the key adults in the early years of life may come to be focused on God. Thus Job accuses God of preventing him from (re)discovering the joy – and resulting inner unity – of being himself that comes through self-knowledge.

Biblical language encourages us never to dissociate the psychological underpinnings of anger from its spiritual density: in fact, they are one and the same reality. Yet it is striking that the first biblical words about anger should be pronounced in the context of the relationship to God. Without the help of Freud, the author of Genesis 4 understood that Cain needed an OTHER to be able to name his anger, to own it, so that he might no longer lose his identity as one loses face, as the "countenance falls." God did not tell Cain that it is good or evil to be angry. God knows since the beginning of time that if a human being loses his countenance and consistency through being deprived of his ability to face the OTHER, his or her very identity is threatened: what could be more distinctive, more easily identifiable than a face?

The first lesson of Genesis 4 is that all humans are capable of addressing their anger to someone. Elie Wiesel stressed that Abel had not come to Cain's assistance but remained deaf to his pain and his anger.[7] Yet even when, as is often the case, no human being faces up to the person who is overcome with anger, there is Someone who says he is ready to listen. But what if one does not believe in God? How do we address our anger to Fate, to Nature, to Life, to the Cosmos when what we really need is an encounter with someone? "The Lord" had never spoken to Cain, who appeared only five verses earlier. It does not seem very important that Cain should know exactly to whom to address his anger. What matters above all is that he not censor himself. "If there is someone up there, he deserves to be punished," a rebellious person once said. This is more or less what God expects of Cain: turn your face towards me and cry out that you are mad at me. Even if you do not know me and even if the heavens appear empty to you, spit out your anger in the face of this Someone who made your life so unfair! And if you hear within yourself this twofold question, it is perhaps because you need to believe that there is, after all, "somewhere" someone solid enough to endure the violence of your rage!

With one and the same movement we censor ourselves and we censor texts, placing in quotation marks or simply deleting passages of the Psalms whose violence offends us:

> As Christians, biblical critics want us to endure passion with-
> out complaining. But the voice of the Psalms calls upon God
> to come to our aid, asks God to strike down their enemies! ...
> What are these texts talking about? It is the story of a man who
> is persecuted, who knows he will die. He is alone. He is afraid
> ... Does he not have a right to complain, to call for help? To call
> for assistance obviously means to call for violence. But the point
> of these texts is not that they are violent. On the contrary, they
> express the need to escape violence.[8]

The Psalms are in harmony with the story of Cain and Abel. Nowhere does God censure the verbal expression of anger; what is more, he encourages it. The great masters of prayer who composed the Psalms regularly experienced anger and did not shy away from expressing it: "You answered me!" The prohibition against complaining – and against anger – is still widespread in our Western societies, especially in Christian circles. As if we had never read Job or the Psalms or the Lamentations of Jeremiah! You often hear people who would have every reason to complain of their calamities affirm fervently, "I can't complain." A reflection often heard at funerals is that the deceased person's greatest quality was that he or she never complained. In the same way, we might be astonished that the verse that is often chosen for an obituary or an epitaph is Job's declaration the day after the death of all his children: "The Lord gave, and the Lord has taken away; blessed be the name of the Lord" (1:21b).

Is it really possible to accept misfortune so quickly? Is such a spiritually admirable attitude not suspect, precisely because we think it pleases God? Immediately after repressing his complaint, Job is said to have fallen ill with a "serious inflammation" diagnosed as the symptom of a fatal disease, generally attributed to a curse.[9] Did Job curse himself by censuring his feelings and emotions? Did his body cry out that which he did not allow to "dance on his lips," as C. Bobin put it? It takes a seemingly endless time of depression

("seven days and seven nights" of total silence[10]) for Job at last to
begin to complain. And it would take still longer for him to cease
"cursing the day" (of his birth): that is, to turn his complaint and
anger away from himself, and dare to point the finger at God.

Listening to the story of Job and to other biblical narratives, we
might be justified in expecting that sooner or later the day of wrath
will come. Yet what the Bible prophesies as the "Day of the Lord"
is the day of God's anger against all that impedes the fullness of the
relationship God longs to have with humanity, with his people
and with the nations. The first obstacle to the divine relational life
within us and among us – to the reign of God, as the texts put it
– is this censorship of complaint which, while leaving the wound,
intact, prevents healing and poisons all relationships. This is why no
matter how hard we restrain ourselves from having our own day
of anger (even if we fail, despite our best efforts), it is God who,
as the Bible says, sees to it that in the end – in any case at the end
of time, say the texts – our complaint is expressed and our anger
purged. Our anger from now on is his anger as well, for that face-
to-face encounter (to which God aspires infinitely more than we
do) depends on that anger.

What happens to anger once it is censured? René Girard rightly
shows how, on the collective level, the repression of violence always
leads to the creation of scapegoats:

> Behind the ritual scapegoat there is not only superstition but the
> tendency, universal among human beings, to unburden their ac-
> cumulated violence on another, a substitute victim ... Scapegoats
> continue to exist, albeit in a generally attenuated form that is
> nevertheless fundamentally identical to that of archaic religion.
> *Everywhere and always, when humans cannot or dare not attack the*
> *object of their anger, they unconsciously look for substitutes, and most of*
> *the time they find them.*[11]

Repressed anger falls upon an innocent person: the anger of the
employer falls on the employee, of the parent on the child, of the
child on the youngest brother or sister, who takes it out on the
cat! Girard notes that mythical stories reflect what still goes on in
schools today: the one "chosen" as the scapegoat is someone who

is not physically attractive, is a foreigner, a person with a disability, or even someone exceptionally beautiful, flawless, wealthy. In short, it is people with extreme qualities who, in world mythology, are most often used as collective lightning rods for an anger that has long been kept under wraps.[12]

The choice of victim is generally unanimous, and falls upon those who are likely to cause no grief, pose no threat of reprisals. It may be true that unloading one's anger on them can give temporary relief. But does this mean that in the process every individual will have done with his or her own complaint, with the anger that arises out of his or her own particular life story? To bring our anger to bear on an innocent person or persons is no solution at all: in doing so, we have not even begun to own up to an anger that is constitutive of the self, of our wounded identity. It is very likely that by acting in this way, we refuse to acknowledge our own truth in face of the person who has denied it by his or her violent or unjust behaviour. This way of behaving means losing the opportunity to grow in consistency *in our own eyes* and to emerge more mature from a confrontation that might have begun with the simple, authentic statement of "what was burning us up" so painfully.

The same was true of Cain. His censured anger turned against his younger brother, who was so puny and weak that the very name he is saddled with – Abel [hevel] – means breath, or wind. A brother who is nothing but an appendage of the elder son, as the text implies: "And again, [Eve] bore his brother Abel." (4.2) After the murder, God saw that Cain was no further ahead. Once again God tried to put into words what Cain is unable to express: "you shall be a fugitive and a wanderer on the earth" (4.12), you realize that you are like Abel and like every human being in frailty, a passing "breath," without solidity and without any bonds, all alone. This time it was Cain himself who made the connection between his experience of insolidity (he even echoed the same words that God used) and his incapacity to confront the OTHER, to direct his anger towards it, to reproach it for the injustice: "from your face I shall be hidden; and I shall be a fugitive and a wanderer on the earth" (4:14).

What could have been preventing him from facing instead the One who refused his offering? Why did he choose to hide from God, as Adam and Eve hid in the garden, and for such a long time? The end of the story uses the language of wandering to evoke the experience of one who has censured his or her anger and avoided coming face to face with the OTHER and thus with himself or herself: "Then Cain went away from the presence of the Lord, and dwelt in the land of Nod, east of Eden." (4.16) *Nod* does not exist (this is in itself revealing), but its name recalls *nad*, meaning "homeless, wandering."

"It was his refusal of God and of his own need that made [Cain] into a murderer and changed for him the face of the Other," writes L. Beirnaert.[13] For thenceforth it was in the Other that he perceived rage, as if it were turned back against himself, and therefore he became a "wanderer." It is undoubtedly in the book of Job that we can best grasp the subtle shift from concealment of anger to the demonization of the OTHER: anger that is censured will re-emerge somehow, but now attributed to God. Job had every reason not to be able to acknowledge his own counter-violence. Some of those responsible for his misery are human beings, nomads and thieves, but these were passed over in silence and never aroused his anger. Why? The only witnesses to these injustices did not take his side – neither his wife nor the four friends who remained. God seemed to have disappeared completely: no inner voice spoke to Job with concern, as it had done to Cain. Since he received no support or encouragement from the OTHER to name what was burning him, all Job could do was hide his anger. As a result, it turned into a caricature of God, a sort of deified Wrath that seemed determined to break him:

> I was at ease and he broke me asunder;
> he *seized me by the neck* and *dashed me to pieces*. (Job 16:12)

Is it a coincidence? We find the same two verbs in Psalm 137:9, in a verse addressed to Babylon, the foreign power responsible for Israel's misfortune – looting and deportation:

> Happy shall they be *who take your little ones*
> *and dash them* against the rock![14]

The Bible gives a realistic illustration of our desire to reproduce the violence that we have first endured ourselves, a desire that is exacerbated by the lack of empathy around us. What can we do about a counter-violence that has been provoked by a violence that no one is able to recognize as such – a verbal violence that remains the only "act" still possible before either taking action or else stifling our anger completely? There remains the possibility of attributing our counter-violence to God. That is what Job did, unlike the Psalmist, who would have been happy to reproduce himself what he had endured: "Job imagined God seizing him by the neck and dashing his head against a rock, just like the Babylonians did to the innocents, the young children of Israel" in 586 BCE.[15]

We experience the same psycho-spiritual loss of control that Job felt when our representation of Almighty God collapses, and we conceal our anger against a God who is unable to preserve us from misfortune. The convergence with the experience of abandonment, as A. Vergote describes it on the psychological level, is striking: the day when our unconscious representation of an ideal, all-powerful father collapses, and if we do not take responsibility for our hatred and disappointment, we may turn it against God without even realizing it. At that moment we notice that we no longer have confidence: He has become ambivalent, God and the Devil in one.[16]

If Job did not fully own his anger, and perceived God as increasingly diabolical, this was essentially because those around him were convinced and tried to convince him that his anger was unjustified. The more his friends remained outside what he was going through, the more they addressed him with an anger that they were too weak to simply accept: "you tear *yourself* in your anger," (18:4) they accused him from the lofty perch of their serenity, just as elsewhere they told him, in essence: "*You* are the cause of your misfortune." What a way to encourage self-destruction, when what a person weighed down by pain and anger desperately needs is a real opponent he can face. It is possible, however, that on account of their incomprehension, his friends in fact held up against Job a sort of irreducible constancy that, for lack of anything better, could fulfill the function of the OTHER – the "punching bag" that is better than the total absence of a counterpart.

Psychology today would speak of projection. The violence attributed to God increases steadily in the Book of Job, reaching a climax in chapter 16; according to Job, God is a breaker of heads, a wild animal that tears its victims apart, an archer pulling his bow, a warrior leading an assault:

> Yes, he has torn me in his wrath,
> He has gnashed his teeth at me
> My adversary sharpens his eyes against me …
> He breaks me with breach *upon* breach;
> He runs *upon* me like a warrior.
> I have sewed sackcloth *upon* my skin,
> And have laid my forehead (lit. my horn) in the dust.
> My face is red with weeping,
> And *upon* my eyelids is the shadow of death[17]
> *Upon* non-violence in my hands and my pure prayer.
> (Job 16:9, 14-17)

Sackcloth was a sign of mourning or of imminent punishment, an attitude of supplication in order to ward off the wrath of a conqueror. One might say that Job sewed sackcloth upon his skin as if upon his restrained anger or apparent non-violence – "upon non-violence in my hands." At the same time, he buried ("laid in the dust") his ability to face the OTHER (his "face" or his "horn," eloquent symbol of the strength of the counter-violence and combativeness that he had renounced).

The fantasy of being protected from his own anger (of being perfectly non-violent) will nourish over several chapters the fantasy of the incomprehensible anger of God towards Job:

> He demolishes me down on every side …
> He has kindled his wrath against me and counts me as his
> adversary. (19:10ff.)[18]

No doubt only the awareness of his own anger could deliver Job of the memory of the violence he endured. Yet he is still suffering too much and is too broken not to project onto God a counter-violence that terrifies him as much as the actual violence he has helplessly had to endure. But there is worse to come: remaining crushed by what has happened, while continuing to say and to repeat: if I gave free rein to my anger, it would be completely destructive. For if this happened even once and the experiment was not conclusive, we could definitively censure our own violence, ascribing it instead to those close to us; the more we are fascinated by the violence of another, the less we will be aware of the one we have censured in ourselves!

Ascribing our own anger to God offers at least two advantages: it allows us to feel less threatened by an interior violence that we think we are unable to curb, and by the reprisals that might follow an inter-personal confrontation. We prefer to suffer from divine wrath rather than expose ourselves to fresh human wounds. Moreover, when it is fate that is against us – that is, life with its share of injustices – we might at times prefer to suffer from the wrath of Someone (even if we had not believed in his existence previously)[19] rather than from a Nothing or a Meaninglessness. If Someone sends his wrath upon me, this may have a meaning; in any case, I have someone face to face, even if his face is disfigured.

In the history of the Church, as in certain current theological trends, self-censorship of anger goes even further. The authors, failing to be in touch with their own anger, charge "God" with the task of expressing it and enacting it in their stead. Thus we see Tertullian "transfer to God his anger and his desire for revenge, given that he was unable to act himself … At the end of *De spectaculis*, in a famous passage, Tertullian declares his joy at the thought that his adversaries, on the Day of Judgment, would suffer the worst possible chastisements." As for Lactantius (230–325), "it is indisputable that fundamentally, he is preaching the expectation of divine vengeance as a subtitute for personal vengeance."[20]

But from God as judge to a God who is gratuitously cruel, there is but a short step, easy to take given that both are the fruit of our rebellious imagination. In either case, we avoid owning up to our own anger, and we fail to accept it as a legitimate reaction, one that is full of meaning. By transposing it onto God,[21] we maintain the illusion that the great thing would be simply to punish the guilty. Yet the entire book of Job points us to another perception of suffering. It matters little, in the long run, what it is that hurts or angers us; it makes little difference who are the guilty ones (God, human beings, or ourselves); the only thing that counts is to react to what is happening. How would we know that we have any resilience if no one ever pressed down on us, "laid [our] foreheads in the dust" (16:15)? Therefore transferring our anger onto a judging God does not really liberate us. We easily fall back into a pain that has no visible source, and into the fantasy of a God who is gratuitously cruel.

A few minutes alone suffice, perhaps – through a dream, someone's remark, or a word involuntarily issuing from our own mouth – and we realize that we are in fact resilient. It is up to us then to remain in contact with this capacity to react, this "guarantor," this refusal to simply die, suffer and endure, this combativeness: in a word, this life-giving anger! The more difficult it is to remain in touch with it, the more we can measure just how much we have censured it until now. Yet the more "they" push down on us, the more "they" press us down, the more we feel that someone or something is exerting pressure in order to break that censure. "They" push us to the limit … until we finally cry out to the empty heavens: "Is anyone up there? Come down here if you are a man!" as the cartoonists say.

Thus, Job would go to the limits of the most violent confrontation with God in the whole Bible, until he perceives that, after all, God was never really hostile or ill-disposed towards him. As M.-D. Molinié observes:

> The most cruel aspect of his situation is that even in the most profound moment of darkness, divine pressure was not absent … Yet still, something in him prevents him from ceasing to believe ("I know that my Redeemer lives," etc.), but it is precisely this hope that is the most painful, confronted with the spectacle of a divine behaviour that cannot, it seems to him, be love nor even, alas, indifference, but rather a merciless malevolence justified, moreover, by an inaccessible transcendance that Job continues to adore even while railing against it … The temptation is great

to see in this [divine] love a pitiless enemy, and to call a burden-
some espionage that which is instead an unceasing solicitude, the
maternal nature of which completely escapes us.[22]

In the end, Job had to lift up his head, look God in the eye, so to
speak, assume fully his anger, in order to recognize that the OTHER is
benevolent. That is the price to pay: to work at no longer censuring
his anger. As the Psalmist cries out, in a marvellously ambiguous
phrase: "*You* pushed me hard, so that I was falling, but the Lord
helped me. The Lord is my strength and my battle cry, he gives
me victory" (118:13ff, following the TOB). Who is this "you"?
The Jewish tradition is divided on the matter: for some it is God,
for others, the Enemy;[23] it makes little difference who is guilty, we
used to say. In any case, without my "battle cry," that I alone can
utter, how could the Lord help me?

Our aspiration to lift the ban on anger raises the question of why
this interdiction exists in the first place. Where did this censorship
come from? Some rightly invoke the early permeation of Western
Christianity with the Stoic ideal of ataraxia – this tranquillity of a
soul is sheltered from the passions – and with a Platonic dualism
accompanied by a tenacious contempt for the body, and thus also
for the emotions and feelings, right up until modern times. Others
attribute it to a traditional education based on obedience and on
a muscular concept of authority. Finally, some see it as a personal
choice that consists in exerting true control over oneself at a time
when the free expression of emotions is not tolerated. More than
one person, mistreated from childhood, recalls having decided at an
early age never to cry again or to get angry, in order to make the
abusive adults believe that "I don't care." That is the sole dignity
left to such children, the only hold they can keep over their lives:
their last resort, we might say.

The first time anger is mentioned in the Bible, God tried to prevent
the self-censure of Cain. To this end, God discreetly invited Cain
to challenge Him: Why are you angry? *Why don't you look at me
face to face?* An excellent test of our interpersonal relationships! The
rabbinic commentaries make great efforts to justify God's favouritism towards Abel. They show us why Cain's offering was not

acceptable, and how God is above all suspicion of partiality. They are often convincing, but the problem does not really lie there, it seems to me. The absence of an explicit reason in the text – we really do not know why Cain's offering was rejected – is rich in meaning. It reminds us of the impossibility of evaluating suffering: the same event can be experienced as the worst injustice by one person, and quite differently by someone else, who would see in it a blessing! Pain resulting from an event will take on a different colouration depending on what we do with it, for what matters ultimately is never to lose contact with "what it does to us."

Now this "burned Cain badly," all the more so since if he had not had confidence in a just God, like the rabbis, he would not have sought to accomplish the first religious act of the Bible. He certainly fell from a great height! The first human anger was provoked by this God whom we thought just and who showed Himself to be as absurdly arbitrary as any human. But after all, how do we know that God refused Cain's offering? How do we go about seeing God "turn His face" from one side to another? And who was it who taught the two brothers to decode the divine response to the offerings, since no one until then had ever offered a sacrifice to God? The conclusion is astonishing: the first human anger was provoked by an injustice that cannot be measured in any objective way. Given the absence of any external sign – we do not really know how Cain established that his offering has been rejected – we might say that the text focuses exclusively on the *sense of injustice* that strikes Cain down. Once again, it matters little who is guilty of what hurt Cain (God, Abel, himself[24]); one question is put to him, and only one: What do you feel that is revolting in *your* life – in your personal way of living through what happens to you – which prevents you from looking at me face to face and speaking to me?

When we begin to make the text say what it leaves unsaid, we feel compelled to continue. We have a nice illustration of this from the pen of Saint Augustine, who comments on the rejection of Cain's offering as follows:

> ... which was doubtless intimated by some visible sign to that
> effect; and when God had done so because the works of the one

were evil but those of his brother good … God did not respect his offering because it was not rightly "distinguished" in this, that he gave to God something of his own but kept himself to himself … For God saw that he envied his brother and of this He accused him … But God, in giving the reason why He refused to accept Cain's offering … shows him that though he was unjust in "not rightly distinguishing," that is, not rightly living and being unworthy to have his offering received, he was more unjust by far in hating his just brother without a cause.[25]

No, that's just it! The absence of "visible sign" made Cain turn back all the more to what was happening within him: where could this feeling come from that he was not recognized or valued? Here was the ideal opportunity to express a revolt that he had never allowed to burst forth before a dominant mother because she was "ruled over by her husband"[26] (Gen. 3:16). And to do so even if it meant attacking God, since He said he was prepared to "take it" face to face: "Why has your countenance fallen?" You can look me in the eye with your anger!

No, God did not "reproach" Cain for anything. God did not "explain" anything, nor did He show Cain what he "must" do. Precisely because God is not a human being. He began by giving Cain some space, saying He was ready to listen. Nothing is more urgent than putting Cain in touch with his anger, and having his anger be heard. If only Cain had chosen to speak, dreams Elie Wiesel, he would have said:

> Admit though that I have had every reason to cry out to you my anguish and my wrath; I have every means to oppose my injustice to Yours. Admit that I could strike my brother as You Yourself punished my father … I could drown mankind with tears and in its blood. I could bring this farce to an end; that may even be what You want, what You are driving me to. But I shall not do it, do You hear me, Master of the Universe, I shall not do it, I shall not destroy, do You hear me, I shall not kill.[27]

In that case Cain would have learned a great deal about justice: that it cannot just fall from the sky like a meteor, that no one can know exactly what it is, and that from the very first pages of the

Bible, it has to do with anger, since it unfolds completely within
the domain of the relational. It is no coincidence that the famous
invitation by Christ gives pride of place to the "kingdom of heaven,"
before justice:

> Seek first *the relational* with God and his justice,
> And all these things shall be yours as well. (Matt. 6:33)

Why the "relational"? In the New Testament, the kingdom of
heaven is spoken of as an exceptional kind of life, when relations
between humans and God will make it possible to live "heavenly"
moments. To live in an age when peace and justice reign, there need
to be at least two of you. What prevented Cain and Abel from living something heavenly? Is it not the fact that Cain wanted to place
justice (or rather, his conception of justice) before the "relational"
with God? By lowering his head, by remaining mute and turning
his anger inward, he withdrew from the relationship with God and
then with Abel. To the Cains of every age, the Gospel might say
the following: seek first and above all the Relational, for it is "of
God"; seek it at the expense of a face-to-face encounter, one that
is difficult, painful, demanding. It is in and through relationship
that Justice is inaugurated or restored as God desires it for us and
for Himself, and never any other way.

# 2 Furyand complaint, on a par with pain

Where can we readily find a man who holds in fit and just estima-
tion those persons on account of whose revolting pride, luxury,
and avarice, and cursed iniquities and impiety, God now smites
the earth as His predictions threatened? Where is the man who
lives with them in the style in which it becomes us to live with
them? For often we wickedly blind ourselves to the occasions of
teaching and admonishing them, sometimes even of reprimand-
ing and chiding them, either because we shrink from the labour
or are ashamed to offend them, or because we fear to lose good
friendship, lest this should stand in the way of our advancement,
or injure us in some worldly matter, which either our covet-
ous disposition desires to obtain, or our weakness shrinks from
losing[28]

Fear of clashing head on: that was the problem the future patriarch
Jacob faced until he was getting on in years. According to Genesis,
he was a kind of add-on, having come into the world clasping the
heel of his twin, Esau, the strong man who would become a hunter.
As an adolescent, Jacob "dwelt in tents" and cooked (Gen. 25:27,
29) – always clutching his mother's skirts, one might say. He did
nothing but obey those around him: Esau, even though he bargained

with him; and his mother ("obey my word as I command you"). He went so far as to state: "I am a smooth man" (27:8-11), but his timid objections did not prevent his mother from making a decision for him and thus stripping him completely of responsibility. She decked him out in Esau's clothes and goatskins, and sent him in to repeat his lines to his father Isaac, who was blind, so that he might obtain for himself the paternal blessing reserved for Esau, the elder son (vv. 15-17). From that point on, Esau would "treat him as an enemy" and plan to kill him; but this elicited no response from Jacob. It was once again Rebecca who ordered him to flee "until your brother's anger turns away" (she says this twice) and "forgets what you have done to him": *then I will send and fetch you from there,*" she added (vv. 41-45).

Yet it appears that Jacob was over forty years old at the time of these events: since Genesis 26:34ff. had told us that his twin brother married two foreign women at the age of forty. It is only in 28:8, however, that Esau became aware of his parents' disapproval, at the point when Jacob "obeys" them (v. 7) by fleeing to Harân to his uncle Laban. The official reason for this exile, as Rebecca told Isaac and Isaac told Jacob, was so Jacob could marry one of Laban's daughters rather than a foreign woman. The underlying motive, however, was that Rebecca was afraid Esau would kill Jacob. The least we can infer from this course of action is that this very ordinary family was susceptible to manipulation and left much unsaid, for no one learned to express opposition to another openly, with authenticity and with respect for difference. This is the human mass within which the Word of God has been at work since the very first pages of the Bible.

Psycho-genealogy today makes us aware of the burden Isaac no doubt placed on his entourage as a result of nearly being sacrificed on Mount Moriah.[29] Elie Wiesel sees in him the "first survivor" in Jewish history, who "had to make something of his memories, his experience … He felt neither hatred nor anger" but founded a family, and "knew how to transform [his suffering] into prayer and love rather than into rancor and malediction" and "defied death,"[30] as his father had defied God, by obeying Him even to the point of

absurdity. Indeed, Isaac would never free himself from "the trau-
matizing scenes that violated his youth; the holocaust had marked
him and continued to haunt him forever. Yet he remained capable
of laughter. And in spite of everything, *he did laugh*,"[31] according
to the etymology of his name. An idealized portrait?

Defying death by laughter is certainly a way of "living in spite of
everything." But Isaac's silence about his past, when added to the
dysfunctionality of his family life, implies that something in him
may have been broken since his childhood. Wiesel says that Isaac
"remained the defender of his people ... pleading its cause with
great ability."[32] It is all the more striking, then, that at no time did
he take up the defence of his children, as if something were preventing him from doing so. He abandoned Jacob to the manipulations
of his mother. He "preferred Esau," the hunter, for "he had a taste
for game" (Gen. 25:28, as the TOB and the New American Bible
translate it). In other words, he loved this son because of what Esau
brought him – a love that appears even more fusional in André
Chouraqui's translation: "Isaac loves Esau, or the wild game in his
mouth." Is this compulsive need for bloody meat not a sign that the
old story of bloody sacrifice linked to filial love has still not been
resolved? That he had never been able to distance himself from the
violence he had had to endure, or to lay the blame on his father,
or God, or both?

But there is something even more striking: when Isaac noticed that
Jacob had taken advantage of him, usurping the blessing owed to the
elder son, Esau, he did not get angry. As Augustine comments:

> Yet [Isaac] does not complain that he has been deceived, yea
> ... he at once eschews anger, and confirms the blessing. "Who
> then," he says, "hath hunted me venison, and brought it me, and
> I have eaten of all before thou camest, and have blessed him, and
> he shall be blessed?" Who would not rather have expected the
> curse of an angry man here, if these things had been done in an
> earthly manner, and not by inspiration from above?[33]

That may well be, but this interpretation is too edifying to be
embodied fully. Isaac himself had once been duped, by a father
whom he had trusted completely and who never told him what he

was preparing to do on Mount Moriah. If he now did not allow his fury to explode at having unwittingly *sacrificed* Esau, is this not because he never challenged the "sacrifice" which he himself had at one time experienced? Are we not impelled to reproduce what we ourselves have undergone, so long as we do not reject it as an act of violence that ought never to have happened? But even if he did not give in to anger, Isaac was nonetheless deeply moved, and "trembled violently" (Gen. 27:33).[34] The poet Pierre Emmanuel seems to me to have been very attuned to the repressed drama within Isaac and to the stakes involved in this family story:

> The impenetrable memory of Isaac,
> Rebecca was worn down next to it like a flint
> Without the blade ever shining, even in a flash.
> On the spouse whom she is horrified to see bound
> To the stake of his funereal childhood,
> What she enkindles in her son and causes to burst forth,
> An adult flame that engrosses anger,
> Is the cry, the rush of blood in the arteries,
> Breath to breath body to body coupling
> God man.[35]

It was impossible, therefore, to awaken the anger of Isaac, still "bound to the stake of his childhood." Jacob went into exile without ever confronting his father nor, as a result, assuming his own status as a man.

Everything continued as before: Jacob endured twenty years of multiple manipulations and deceptions on the part of his uncle Laban, at work and in family life, and even by his wives, Leah and Rachel, who used his body as they wished, making him into a veritable "object" without ever arousing the least anger in him (cf. Gen. 30, and especially 30:15ff and 31:7). This went on until the day when Joseph was born, the second last of his twelve sons. The time had come, it seemed to Jacob, as often happens in life, when we suddenly say, "It can't go on like this." At last, Jacob complained to Laban that he had still not been able to set himself up on his own, despite the considerable wealth his labour had brought his uncle (30:25-30). Yet when Laban deceives him to get out of an agreement, Jacob does not confront him but once again acts by stealth. Through a clever trick he augmented his flock and prepared to leave Harân without telling his uncle. Once again he seemed to be fleeing, a point that is made all the more forcefully since the narrator repeats it three times (31:20).

Yet something has shifted. If for the first time in his life he was not following the dictates of another human being, this was because the birth of Joseph awakened in Isaac a desire that truly came from within him: "Send me away, that I may go to my own home and country," he said to Laban (30:25). This time he did not wait for his mother, though she had told him: "I will send and fetch you from there" (27:45). Once his material preparations were complete, he "*saw* Laban's face"; he said to his wives: "I *see* that your father does not regard me as favourably as he did before" (31:3, 5). But it is precisely between these two mentions of a new and clear perception of reality that Jacob hears the voice of God confirm his own desire: "Return to the land of your ancestors and to your kindred, and I will be with you" (TOB) or, in an even more symbolic phrasing, "return to the land of your fathers, towards your birth. I am with you" (Chouraqui). In other words, retrace your life to its roots, to the place where you left it untilled. Certainly the departure would seem a kind of flight, for one cannot change so quickly; but this return to the fold, though it seemed to begin with a step back, represented the greatest leap forward that Jacob had ever made. Regardless of his fears, God had given him the assurance that this was not an escape.

Chapter 31 is one of awakenings, of the first open conflict and the first reconciliation or covenant in Jacob's life. The biblical texts tell us this more than once: we cannot change our behaviour, much less our mentality, unless there is someone we can lean on. Even in the most extreme cases where we have no human support, there is that inner Voice that we finally hear and, especially, believe. There is something solid within you – at the very spot where you were born, you can move. Starting from this experience of the inner Voice, Jacob reviewed all his years living with Laban and opened his eyes to what he had endured. It was no longer the Lord, but his "angel" – that is, this voice of intimacy blended with the Voice – that impelled him to open his eyes: it was Jacob himself who has now "seen [at last] all that Laban is doing" (31:12). No, this was not paranoia; the Voice confirmed it … as did other human beings, namely his wives, Rachel and Leah, who in turn "saw" what they had had to endure from their father. These awakenings have a contagious quality about them. "Do whatever God has said to you," they added (v. 16), thereby pointing to the OTHER bursting into Jacob's life and into their life together. We have moved far beyond blind obedience to mere human beings!

But all this support does not prevent Jacob from acting as he has always done. "Why did you flee secretly?" his uncle asked when he found him. For fear of reprisals, Jacob acknowledged (v. 31), allowing Laban to search the entire camp for statuettes (household gods) that had apparently been stolen from him. The search proved futile, and it was at that point that Jacob exploded for the first time in his life.

> Jacob became angry, and upbraided Laban.
> Jacob replied/was defeated/mastered[36] and said to Laban …
> (v. 36)

Where Cain, in the fire of his anger, lost face and would not enter into dialogue, Jacob, although he was equally ill prepared by his past to accept the unfolding of his fury, succeeded in getting in touch with his pain, in feeling his long-standing "defeat" and thus in "mastering" violence and counter-violence by tranforming them into a "response." In the span of seven verses (36-42) he unloaded on Laban all his reproaches and complaints, in an authentic face-to-face encounter that brought an end to twenty years of shameful exploitation by his uncle and put a stop to his position of self-enslavement. Suddenly, he no longer had anything to lose and no longer needed to prove himself or be deserving of anything. "For twenty years" this had been going on (v. 41); now it was over. How can we fail to recall the elder son in the parable of the so-called prodigal son, who "became angry and refused to go in" there, as a "slave" of his father, which he felt he had been forced to be "these many years" (Lk. 15:28ff)?

A sort of miracle then occured, which speaks eloquently of the relationship between anger and truth: this was the first time in his life that Jacob grew angry, and it was precisely in this explosion of anger that he gave expression, if unconsciously, to the drama of his father Isaac. This drama had up until now weighed upon his own existence without his ever having been able to name it:

> If the God of my father, the God of Abraham and the *Fear of Isaac*,
> had not been on my side, [he says to Laban]
> surely now you would have sent me away empty-handed.
> God saw my affliction and the labour of my hands.
> (Gen. 31:42)

What the TOB version considers a "divine title," Chouraqui translates with a more human expression: "the trembling of Isaac." As if Jacob had always felt, without realizing it, that the "God of his father" inspired fear and trembling in his father. As if Jacob had felt that his father was still living under the threat of an incomprehensible sacrifice.

But the miracle is not in the awakening of Jacob's consciousness – which in any case is purely hypothetical, since when one speaks truthfully under the effect of a liberating anger, it is as if something were speaking louder than oneself, the meaning of which we may not fully grasp. The miracle lies in the fact that the burden of his father, having become his own burden as well, now seemed in Jacob's eyes to be indivisible from God who saw his "affliction and the labour of his hands": the God of his grandfather Abraham, the God of promises kept who ultimately delivers justice – from the moment when we are prepared to fight for justice to be done.

The rest of the miracle is that Jacob's first confrontation leads to the conclusion of a covenant proposed by Laban, a non-aggression pact with the demarcation of a line that is not to be crossed in the direction of the other's territory. But the most spectacular fruit of Jacob's development is in what follows: Laban swears to keep his word "by the God of Abraham and the God of Nahor – the God of their father,"[37] while Jacob swears by "the Fear of Isaac" his father (v. 53). This no doubt suggests that, in Jacob's eyes, there was no longer any need to fear or to flee from this God who had aroused fear and trembling in his father; what is more, Jacob could henceforth put his trust in God even to the point of invoking his Name in order that justice might be respected between himself and his uncle. The following verse, which concludes this key chapter in the patriarch's development, could give the impression that Jacob has exorcised his father's traumatic past, of which he had until then been a prisoner. It was he who now organized a sacrifice on the mountain, but in the most reassuring and convivial of celebrations. The threat of sacrifice on Mount Moriah had been eradicated from Jacob's spiritual space for good:

> So Jacob swore by the Fear of his father Isaac,
> and Jacob offered a sacrifice on the mountain.
> He called his kinsfolk to eat bread.
> And they ate bread and tarried all night on the mountain
> (v. 53ff).[38]

This time Jacob verified that his dream spoke the truth: twenty years before, on the way to his exile, he had dreamed of a ladder on which the angels of God were ascending and descending, and the One who spoke to him then was "the Lord, the God of Abraham your father and the God of Isaac" – a God full of concern for Jacob, the same God who was the God of his father and his grandfather, the God who keeps His promises. Upon awakening, Jacob felt so good in the presence of this God that he called the rocky spot Bethel, the "house of God," and made a vow that if he should return safe and sound to the house of his father, "then the Lord shall be my God" (28:10-22). It would take him twenty years to find this God of Abraham and Isaac once again, this God who at the end of Jacob's stay with Laban came to confirm that He would continue to support Jacob's desire for a free life. Twenty years to rid God of the "parasite" of the death-dealing image with which he had saddled Him as a result of the "trembling of Isaac" and of his family history.

If he had never gotten in touch with and allowed his anger to come out, how could Jacob have "slain" this Fear of Isaac, which prevented him from being himself? Certainly he had not yet done with fear entirely. The imminent confrontation with his brother, Esau, caused him far more anguish than the struggle with Laban. But there is no doubt that the archaic – almost sacred – source of his fear of affirming himself had been uprooted for good. Indeed the night before facing Esau, this is how Jacob invoked God:

> God of my father Abraham and *God of my father Isaac*,
> O Lord who said to me:
> Return to your country and to your kindred, and I will do you good ... (32:10)

From now on it would be impossible to flee. There was no other option but to trust in the word of this God – as we would say today, "you will get through it." The story makes us think of our own experiences. It is the crucial moment when we can no longer turn back – there is something irreversible that prevents us from going backwards (in this case, the pact made with Laban) – but when we feel unable to overcome the obstacle looming ahead. We are stopped short by the inevitable, we are convinced that the road leads in that direction, but to follow it seems to require no less a superhuman effort than moving a mountain. Yet the point is precisely that Jacob is not asked to move Mount Moriah, but to climb it, to sojourn upon it and to invoke there the God of covenants and of companionable meals! For the moment, the panic of finding himself face to face with the brother who had wished to kill him twenty years ago, when they last saw each other, erased all the pain and frustration of the past. The simple announcement of Esau's imminent arrival with "four hundred men" made Jacob "greatly afraid and distressed" (32:7). One might say that he was no longer in touch with his anger. He could see nothing but his own wrongs towards Esau.

Many commentators have struggled to paint a picture of a Jacob who is cunning, weak and irresponsible. No doubt we show greater understanding when we have (had) the same problem of fear of confrontation and were aware of it. If we do not feel obliged to find, at all costs, in Jacob's actions and gestures proof of his need to manipulate, we will be all the more sensitive to his desperate search for peaceful solutions that takes up all of chapter 32, until he decides to cross the Jabbok himself to meet Esau and his four hundred men. Let us not try to imagine that his pathetic prayer addressed to the God of promises (vv. 10-14), as well as his decision to spend the night alone before crossing the torrent, were final efforts to put pressure on God to manifest Himself and place Himself clearly on Jacob's side.[39] Let us simply note that certain confrontations can seem so terrifying, in view of the emotional charge they acquire over time, that we only resolve to take them on if pushed by events that have us up against the wall – the wall in Jacob's case being the pact with Laban, and thus a promise that has for the first time been given and received in an irreversible manner.

Reformulating the question God put to Adam in Genesis 3:11 after he had eaten the fruit in the garden of Eden ("who told you that you were naked?"), M. Balmary puts it in terms that could be addressed equally to Cain red with anger and to Jacob bowing down before Esau: "Who made you swallow this humiliating word? Who harmed you by words, with so great a harm that you no longer believed in yourself or in me?"[40] The fear of confrontation is not necessarily the sign of a cowardly nature. If I am paralyzed by the fear of confronting another with my truth, I have other things to do than to hold myself in contempt. The God of the Bible does not do so. Each time, He questions human beings: What happened? Why are you suffering? You, Adam, what is it that destroyed the trust between us to the point that you can no longer look me in the face? On what sore spot has the serpent cleverly put pressure in your innermost being? And you, Cain, what kind of burning pulls you downwards, preventing you from spitting your rage in my face?[41] And you too, Jacob, you will soon have to raise your head – and "I shall be with you" as I promised. Even if it takes a whole night, you will end up confronting me as one finally ends up taking on one's past; your body, breaking free of its chains, will cry out to me at last of your suffering as a son who pledged allegiance to your mother, your wives, your father-in-law; your distress at not having had access to a father who was cruelly absent (all the more so since he was in fact right there); your sense of being torn as a son caught in a conflict of loyalties that could find no other solution but a long exile.

To be forced to face up: that is the sign of each individual dysfunction. One can look upon all these years spent in foreign lands, on marriage, family and work, as the time needed for what I like to call "suffering without." The time had come for Jacob to move forward, to take his place in society, but by locking up his past suffering while continuing to behave under its influence. There had never been any OTHER to help him live autonomously in his difference; he had always "suffered without." No complaint, no anger … twenty years and not a day more: when the fruit is ripe, it falls from the tree! Esau was drawing near, and Jacob could already feel his presence in his surroundings – the very existence of this OTHER – as an aggression. Yet he knew nothing of his brother's true intentions. The messengers he sent to Esau with a greeting of peace brought back a terse report: "He is coming to meet you, and four hundred men are with him" (32:6). Were they armed? Did Esau get the message? What was keeping Jacob from finding out? If he gave in immediately to panic, it was because his inner world had always made him see others either as submissive people, easily manipulated, or else as aggressors whom one did best to avoid.[42]

The state of unknowing in which he remains informs us that it is over. The moment comes when we can no longer (as we have always done) eliminate the OTHER, whether by consuming it or by fleeing. The hour comes when we are offered a way out of our usual manner of "suffering without" the OTHER. By his mere appearance in the vicinity, Esau "exists against" Jacob, all the more so because he had indeed been very hostile towards him twenty years earlier. If it never occurred to Jacob that Esau might have changed, it is undoubtedly because he now had the need to feel that an OTHER is looking for him, as we might say. Someone was taking interest in Jacob and in his existence, even if for the moment he perceives nothing but hostility in such an interest. This is all I need, we sometimes say when we find ourselves backed up against a wall, forced to confront a situation on our own. It was useful, therefore,

for Jacob to imagine that Esau was coming to make trouble, for
in this way he was impelled to continue what he had begun with
Laban; an OTHER, more and more substantial before him, aroused
and called forth from him a capacity to confront the situation that
would surprise even him, as long as he did not look back, to the
"good" old days when he fled all conflicts.

"Someone is knocking at our door – insistently, with knocks that
hurt, 'the blows of fate' ... Afterwards, we understand that this
insistence on the part of others, of life, of the Other, was necessary
in order to awaken all our capacity to react, to arouse a new source
of energy unaware of itself as long as it did not hurl itself against
*the existence* of the OTHER."[43] The worst of it is that everything
unfolds as if, at a certain point, we were seeking or provoking this
confrontation ourselves, unconsciously. Struck down by anguish,
Jacob called upon God's help, telling him, more or less: "It is You
who has pushed me to return to my country. Until now you have
saved me, so now finish what You started, for I am afraid of Esau!"
Fear is a liar: it does not acknowledge that returning to his country
was just as much his own desire and that he would certainly have
expected to meet Esau sooner or later.

There is already something of "the OTHER" at work in the depths
of our being when, forced into a much-feared encounter, the
thought comes over us, or even slaps us in the face, that we have
given someone the very stick with which they will beat us. What
possessed me to wish to return home? Jacob may ask himself. What
possessed me to make this offering to the Lord, Cain might think, as
if I needed recognition, reassurance of my worth? This is precisely
L. Beirnaert's interpretation:[44] on that day, Cain ceased to exist only
for the sake of securing his mother's satisfaction, "undertaking to
engage himself in the way of loss," agreeing to renounce a part of
his enjoyment (of the fruit of the land he cultivates) in order to
offer them to the OTHER. Yet "oblation is a request: does it please
you? ... What am I worth to you? ... Cain is on the way to an
unforeseeable success, for through the very impetus of his rage, he
gains access to what he has been seeking without knowing it." It is
as if he had sought opposition: Someone facing him, "the Other"

against which he can throw himself, he the "son of an unknown father."[45]

The same astonishing process took place with Job, who continued to speak to his friends in spite of their deafness and their poisonous words. One would think that he needed to "rub against" them in order to feel that he is alive. To the degree that they resisted him and presented an obstacle, they constituted "the OTHER" who confronts him, and this "existence against" undoubtedly saved him from the worst pain of all: the one that engulfs all cries and all anger. His friends have one quality that is rarely found in our own societies: they allow themselves to be insulted by Job without abandoning him, and without letting him have the last word, as if their mission were to fan the flames of his anger so that he might, in spite of everything, remain in touch with his capacity to react.

> You whitewashers with lies!…you worthless physicians!…
> Your maxims are proverbs of ashes,
> your answers are answers of clay …
> How dare you comfort me with empty nothings?
> There is nothing left of your answers but falsehood.
> (Job 13:4, 12; 21:34)[46]

In other words, your way of speaking to me and answering me, your pretense of consoling me is nothing but a way of abandoning me, of being "false" to me, of betraying our friendship. This experience is fairly widespread: we say that it is in the difficult times that we find out who our true friends are, on whom we can really count. Job was neither heard nor supported, but he did not stop talking to his friends, as if his anger needed to be sharpened against their armour in order to push him more and more forcefully to address God directly. For a long time, Job had been entertaining the hope of being vindicated with God against the "whitewashers with lies." By talking to them, perhaps he was practising to speak to God: "But I would speak to Shaddai [the Almighty], and I desire to argue my case with El [=Elohim, God]."[47]

A perpetual merry-go-round of complaints and fury: the witnesses declare inadmissible the expression of a pain that they judge to be illegitimate. If the pain ought not to be (you're getting what you deserve; "that's your problem," we would say today), then complaint and fury are not permitted either. All of a sudden, the wrath of Job aggravated the violence of his friends. "Their hostile speeches are not merely an image of collective violence," René Girard writes, "they are a form of active participation in it. Job is well aware of this and denounces the verbal dismemberment to which he is subjected."[48] But the friends did something even worse, it seems to me: they used God to justify their own violence without even realizing it, unlike Job, who expressed his own anger authentically. The "mythology of divine vengeance" that Girard denounces[49] seems to me to explain quite well the poor interpretations of fundamentalists on all sides: it is so much easier to make God shoulder one's own fury and to sit in judgment over another person's anger!

In short, this is the ultimate form of moral harassment: God himself is involved, if we are to believe Job's entourage. Job's fury only aggravated the blindness of the witnesses regarding their own violence, and reinforced the self-satisfaction that is typical of those who imagine they have God on their side. In the end it became a spiritual harassment, the worst thing of all insofar as God ought to have been the last resort, a true "other" able and willing to accept complaint and fury, to take them seriously and transform them into the basis of a dialogue among equals.

This is why the Bible never ceases to denounce the kind of violence to another that involves taking God hostage to stifle untimely complaints and cries. Harassment causes the total isolation of the person through the destruction of any dialogue partner, of any face-to-face encounter. Thus we can understand that the enemies of Jesus hid behind the commandments of God in order to conceal (from themselves) their own violence, and what is more, to try to convince Jesus that if everyone has abandoned him, including God, it is because he no longer has the right to exist. Spiritual harassment can go that far. Yet, to a lesser degree, it can be said to begin as soon as we refuse to hear the complaint and the fury of a suffering person, and thus block the way to God by suggesting to him or her that it is ungrateful and unjust to be angry with God.

The unrelenting force of misfortune throughout life pushes many people to turn against Someone, even if they have never really had a relationship with him before. It makes no difference what name we give him. There is someone above us, something greater than us, there is He/She, *a Life* and *a Living One* whom we suddenly need to call to account. Did we invent this Someone? Could it be a fantasy? No, because for the moment He is too closely linked to whatever is boiling within us. He is within us, the first trace of a face-to-face encounter: this diffuse combativeness, this saturation and this energy of rebellion that pushes us to seek an OTHER on whom we can pour out what is overflowing in us. We may not necessarily be aware of it. Another human being can act as a mirror for us, reflecting back to us this complaint or this fury as being well and truly ours, and thereby confirming in us this teeming life that we do not yet realize is a longing to throw ourselves at an OTHER.

This is what Abel failed to do. Cain did not see his own ravaged face in the mirror that God held up to him. He thus addressed Abel, who seemingly did not hear him: "Cain said to his brother Abel, 'Let us go out to the field.' And when they were in the field, Cain rose up against his brother Abel and killed him" (Gen. 4:8). We do not know what Cain said, but he certainly engaged in dialogue. Elie Wiesel notes that Abel did nothing to help him, to make him feel his presence, to be his "ally before God":

> In the face of suffering, one has no right to turn away, not to see … When someone cries, and it is not you, he has rights over you even if his pain has been inflicted by your common God. Though too weak to oppose God, man is strong enough to defend his fellow-man or at least to dress his wounds.

As for Cain,

> [he] should have understood his brother's tragedy … to live with God causes no less anguish than to live without Him or against Him … Cain should have felt sorry for him, for man pays dearly for God's favors.[50]

Why is it that confrontation seems so terrifying, when the one we face finds it trivial, and when later we can even smile about it ("to think that I was sick with fear at the thought of opposing this person")? Why is there such a discrepancy between emotions and reality? We have alluded to the novelty of the thing: if it is the first time, there is good reason for being apprehensive of the least encounter that may be loaded with challenge or discord. But there may be an additional reason: the more the evil suffered was destructive and the pain repressed, the greater the risk that the accumulated anger will explode without warning like a fuse that blows. An excessive anger is probably on a par with the pain endured. It is easy today to see a person who is suffering greatly as a victim who always needs to complain. But are we so sure that his or her complaint has truly been heard, accepted and taken seriously? The refusal of the complaint of another is almost inevitably the sign of an intolerance that is at least as great as the expression of anger.

Seen from this perspective, the attitude of Job's friends may seem much more positive. Each came from his own country to "console and comfort" his friend. They wept aloud and raised their voices, mourned and sat with him on the ground for seven days and seven nights, and no one spoke a word to him, "for they saw that his suffering was very great" (Job 2:13). Seven is the symbolic number evoking completion, fulfillment, totality – all the time it takes Job to go to the final point of annihilation of words through excessive suffering. It is the silent presence of these loving human beings as long as is necessary, and the faithful density of their bodies beside him, that will eventually enable him to breathe forth his complaint in words. Why, then, could they not accept, with the same unconditional availability, the fury that would subsequently issue from Job's mouth? Instead of losing control for chapters on end, why do they not see that this fury makes it possible for Job to take a great step forward?

Yet, is silence appropriate here? What would happen if the author had said "and they kept silent for seven days and seven nights for they saw that his *anger* was very great"? No doubt Elie Wiesel would say that this would be to behave like Abel, pushing the other back to his incommunicable violence and impelling him to take action. We can no longer simply accuse others of being violent and refuse to respond to them. If we treat their anger as inadmissible, we put them in danger – and ourselves, too, in the end. The friends of Job at least confirmed the anger that dwelled in him. Even if they sought to ban it, even if their words were rather inauthentic, they answered him, they were thus "the OTHER" against whom the inner violence of Job could find support. Without this limit that they imposed on him, Job might have been swamped by the excess of his fury, to the point of being paralyzed by it. His friends appeared to be short-sighted precisely because they acted as limits in the face of a Job who was threatened by a devastating anger. Are we really so far from these sorts of dramas, recurring in our societies, where individuals who are known to be gentle suddenly turn into killers when they reach the point where they can no longer bear to suppress the anger that is in them? By being unable to endure the verbal violence of another, we deprive them of that face-to-face encounter, and send the person back into the depths of his or her anger. Acknowledging this fact might make us aware that we also need confrontation, and that his or her problem points to our own.

Returning now to Jacob, we should recall his legendary physical strength, often mentioned on the basis of Genesis 29:10[51] and the nocturnal struggle at the Jabbok (32:23-30). The Jewish commentators certainly move in the direction of this fear brought about by the rise of the counter-violence within us. Beneath the fear of confronting another may lurk the fear of "killing" them. This is how the Midrash Rabbah understands the great anguish felt by Jacob in 32:8: "For he thought: If he [Esau] prevails against me, will he not slay me; while if I am stronger than he, will I not slay him?"[52] For A. Abécassis and J. Eisenberg, the question is phrased exactly in these terms, in society as in one's personal life:

> Jacob returns to his country and in order to be able to live there, he would have to *kill* or *be killed* ... All relationships are aggressive. We are always obliged to struggle to be recognized, to exist. In politics as in the economy, either you kill or you are

killed! If you do not devour your opponent, he is the one who will engulf you ... [Co-existence] constitutes the veritable goal of the human adventure, which Jewish mysticism refers to as the "world of Reparation."[53]

Before he was capable of naming his fear, Jacob yielded to panic. Yet along the way he had just "seen the messengers of God" – a powerful and reassuring experience of the Presence at his side: this is "God's camp," he had exclaimed. Resolved to join God's side, one might say, he called the place "Mahanaim," meaning "the two camps" (32:2ff.), as if to say, perhaps, "together we will face Esau." But afterwards the messengers went away and returned with the news that Esau was approaching, in the company of four hundred men. Jacob's panic caused him immediately to forget that he had joined sides with God. He divided his whole caravan into "two companies" of a very earthly nature, thinking to himself: "If Esau comes to one company and destroys it, then the company that is left will escape" (32:9). God's camp slipped his mind entirely, and Jacob was reduced to his horizontal vision of things: it is not surprising that he fell back into his usual rut and quickly thought up a strategy of partial flight!

Yet Jacob had changed. No sooner did he obey his dysfunctionality as a man condemned since time immemorial to cope on his own, but he began, without warning, to pray, as if God had mysteriously established his camp in him after all. The company that is left will escape? Escape? Always and evermore? No, Jacob, pray and face up! The time of prayer (32:10-13) allowed him to review the road he had travelled, to remind himself of the promises of Life, to name his emotions and feelings, in all truthfulness, and thus to take stock of his own powerlessness. Authentic prayer leads to the (re)discovery of the reality principle. It is useless to try to flee: this is the way things are; I feel incapable of facing it all alone. "Deliver me, please, from the hand of my brother, from the hand of Esau, for I am afraid of him; he may come and kill us all, the mothers with the children" (32:11). By admitting the worst-case scenario – that it is possible no one will escape – Jacob was able to go to the depths of his fear, where all that was left was the promise made by God: "Yet you

have said, 'I will surely do you good'" (32:12). At last there is an
OTHER face to face with him, and if he believes, if he trusts that this
OTHER wishes to do him good, then he will have the strength to
confront the OTHER who, in his eyes, wishes him ill.

The first fruits of prayer are peace (Jacob would no longer speak
of his fear, but was completely absorbed in the preparations for the
encounter) and discernment, linked to the fact that he could now
recover his footing in his own desire. For his was a desire for peace
and reconciliation. He would thus replace his military strategy with
a peace offering: sending numerous flocks, one after the other, in
the form of a gift to Esau. His intention may be revealed by the two
verses (21ff.) that precede the struggle on the banks of the Jabbok.
In the message destined for Esau, Jacob insisted that his servants
say: "moreover he is *behind us*," and at the end, the text says, "So
the *present* passed on ahead of him" (or above, or before him), as if
Jacob had wished to shelter himself behind his gifts. And indeed,
all these flocks became but one gift: for it is the act of offering that
counts here.

Until this point, Jacob had always expected to be given things. For
the first time it was he who was offering, and this amounted more
to a choice of life than to a behaviour dictated by fear. Offering is
indeed a way of saying yes to a lack, to a loss, to the risk of "not
having enough" and to seeing death looming on the horizon. Was
it not the time spent in prayer that opened Jacob up to this third
way? We do not have to resign ourselves helplessly to the sole
alternatives of "kill" or "be killed." We can go to face the OTHER
with a face that asks. It should be possible to read on our face that
we lack the OTHER and that we are willing to risk *ourselves* in the
relationship, for in choosing the face-to-face encounter we choose
to be in relationship. This is a strong echo of the Jewish tradition,
in which we find an explanation for the rejection of Cain's offering
in his inappropriate manner of offering: by offering "the fruit of the
earth," Cain did not risk his own person, whereas Abel gave the
best of himself by bringing "firstlings of *his* flock, their *fat portions*"
(Gen. 4:3ff.), and thus of the best of what he had – as they say, "the
crème de la crème," as M. Balmary aptly observes.[54]

It may be said that the gift of Jacob served both to protect him
from the violence of Esau and to protect Esau from his own anger,
as if the act of offering opened up a space, creating first of all a safe
space for the person offering. Long suppressed, the anger of Jacob
towards the whole world – everyone else! – could make him turn
completely against Esau. It was because of Esau, after all, that Jacob
had had to spend twenty years living in exile, paying a high price
for the dysfunctionality of his parents, of whom all that time he
heard nothing. If the gift was to *precede* Jacob, this was because it
constituted a boundary, a demarcation, a signpost able to contain
his counter-violence. We speak of "fleeing forward" when we are
faced with behaviours we can no longer master. Jacob did not wish
to flee forward in a cycle of violence that would make him destroy
the face of Esau even before having seen it. But he would not turn
back, either, for fear that the face would be destroyed before he
had come face to face with his brother. And so the gift – the act
of offering – bought him some time: they were not yet ready to
meet each other directly, but they were moving closer in a *climate
of gratuitousness* that suggests the possibility of an OTHER life.

Jacob never before envisaged with as much lucidity and realism the
scene of his encounter with Esau. Only two verses remain before
the nocturnal combat that precedes this scene:

> and you shall say, "Moreover your servant Jacob is behind us."
> For he thought, "I may appease him with the present that goes
> ahead of me [literally, *which goes for my face*],
> and afterwards I shall see *his face*;
> perhaps he will accept me/accept my face."
> So the present passed on ahead of him [literally, *on his face*];
> And he himself spent that night in the camp. (32:20-21)

The movement back and forth between "his face" and "my face,"
and the role of the gift in this story, perhaps show us how to clear
this third way. The gift – my acceptance of the loss, of the risk of
being without and of dying – goes before me, "to [protect] my
face" and at the same time to appease Esau and soothe the burning
of his past wounds. "I will cover his face [with the gift]" is indeed
a Hebrew formula to say "I will appease him," as one might say,

"whatever you do or whatever you may have done, I will shield you": in so doing, Jacob was also seeking to protect Esau from his own counter-violence (even if I am mad at him, I will cover him). Then – and only then – I will look him in the eye, "I will see his face" and the reflection of the gift will still be on his face, and perhaps he will "accept my face" because he will see the reflection of the gift on it as well. Something in the nature of a gratuitous relationship may have refashioned both our faces. And indeed that is what would happen.

Many commentators have stressed the proximity, in Hebrew, of [mahanèh], the "camp," and [minhah], the "gift." These are the last words before the famous struggle. "The gift passes on his face," as the text literally reads – this will be visible on his face, that he is offering himself to the relationship, whatever its risks and perils – and therefore "he spent that night in *the camp*." The military strategy, born of fear, was abandoned once and for all. Jacob gave up the notion of founding two companies and recovered his unity – a single "camp," which he knew from the very beginning was also God's camp. Remaining with only one camp, being on one side only, the one that God invested with our consent, escaping internal division as well as division with others, is to experience an unexpected gift, one that strangely enough comes from our own initiative.

But if the camp is like a gift, the opposite is also true: the gift is like a camp, a protected space where we can relax and meet others with the best that is in us, addressing ourselves first of all to what is best in them. The gift – the act of offering – comes from beyond us. As the text suggests, this is "what we have in [our] hand" once panic has stripped us of everything, and our confidence in the word of the OTHER suddenly calls up before our eyes a future that is truly ours and a life that is abundant. It is as though by praying, Jacob chose to put an end to his flight: before being forced to confront Esau, he wanted to learn to receive a gift, without usurping it and without deserving it. This is the only alternative: to flee once again, or to receive the word of an OTHER as one receives a gift. How do we know that Jacob made the right choice? He stayed alive, he

saw his being bear fruit in countless seeds of life, he would have an
abundant harvest, and he would have only to "take" the gift that
was already in the process of "passing on his face." God's camp was
once again his own.

> Yet you have said, "I will surely do you good,
> and make your offspring as the sand of the sea,
> which cannot be counted because of their number."
> So [Jacob] spent that night there,
> and from what he had *in his hand* he took
> a present for his brother Esau
>
> …
>
> So the present passed on ahead of him;
> and he himself spent that night in the camp. (32:12ff. and 21)

It is in prayer – the invocation of the OTHER – that he said yes to
loss, to a lack, to the risk of death, and thus a decisive yes to life,
his own and that of others, at the same time pushing away the violence of suicide and homicide. "When [violence] appears," notes
L. Beirnaert, "it is the sign that the fundamental question has been
raised, in the 'no' that we say to death."[55] This is the inevitable
moment that every human being must face one day. To choose
oneself, to prefer one's own life – though without having to "kill"
another – is to say yes to *oneself in one's incompleteness*. That is without a doubt the third way: instead of killing or being killed, getting
rid of some ballast, choosing to stay alive while under the threat
of non-life … and discovering that this choice gives us the Living
One himself, in abundance.

"I have set before you life and death, blessings and curses. Choose
life so that you and your descendants may live, loving the LORD
your God, obeying him, and holding fast to him; for that means life
to you…" (Deut. 30:19ff.). And you, Jacob, and all those who are
under reprieve from death – which is the majority of your brothers and sisters – you are perfectly capable of making your own this
blessing that is your life as it is. At the very moment when you risk
locking yourself into the illusion that Life is not big enough for
both you and the other, you can always, unlike Cain, choose to
look at me and to speak to me, the Living One, for I have room

to spare. Your blessing is "what comes in your hands." It is to be seized as one seizes a lifeline: an OTHER relationship is constantly being offered at the point where all relationship seems destined to meet a violent end.

Jacob, here, said yes to Jacob. He had to choose himself for he had already been chosen. In Romans 9:13, the apostle Paul recalls the declaration God makes in the Hebrew Bible: "I have loved Jacob, but I have hated Esau" (Mal. 1:2) – a Hebraism that signifies God's preference for Jacob. In fact, Esau also received a full blessing, and said so himself (Gen. 25:23; 33:9), while Jacob would not be favoured during his life's journey. We might say that we are all the preferred ones of God, but that it is up to us to prefer *ourselves*; some of us seize hold of this preference and others do not believe in it, or not very much. Thus it is that the Church Fathers disapproved of Esau for having had contempt for his rights as the first-born, preferring a mess of pottage to this great blessing. As St. John Chrysostom explains: "Esau considered himself to hold pride of place, by birthright or by his father's preference for him, and yet was suddenly found to be bereft of all this ... because of the evil of his ways."[56]

Along the same lines, A. Abécassis notes that God could have preferred Cain, but refused to have a relationship with him founded on fear of death and of suffering.[57] It seems to me that it was up to Cain to choose life, and the blessing that is in itself life, by responding to God, showing him his face ravaged by shame and the fear of death. Is this not the way he chose himself, since he doubted that God had chosen him, and is it not at that point that God's preference would have come upon him? Through the story of Cain, God may be telling us in the end about our own self-election: it is up to you to choose to be "the preferred of God," rather than the murderer of the other and of yourself! But "preferred" in the sense of "chosen to face Him," the One who can endure the violence of your emotions.

By the simple fact of praying, Jacob could be said to have chosen to be God's preferred one: that is, loveable enough to be taken into account. To name this fear that pushed him towards a blind violence was enough to deliver him from its grip: complaint had replaced explosive emotion. Throughout the Bible, God shows himself to be the sole OTHER who is never tired of our "Jeremiads" – Jeremiah having been the most pathetic of the suffering prophets, in spite of the pejorative meaning of the word. In the story of Jacob, the time for complaining is expressed in spatial terms: he prayed and he "spent that night there, and from what he had in his hand he took a present for his brother Esau" (32:14). "There" was no doubt also the place of his complaint, addressed to the One who receives and accepts these emotions that we do not know what to do with.

There is a privileged place, explicitly offered by Christ to "all you that are weary and are carrying heavy burdens" (Matt. 11:28), tired of carrying a past of injustices suffered, of compromises, of more or less contained violence, and crushed by an anger that you turn back upon yourself: in short, in danger of exploding. And the "I" who is ever alive, of whom Christ becomes the word, adds something that resembles the word given to Jacob ("I will be with you," "I will do you good"): "And I will give you rest." If this rest that Jacob tastes while praying is transformed immediately in his hand into a gift for Esau, this was because the most intimate of his prayers of complaint addressed to God had opened, without delay, a space for himself and for others. Confessing our complaint to the OTHER is the best possible way to channel our anger.[58]

# 3 Instead of murder, a violence that speaks the truth

> This awareness of emotions is the fundamental emotional compe-
> tence ... When we say "stop that!" to a child whose anger has led
> him to hit a playmate, we may stop the hitting, but the anger still
> simmers ... Self-awareness has a more powerful effect on strong,
> aversive feelings: the realization "This is anger I'm feeling" offers
> a greater degree of freedom − not just the option not to act on
> it, but the added option to try to let go of it.[59]

"Emotion" − (with the Latin root *motere,* "to move," plus the
prefix *e,* connoting "to move away") as the etymology suggests,
and as a scientific psychology that is far from having explored the
entire landscape of feelings has already confirmed − is linked to the
tendency to action. "Each emotion prepares the body for a very
different kind of response: With *anger* blood flows to the hands,
making it easier to grasp a weapon or strike at a foe; heart rate
increases, and a rush of hormones such as adrenaline generates a
pulse of energy strong enough for vigorous action."[60] Today there
is neurobiological information that allows us to identify how our

brain centres govern and temper our emotions. From this it appears
that we have sufficiently diversified physiological resources to be
able to free ourselves from slavery to our emotions (or passions,
as they used to be called). Indeed, the increase in connections between the neurons gives us a wide range of possible reactions – for
instance, in face of anger:

> The neocortex is the seat of thought: it contains the centers that
> put together and comprehend what the senses perceive. It adds to
> a feeling what we think about it – and allows us to have feelings
> about ideas, art, symbols, imaginings ... The neocortex allows for
> the subtlety and complexity of emotional life, such as the ability
> *to have feelings about our feelings* ... The amygdala's extensive web
> of neural connections allows it, during an emotional emergency,
> to capture and drive much of the rest of the brain – including
> the rational mind ... The prefrontal cortex seems to be at work
> when someone is fearful or enraged, but stifles or controls the
> feeling in order to deal more effectively with the situation at
> hand ... The right prefrontal lobes are a seat of negative feel-
> ings like fear and aggression, while the left lobes keep those raw
> emotions in check, probably by inhibiting the right lobe ... The
> left prefrontal lobe, in short, seems to be part of a neural circuit
> that can switch off, or at least dampen down, all but the strongest
> negative surges of emotion.[61]

The slap in the face that seems to come of its own volition is thus
not inevitable, even if our hand is truly itching. Our anger does not
condemn us to kill (with or without quotation marks). It pushes
us to act, certainly, but in more than one possible direction. In this
case, scientific knowledge might stop us in time: "Oh, it's my right
lobe that is acting up!" It is reassuring at such a time to know that,
in order to gain this sort of perspective, we are basing ourselves on
the real – our left frontal lobe – without denying the reality of the
anger we have experienced. This sheds new light on the story of a
slap in the face that has always posed a problem.

> You have heard that it was said, "An eye for an eye and a tooth
> for a tooth." But I say to you, Do not resist an evildoer. But
> if anyone strikes you on the right cheek, turn the other also.
> (Matt. 5:38ff)

This behaviour is as unexpected as it is unimaginable. During his trial, Jesus himself would not put this into practice literally, but rather symbolically, yet in a way that was very real.[62] The point is that human beings are capable of reacting to anger in other ways than impulsively. Remaining at the stage of the burning cheek would be a way of fleeing, of self-destructing and of consenting to being reduced to an object that is beaten and humiliated. Returning violence blow for blow – a tooth for a tooth – is not a solution either, even if Jesus does not in that context evoke the spectre of the escalation of violence, no more than God saved Cain from the risk involved in turning his anger into an irreparable act. It would be very motivating, however, to hear good, convincing reasons for restraining ourselves from entering the vicious circle of "anti… anti …" Why did Jesus not say more clearly what could automatically defuse our need for vengeance? Perhaps because he wanted us to find out for ourselves? Or perhaps because non-violence does not need legitimation, any more than human life itself does?

What Jesus does say clearly, however, is "evil" – in Greek, a masculine or a neuter noun – that does violence to me and awakens a reaction on my part. Just before the scene in question, he had been speaking of taking a position: "Let your word be 'Yes, Yes' or 'No, No'; anything more than this comes from the evil one" (Matt. 5:37). Non-violence cannot exist, then, unless one rejects all compromise or distortion of the true word. "Evil" is "evil" even if it is someone close to us and whom we would prefer to consider a friend. To banish violent behaviour, we must call it by its real name. We could designate a moment of pause: "Do not rise up against the evil one"; in present-day terms, let your left frontal lobe act on your rush of anger by repeating within you "no to the evil one!" or "it's your violence, not mine!" or even "evil is before me, it is not me." A few seconds may suffice to allow me to "turn myself around" before it is too late, and this is precisely the verb Matthew uses here, as he does in 18:3 as well, where we are told that in order to forgive, we must "turn back and become like little children."

If I have a bit of time to turn myself around, I become capable of "turning *towards him also* the other [cheek]."[63] If someone strikes me, if he needs to eliminate me in order to take my place, it is because without realizing it, he feels threatened. By turning towards him this *other* part of myself (connected with the famous left lobe!) with which I have got in touch with myself, I present another facet of myself: temperate, welcoming, unarmed. He may never have seen me in this light. He wanted to take me by force, yet I offer what I have no fear of losing: face, that is, an uncovered, open face.

Here the parallel text in Luke reminds us of the famous gift of Jacob: "If anyone strikes you on the cheek, *offer* the other also" (6:29). What we have here is the double meaning of presenting (or offering) – becoming present to the adversary (present your other cheek also) and offering him the other cheek. What it amounts to, then, is giving the other voluntarily the place he or she wanted to take by force. If the words spoken by Jesus are not simply a "clever trick" to disarm the violent, it is perhaps up to us to see what advantages they hold for us. That is the place of security that prayer opened up in Jacob – an impregnable space that he could offer also to Esau, immediately after his prayer. Jacob's gift – several kinds of livestock – itself bears the traces of this space that is indispensable to the lives of all beings. In giving his instructions, Jacob specified: "put a space between drove and drove" (Gen. 32:17b). To break down the symmetrical violence, Jacob chose to present to his brother, or to offer him, this OTHER space where there is room for everyone. And if he is able to do so, it is because he has himself entered there during his time of prayer.

As for Cain, the Midrash seems to grant him extenuating circumstances, for, as it affirms, he did not know that murder could exist, nor, therefore, that he himself was capable of killing, nor that the law of God forbade it: "He did not know what he was doing," comments J. Eisenberg.[64] That is indeed the reaction of many murderers, taken aback by what they have done without wanting to, without having had the least notion beforehand of what they would do. By contrast, anyone who lucidly accepts his or her own anger looks to the day when he or she will be capable of killing, under the sway of violent emotion, and realizes that the responsibility would not necessarily fall on those primarily responsible for his or her own misfortunes. Courage and a great deal of honesty are needed to admit that "we could kill our father or mother" or someone else close to us, so all-encompassing is the violence we experienced. But to *say* this (and preferably to someone who is empathetic) is precisely what opens up a space that will prevent us from *doing* it.

This does not necessarily mean that "we know what we are doing." In effect, we are still eating the fruit of the tree of knowledge of Good and Evil when, even if we see ourselves clearly, we believe we can hide behind a murderous rage. If God did not alert Cain to the murderous act that was lurking in him, it is because only the relationship with God could dissuade him from committing it. To know intellectually the risk of killing is far from being enough – this happens only to other people, we think. Cain's parents were warned of the danger of a violence that was doubly murderous: "You may freely eat of every tree of the garden; but of the tree of the knowledge of good and evil you shall not eat, for in the day that you eat of it you shall die" (Gen. 2:16ff). When we think we know Good and Evil, those who are good and those who are evil, thus eating of that tree without even realizing it, we face the threat of reducing others and ourselves to the image we have of them, deformed by the anger that controls us. This anger is fearsome, for it adds to our fantasy of knowing others and ourselves: "I know you, you are a liar, you are warped, and you will never change." We die twice: once by being deprived of this other who is so well "known" that he or she has disappeared as other, and secondly by no longer knowing who we are ourselves, since, having hidden our own violence, we are disconnected from our most profound being and are no longer in relation to any other person.

We are no doubt justified in thinking that the prayer of Jesus on the cross concerns all human beings, insofar as even neutrality does not shelter them from violence: forgive them for none of us, ever, knows exactly what we are doing, what we are allowing others to do, much less what we are capable of doing. Ever since the Garden of Eden, in place of this unknowing, God offers a relationship of trust with Him to those humans who imagine they can leave behind their relationships of violence through their own ideas of Good and Evil. If Cain is not aware of what he will do, this is because God relies entirely on Cain's capacity to enter into a relationship of trust with Him. If Cain had foresworn killing Abel only for fear of punishment – thus under the constraint of a greater violence – this would have meant for him another kind of death: left intact, his rage would have continued to fester within. If no OTHER receives our anger that bears the truth that is ours at that moment, if an OTHER asks us to share the anger but we lock ourselves up within it, then we truly place ourselves in danger ... and let us remember that there are many ways of killing and being killed!

In other words, our freedom is complete, but not where we expect to find it. God himself cannot but stammer into Cain's ear: "If you do well, will you not be ... lifted up? And if you do not do well, sin is lurking at the door [= the relationship with God is broken]; its desire is for you, but you must master it." (Gen. 4:7) The somewhat laborious style suggests that in the eyes of God, human freedom is not easy to accept. The passage is in an elliptic form that is almost impossible to translate, according to J. Eisenberg,[65] who understands this key verse of the Bible to be a strong affirmation of our free will. If ... if not ... and you must master it or it will master you: what can make us believe in our capacity to dominate our impulses?

The physiology of the human brain confirms God's trust in Cain's capacity for analysis and understanding. We really do have what it takes to observe and decipher our own fits of anger. As Augustine wrote:

> [Scripture] subjects the mind itself to God, that He may rule and aid it, and the passions, again, to the mind, to moderate and bridle them, and turn them to righteous uses. In our ethics, we do not so much inquire whether a pious soul is angry, as why he is angry; not whether he is sad, but what is the cause of his sadness; not whether he fears, but what he fears. For I am not aware that any right thinking person would find fault with anger at a wrongdoer which seeks his amendment, or with sadness which intends relief to the suffering, or with fear lest one in danger be destroyed.[66]

It is as though, from the very start, God Himself sets an example: "Why did this burn you and why has your countenance fallen?" And in the face of Cain's silence, God seems to be looking for the words to bring this human being out of his powerlessness: if … and if not … Your future is in your hands, you are free to turn in a different direction. You can "do well" – the text does not say what, since it is not trying to provide a recipe – you are equipped to "lift up," referring to his fallen face. What matters is what you want. If the goal you seek is to lift up your head, it is this goal that will show you how to "do well." And, indeed, this verb "to lift up" (na'sa'] is rich with meaning:[67] it means at one and the same time to accept, take into consideration, raise the eyes or the voice, look someone in the eye and speak, desire, endure, carry and forgive. Thus, you can act, work at accepting yourself with the negative image you have of yourself at the moment, take yourself into consideration (devote time and attention to what you feel), *raise your eyes* by turning (once again, this image) towards the OTHER, by *desiring* in spite of everything the face-to-face encounter, by *enduring* humiliation (or burning), by *carrying* your head high and thus *forgiving* (or letting go of) the evil that was done to you. All this is within your reach.

It is here that God adds: "sin is lurking at the door and its desire is for you, but you must master it!" Like a wild animal ready to burst into your home, sin (the rupture of the relationship) obeys only your orders. According to the rabbis, it stands at the door to your heart and not within your heart – a way of saying that you have complete freedom. And we should remember that in the Bible, the heart is the seat not only of the emotions but also of the intellect – or, more precisely, it is the "decision centre in which emotion and intellect necessarily intersect."[68] As a result, when under the effect of anger and pain, your body and psyche are in a state of "submersion," as Daniel Goleman puts it, give your emotional intelligence the time to express itself. "Be the gatekeeper of your heart," said Evagrius Pontius, a second-century Greek Church Father, "and don't allow any thought to enter without interrogating it first: interrogate them one by one, saying to them: 'Are you on our side or on the side of the enemies?' And if it belongs with us, it will fill you with peace."[69] In other words, is this particular impulse in your best interests? Is it truly likely to bring peace within you? Think of the long-term benefits!

In the Palestinian recensions of the Targum (a translation-explanation of the Bible in Aramaic), the question is raised about the use of anger. Genesis 4:7 is transcribed as follows: "In your hand I have placed power over the evil inclination. Its desire will be towards you, but you will have dominion over it, whether to be innocent or to sin."[70] What will you do with this inner boiling that makes you "desire" to break off the relationship, and thus to annihilate the other in one way or another? In any case, you will be able to dominate it, but will you truly use it to break off all relationship, or will you transform it into an energy for seeking justice?

The text does not say that we are responsible for the existence of the evil inclination – of this natural spiral of anger that *turns* us away from the other – but that God places it under our control. Is this madness on God's part? Or is it rather God's way of associating us with his work of creation? This is the view of P. Beauchamp, based on Genesis 1:26ff:

> 'Let us make humankind in our image ... and let them have dominion over all the wild animals'; God created them male and female, blessed them and said: 'Be fruitful and multiply, and fill the earth and subdue it; and have dominion over the fish of the sea and over the birds of the air and over every living thing that moves upon the earth.' When humans have dominion over the animals, they are in the image of God ... This ruling function will be exercised by means of human language: everyone knows that, to command animals one has to speak to them ... This is a power of command that is not violent; it is given by the tenth of the words of *creation*, which confers upon them the same solemnity as on the nine previous words.[71]

The death-dealing inclination that anger brings to the fore is to be tamed as one tames a wild beast in order to harness its energy without danger.

Now let us return to the Targum. It is as if God were saying to Cain: power to dominate your anger, that you have; sooner or later, you will dominate it. But the question is: will you give up seeking justice and break off the relationship, or do you wish to enter into a process of "justification"? You felt that you were treated unfairly, you need to call someone to account, and *for this* you cannot forgo the relationship. You aspire to justice. Yet the question of justice cannot be asked except within the context of interpersonal relationships. By breaking off your relationship with the other, by "killing" him, you bid farewell to your quest for justification: it is you who becomes guilty, although you still feel that you have been treated unfairly.

Seen from this perspective, anger may be regarded as that which makes our thirst for justice glow with heat: we see red at something we would not even have noticed in a state of indifference. The flooding of our anger backs us up against a wall, whether we like it or not. We have to choose, to come out from our "submersion," give ourselves time to weigh the pros and cons, put a stopper in the anger in order to be able to pursue justice on its own turf (that of relationships) – not to repress the anger in order to end the relationship, thinking that we have thereby put an end to the suffering caused by this or that person.

At no point does God reproach Cain for his anger. We could even say that God is the first to recognize the justice of his cause. By showing that He is willing to listen to the reason for Cain's anger, God gives him the right to live it out. Jesus, too, does not condemn that which, after all, is first and foremost an irrepressible feeling. In a few very explicit verses, he evokes the spiral of anger when, thinking we can "liquidate" it through our insults and aggression, we find ourselves in hell. And then there is the spiral of the other's anger: when we do not ourselves take the initiative to re-establish the relationship, we end up locked into an inextricable situation.

> You have heard that it was said to those of ancient times,
> 'You shall not murder'; and 'whoever murders shall be liable
> to judgement.'
> But I say to you that if you are angry with a brother or sister,

you will be liable to judgement;
and if you insult a brother or sister, you will be liable to the
council;
and if you say, 'You fool', you will be liable to the hell of fire.
So when you are offering your gift at the altar,
if you remember that your brother or sister has something
against you,
leave your gift there before the altar and go;
first be reconciled [literally: change your attitude] to your
brother or sister,
and then come and offer your gift.
Come to terms quickly with your accuser
while you are on the way to court with him,
or your accuser may hand you over to the judge, and the judge
to the guard,
and you will be thrown into prison.
Truly I tell you, you will never get out until you have paid the
last penny.
(Matt. 5:21-26)

Truly you will never get out; it will cost you dearly. So, if you lose
your temper, you are in danger because you are "liable to judgement": you will judge the other and condemn him. And if you
stop there, the other will in turn judge and condemn you – this
is obvious even if not stated in so many words. In this escalation,
there is something worse than a direct insult "to a brother" ("fool"),
namely, to treat him as "mad" by speaking of him in the third person
because you do not even want to condescend to speak to him face
to face. You are "liable" to the risk of being consumed eternally by
anger, of placing yourself in a "fire of hell," subject to hatred, to
an inner violence that you can no longer get rid of since you have
cut off the relationship.

What is striking in the words of Jesus is that at no time does he
say "you have no reason to be angry," nor even "your brother has
every reason in the world to be angry with you." It seems that
the reason for the anger is not important to him: the question is
not at all whether you are right or wrong to be angry. If you find
yourself angry, or if the other is angry with you, that is the way it

is – the reality principle. All that matters is what you will do with this boiling rage. And all of a sudden, you find yourself free again: "When you are offering your gift ... If you remember ..." In other words, if you begin by turning towards the OTHER, as Jacob did by beginning to pray rather than rushing headlong towards Esau, one could say that unconsciously you aspire to offer God this anger that is destroying you. You would like to burn it on his altar like the sacrificial animals; you are capable of offering the sacrifice of your anger, of your resentment, of your self-love, since at that point you are making an offering to God.

Because you have begun this process of liberation, you increase your chances of "remembering that your brother [also] has something against you." Nowadays we would say: you become conscious of it. You begin to see that you are not all white nor he all black, even if you have in fact been the victim of injustice. Whatever his reasons may be, he too feels unjustly treated, and often the whole matter is due to something else, to some previous event, and you have little to do with it. If you are now concerned with *his* anger, this does not necessarily mean you feel it is your fault. It is simply that you are in a good position to know that the other, being angry, is in a bad way, is diminished, "fallen." By "making your offering" to God, by making yourself present to the OTHER in the open space of prayer, you begin to perceive that it is the other person who is in danger, locked within himself or herself, or ready to explode. The face of the other appears before you, and something within you, almost in spite of yourself, begins to pray for him or her.

Such an unexpected reversal is not possible without complete free-dom: "If you are offering ..." As in the case of Jacob, only seeking refuge in this place of safety that is the prayerful contact with the OTHER makes it possible to take a first step, not *towards* the other but *with* the other: that is, in the literal as well as in the figurative sense to "remobilize" the relationship. Jesus says, "go, first be reconciled": literally, "*exchange* with your brother" or "*change your attitude*" towards him or "*reconcile* yourself with him." Inevitably, we are reminded of Cain, whose offering was lacking that authenticity because – as subsequent events reveal – the "exchange" with Abel was lacking. Thus, exchange or change of attitude towards another who is suffering comes first, before any religious practice.[72] Go first ... and only then come and complete your sacrifice at the altar.

Nevertheless, a conflict is a conflict, and an "adversary" remains an adversary even if we begin to journey with him. "Come to terms quickly with your accuser" – literally, think well of him. As if this was possible simply on command. To think well [eunoôn], a term that appears only this once in all of the New Testament, is obviously not easy. Yet a physical movement seems to suffice: go ... and come. It is enough to take one step with the other in order for your thoughts to begin to change. Strangely, it is primarily you who will benefit from these good thoughts towards the adversary: it is you who will "get out" of the prison of anger (v. 26), and thereby you will be able to show the other person the way out as well. Do it "quickly," hurry up, while you are on the way with him or her," for life is short and it is important not to carry the fire of your anger to the next life.

What kind of a trap does anger lay for us? It leads us to believe that it is impossible to take the first step with another because "he/she started it," and then to forget that we can first of all relearn to walk with an OTHER, take a first step with the One who alone can fathom the intensity of our sense of injustice. God alone knows if it really was the other one who started it – this is not something we can ever know for sure. For if it is true that very often we did not start the conflict, we will eventually remember that the other, too, in his or her life, had begun by being humiliated, ignored, killed by others. "If you remember" the other who is also suffering, locked within his or her resentment, if you remember that Jesus himself did not waste time or energy trying to find out who started evil and sin, you will turn towards the other to "exchange," and this concrete gesture will make you think differently, will influence your insight into the situation and your understanding of human beings.

---

In any event, a violent act is unjust. It keeps us under the illusion that Evil originates solely with the adversary who is currently preoccupying our thoughts. Cain experienced the injustice of life. We have seen that his mother, Eve, did not love him for himself but as her possession, and that he grew up with the obligation of doing "good works" according to her wishes. The worst happened: he felt unjustly treated by God Himself; but instead of turning against the author of such an unfair life, he was trapped in the idea that Justice does not exist, and that he thus had to become judge and executioner himself. He then committed the most unjust act possible, pretending to believe that Abel was the enemy to be slain. The Targum provides an interesting elaboration on this subject:

> When the two of them had gone outside [into the field],[73] Cain spoke up and said to Abel, 'I see that the world was created with mercy, but it is not governed according to the fruit of good deeds, and there is partiality in judgment. Therefore your offering was accepted with favor, but my offering was not accepted from me with favor'. Abel contradicted Cain word for word. Cain replied: 'There is neither judgement nor judge nor a world beyond! No reward for the just or punishment for the evil.' Again Abel simply affirmed the opposite. The two of them continued to quarrel about this question out in the fields. And Cain rose up against his brother Abel and killed him.[74]

Our compulsion to act unjustly towards the other is thus said to be on a par with our sense of injustice. What is at stake in anger is indeed justice. Someone who is angry is someone who has not given up on justice: is there such a thing as justice? Will I one day see justice done? Should I take justice into my own hands? Times of reflection or prayer can bring forth our emotional intelligence: someone whom I would like to kill may perhaps be burning with the same desire, deep down; thus he or she too is a human being and no longer this monster who I think is suffocating and destroying me. My anger may thus be capable of bringing me to pass judgment myself: ultimately, do I seek justice for everyone? If so, my judgment will bear on those things that need to be eliminated, and not on people of whom I can never be absolutely sure that they must be slain once and for all. In the fourth century, Evagrius Ponticus put it admirably when he said:

> Whenever a temptation or a feeling of contentiousness comes
> over you, immediately arousing you to anger or to some sense-
> less word, remember your prayer and how you will be judged
> about it and at once the disorderly movement within you will
> subside … When you pray as you ought, you will see before you
> such *things* that you will certainly decide on the righteous use
> of anger. Yet there is absolutely no righteous anger against one's
> *neighbour*. If you look carefully, you will find that it is possible to
> settle matters even without anger.[75]

If there is no "righteous anger" against one's neighbour, this does
not mean that another's action against us cannot be unjust. Nor
does it mean that our anger is not legitimate. It means simply that
we would have to be God to be certain that our anger was capable
of doing full Justice, redressing wrongs without running the risk of
falling into excess and becoming in turn unjust towards the adversary. We do not know and will never know the other well enough
to know whether he or she really deserves to feel the flames of our
anger. That is why our emotional and spiritual intelligence lead us
to judge the situation differently.

We can remove the element of bad faith that was arousing our anger:
no, we do not have absolute proof that another is beyond hope of
a restored relationship and deserves to be eliminated for good. It is
rightly said that anger makes us blind: gradually, we realize that we
have been lying to ourselves by reducing the other to his or her
unjust behaviour. What is more, we may begin to wonder whether
the other's hostile attitude or murderous indifference towards us
has unleashed in us an anger of which he is not really the cause but
only the trigger. This is the phenomenon of the straw that broke
the camel's back. Here we are now, beside ourselves, not knowing
what to do with a rage that seems disproportionate to the incident
that provoked it. There is clearly something else going on inside
us. All it took was this last straw to make us cry out at last our thirst
for justice.

This is the kernel of truth that contains the fruit of anger. Once
the emotion and fury have played themselves out, and we have got
rid of our image of the adversary as embodying Evil, as someone

who must be eliminated at all costs because, as we believed, he or she alone was preventing us from living, what is left but this inextinguishable desire to be justified, rehabilitated, defended by Someone? It is in our interests first to consume the fruit of our anger, no matter how bitter it may be, in order to enter into contact with its irreducible kernel before confronting the adversary, armed with the same truth that our anger contained – our need to have our experience of injustice heard. Our demand for justice would then appear in its true form, purged of its omnipotence. We have given up the desire to become judges, but we insist that our anger impels us to speak the truth: our incapacity or refusal to tolerate what is intolerable in a situation. "If it is in the nature of revolt to attack an existing person," writes B. Bro, "it is just as much in its nature to be totalitarian and to exclude every other presence, every other answer … The most fearsome evil we can confront is undoubtedly the very will to do away with the power of evil."[76] It is in this regard that anger lies (to itself).

If, then, at the point when Cain undergoes the painful experience of anger, God surrounds him with his most attentive care, it is because Cain's freedom is at stake. Is there a better way to liberate someone from the hold of another (here, his mother Eve) than to take away his habitual crutch – his claim to do good, to conform perfectly with another's expectations? Cain's offering is not accepted. It is as if to say that try as we might to satisfy another, despite all our efforts it will never be enough. This is a difficult thing to realize, but it lends itself to raising one's awareness: am I not in the process of losing my soul, although it was created to be free? In the bitterness of this moment, there is a grave risk of becoming a slave of one's anger, in the absence of anyone else under whose power we can remain. If, then, anger is our first step towards freedom, it is up to us not to allow it to become the final step. A dizzying prospect, according to B. Bro:

> It may be that the greatness of this revolt is to reveal just how far our freedom can go. Someone who is unable to revolt lacks the greatness God wishes to give us. [What is] maddening, crushing [is] the possibility – in the name of the very importance of free-

dom – that this rebellion might be eternal. Those who claim to be the most inveterate enemies of God do not go that far, they do not ask for that ... And if they knew that God granted it to them they would be afraid, really afraid.[77]

Every well-meaning person who, when we are in a fit of anger, reflects back to us like a faithful mirror that our face is burning, and tries to talk to us about it, plays the role of the OTHER in the story of Cain. That person occupies precisely the place of the murder, for he or she takes the place of the one we would like to kill. Indeed, this is a dangerous place to be, for murderous rage risks turning against that person. It is this OTHER who, at the decisive moment, chooses to incarnate before us, "on the spot of the murder, the demand for justice," according to the argument in this sub-section. This is why Jesus reverses the problem of anger in Matthew 5:21-26: remember, regardless of your feelings, that you are responsible for holding up a mirror to the person who is angry with you, whether rightly or wrongly, and regardless of what happens, you are to stand in the place of the murder he is about to commit, to stand before him as a living demand for justice for all, to which he too aspires.

But, you might object, if I thus fly to the aid of a human being seized with anger, what about my own anger? The simple fact that I make a move proves that I can get out of it. I am more than my anger – my being cannot be reduced to this anger. If I am able to mobilize and take up this responsibility that God entrusts to me, it is because I have found or rediscovered my freedom and I am no longer under someone else's abusive control. It is when I leave my own territory that I discover that it is well defended. If practice makes perfect, then it is in practising defusing the anger of another that we can defuse our own anger. Commenting on the hermit Evagrius – for whom the passions, of which he considered there were nine, were neither good not evil in themselves – Anselm Grün affirms:

> Anger is a positive force that aims to render me capable of de-limiting my territory, of liberating me from the power of others. But it can also devour me if I allow it to get the better of me ... Anger is the strength to step back from someone who has hurt

us. It allows us to rid ourselves of the cause of the hurt and the irritation ... Anger, even if violent, is a good thing. If we admit this and look it in the eye, if we go to the very heart of the matter, then it can metamorphose into a new vital energy. It may show us that until now we have behaved only in relation to others. We would like from now on to live what we are in ourselves.[78]

We hold fear at arm's length as long as we keep in touch with our anger. But the risk of moving from feeling to action increases, for our sense of powerlessness becomes unbearable. If, at this point, we recall the face of the other and we see that he or she is in the grip of a painful powerlessness and anger that is similar to ours, our fantasy of the other's omnipotence evaporates, and we are somehow reassured, able to feel sympathy for a human being who, like us, feels diminished. All of a sudden, we feel less confined, less closed in on ourselves, and we make room for "the OTHER."

# 4 AccusingGod, even at the risk of death

> Blessed be the name of the Eternal One! Why, but why should I bless Him? In every fibre I rebelled. Because He had thousands of children burned in His pits? Because He kept the crematoria working night and day, on Sundays and feast days? Because He in His great might had created Auschwitz, Birkenau, Buna and so many factories of death? ... and I, the mystic that I had been, thought: Yes, man is very strong, greater than God![79]

The way out for Elie Wiesel and for so many other Holocaust survivors was to hold onto their anger in order to escape both fear and self-destruction. But for there to be anger, there has to be "the OTHER" against whom one can sharpen one's own truth, or simply one's feeling of existing in spite of everything. Not to lose one's anger thus becomes the only way to stay alive: as long as I don't let go of any part of my truth, "they" won't get me! In the life of Kierkegaard, there is an invisible OTHER who plunges him into incomprehensible sense of guilt following a decision he had made in good conscience, and for which he took full responsibility. He moves from despondency to fury:

> I am frantic and travel bewildered from one end of the world
> to the other, to find one person upon whom I could expend
> my wrath ... Though the whole world were to rise up against
> me, though all the scholastics were to dispute with me, though
> my life were at stake, I nevertheless maintain that I am in the
> right. No one shall wrest this conviction from me, though there
> is no language in which I can give utterance to it. I have acted
> correctly.[80]

Two months later, when "the violence and fever had passed," he
compares his own situation with that of Job:

> The secret in Job, the vital power, the nerve, the idea, is that in
> spite of everything Job is in the right ... by his tenacity of pur-
> pose and by his power he demonstrated his authority, his well
> warranted authority ... He buoyantly maintains his conviction
> ... The greatness of Job consists in the fact that the passion for
> freedom within him is not stifled or tranquillized ... the dispute
> with [his friends] is a purgatory in which the thought that he is
> nevertheless right becomes purified.[81]

This is a laborious process of purification of all that is not authentic
in anger. At the end of the process, we gain access to that kernel of
truth that remains once the anger has subsided. We will thus burn
with anger for as long as is necessary to exhaust all the caricatures
and death-dealing "solutions" that anger engenders when it erupts.
It is something like a fever, and it is often a burning in both the
literal and the figurative sense. But in the Bible, paradoxically, it is
God who at one and the same time ignites and seeks to extinguish
the fire. Or rather, we could say that God behaves like someone
who puts a match to the powder keg because he alone sees that the
situation must explode, that anger has to burn off the dross in order
to liberate that part of the human being that has resisted and will
continue to resist all aggression – his or her incorruptible identity
as son or daughter and heir of the God of justice.

In these biblical narratives, the characters end up turning their anger
against God himself, without understanding why God betrayed their
trust. It is striking to see Cain take the initiative of preparing an offering to the Lord, in all innocence, and to see it rejected without

any explanation. It is astonishing to see Jacob trust God in prayer, in preparing his gift for Esau, and finally in accepting solitude – "and Jacob remained alone" or "*safe*"[82] – and then, without any transition, be attacked by an OTHER at the moment when he least expects it. Job, meanwhile, speaks plainly, describing what comes close to the experience of many of us: "Your hands fashioned and made me; and now you turn and destroy me" (Job 10:8). What he echoes is the sense that we can no longer trust God, who betrays us at the very moment when we trust him most completely. Whom can we invoke, to whom can we turn, if God is not the Just One?

The texts hammer it home to us: ask God directly! Go to the very limits of your indignation! You are not worth less than Jacob, exclaims Paul Claudel, who rejected the idea of "Christian resignation":

> Oh, only in combat do we get to know our enemy; he can no longer hide anything from us … and I myself never fully realized this except in this assault on the very fibre of my being, in this assault and in this resistance … And I know that I would not have come to terms with this *God against me* in Justice, if there had not been *God in me* to rescue my justice and my indignation![83]

This is the paradox of spiritual experience, which I have tried to show by means of the words in italics. To defend us against this unjust God who goes after us for no reason, we cannot but invoke this same Justice which we do not doubt for a moment, since it is its absence that is the cause of our suffering.[84] And we will need to get through our revolt in order to see that we have made the injustice we suffered into an all-powerful god intent on having the last word. Another way of speaking of this purification, this cleansing that can lead to anger: it takes time to identify "within me, coming to the aid of my justice," the only living God – the one who does justice to me.

To rebel against God does not seem at first glance to be a life choice. Religious education has a lot to do with this, given its propensity to confuse submission to authorities and submission to God. The biblical God, however, is always in search of the human face, be it smiling or frowning in anger. We have not been taught to face God as we are, and to tell him what we think of him when pain and anger are ravaging us. But there is more than education involved: at such times, it's as if God had disappeared; the violence we are experiencing is such that, since we are unable to take action, we turn back against ourselves. Self-destruction can, for a while, rally all our energy. Job gives a long monologue in which he turns against himself, leaving God in his heaven: "May God above not seek it" (Job 3:4).

We have to wait until the end of the chapter for Job to begin to challenge God, and then only indirectly, at first without naming him ("Why is light *given* to one in misery, and life to the bitter in soul," v. 20) and then designating him in the third person ("whom God has fenced in," v. 23). "Job seems to pronounce the name of the divinity reluctantly. This device conceals the hostility he feels towards him."[85] He does not have enough resilience yet to attack God face to face. For the moment it is [rogez] that comes, that is to say, a mixture of agitation, physical and moral torment, fury and rumblings of thunder. In the Hebrew Bible, it is God who "comes." But for Job, what comes is only pain, terror and rage, without any face-to-face encounter, until such time as he is capable of turning against God himself, since he has no OTHER whom he can address.

The most violent moment of confrontation with God comes when Job gets in touch with his fear of being killed. Psychologists who study emotions will recognize in this a major symptom of post-traumatic stress. Job has received too many blows for him not to expect the worst when he tries for the first time to lift up his head:

> Do not speak, and I will speak,
> and let come on me what may!
> I will take my flesh in my teeth,
> and put my soul in my hand.
> He will kill me, so be it! I await it.
> May I but defend my ways to his face. (13:13ff.)[86]

Anything rather than renounce my truth and my demand for justice! I would rather die with my right to speak and to be heard in my quest for justice than to keep silent. Job tilted the balance towards himself and his life: if I have to choose, I would prefer to be killed by the OTHER than to kill who I am myself. In other words, there is something more important than my life: namely, my right to speak. Hence my truth and my demand for justice. God himself will not make me renounce this: for I have chosen once and for all to defend my cause and have refused to stifle within myself the crying need for justice. Too bad if I am wrong and if there is no justice in the OTHER: I may be the only person and the last person to take my side, but I will confront God with this solidarity in my heart, and we will have to see: I have nothing left to lose.

Luther would put it in almost the same terms: "Even if God wished to kill me, He would do well, as I would live from it."[87] I am never as alive as the day when even my representation of the OTHER as the one who wishes to kill me – in other words, getting to the bottom of who I am – no longer scares me. Because I confront this other face to face (literally, "remove his face"), his mask falls and I realize that it was I who had put it on him. In reality, there was a whole part of me that wanted my own death. With Job, by choosing to stay, come what may, by the side of my truth and my thirst for justice, I have chosen to live.

This confrontation with the OTHER is therefore inevitably ambivalent, involving both a risk of death and yet the possibility of access to life. Whence the existence of the two traditions in the Hebrew Bible, which in my view are complementary: according to the more ancient of the two, we cannot see God without dying; according to the other, the worst trial is when God hides his face, for to see the face of God is to be secure in the joy of his presence. Our experience also tells us something about this ambivalence, when there is "something of the OTHER" at work in us. We always have to overcome a certain fear of death when we face this OTHER that is within us and knocks us around, works us over and wounds us. For we have no proof at all that he is well-disposed towards us and thirsts for justice as well, at least as much as we do. How can we ever know for sure unless we cry out to him, "Do you seek my death or are you on my side?" and unless we hold out against him through our unconditional solidarity with ourselves?

"*And none shall see My face and remain living* means None shall see My face and live as he did before," wrote Elie Wiesel concerning Jacob, who "was never to be the same again." He rethought his life, after having constantly been on the run, and having "lived in ambiguity so long that he could no longer see clearly ... he ached for an ordeal of his own ... no matter how great the risk. It was God he wished to confront ... It was a challenge without precedent... no man before him had ever established relations of provocation with God."[88]

From a psychological perspective, we may emphasize, with Jean-Claude Sagne, the importance of aggression towards the mother, which allows the person to pass himself off as different from her:

> The bad mother incarnates frustration, hatred, in a word, the threat of death. She represents the risk of being torn apart, broken, reabsorbed and dissolved. The subject's projection of his or her internal aggression onto the mother is a key phenomenon ... It provides the opportunity to come into contact with another as she is, by virtue of the fact that she brings the subject to the point of *throwing himself upon her*. This can, therefore, mark the end of a dualistic, co-dependent relationship, one that is saturating and rendered aconflictual.[89]

All one has to do is replace "bad mother" with "wicked God," and we are back in Job's universe or in Jacob's night. It is thus "fortunate" for every human being to have at hand a God who is at once father and mother and who agrees to help bear (or sometimes bear it alone) the brunt of this anger aimed at one's human father and mother and/or at any other substitute father or mother. The result is the same: as I have stressed above, we throw ourselves upon "the OTHER," then discover that this OTHER does not tear us apart. Far from being dissolved, we are well and truly alive, and too angry for there to be any doubt about it!

What is it that has allowed us simply not to accept our representation of the OTHER – this persecutor to whom we had bequeathed all our capacity for opposition, to the point that we believed it to be omnipotent? It is precisely our becoming aware of our own destructive power, which is as strong as our vitality. The wicked OTHER does not seem omnipotent to us once we begin to experience our own counter-wickedness, which we are perfectly aware is not all-powerful. In concrete terms, our confrontation with another human being teaches us that *we are*, body and soul, the limit to all omnipotence by the simple fact that we exist, just as the other is also, body and soul, the limit to our own power of destruction.

Job understands that God will not kill him at the moment when he himself, having renounced "killing" God (that is, eliminating God from his life) throws himself up against the limits of his own destructiveness. Taken up in the fantasy of the destructive omnipotence of the OTHER, he confronts him despite his fear of being killed. Yet in the text, it is at this very moment that this imaginary God melts away: he is going to kill me, fine! I am waiting for him! If only I (could) justify my ways to his face! "This will be my salvation, that a *godless man* shall not come before him" (13:16). The term used also means "the cruel one" or the "hypocrite." What has happened? Instead of giving in to his counter-"wickedness" by taking action and alienating himself from the divine OTHER, in whom all other humans exist, instead of pretending to believe, like the "hypocrites," that one or several humans had single-handedly and without reason or justification authored the injustice for which he, Job, was being made to pay the price, Job chose to demand an accounting from the One who alone can still assure him that Justice exists.

So here he is, without any ulterior motive, fully engaged in the relationship, in solidarity with what he is, with what he is going through and with what he hopes for: the simple fact of being able to stand "before the face of God" in his pain, his anger and his recriminations is "salvation" and his "safety." Job finds in this attitude itself the sense of being rescued and saved. Why? Because at this moment, Job believes in what he is, a being who has a voice and is the bearer of a truth which is his own. What destroys us, in our confrontations with others, is the feeling of not having a right to our own existence and to our own words with which to express it. We are saved when we manage to say to God himself, "You have been unjust to me. The life you have given me has been one long series of injustices. I need to tell you to your face that I shall be just towards my self, that I shall remain in solidarity with all I have experienced and that, whatever you may or may not do, I will never renounce justice, even if I have to die without having seen the sun of justice rise over my head."

---

We have been sadly mistaken about Almighty God. We need to look elsewhere for an Omnipotence that, apparently, is no longer very convincing today. The omnipotence of God is rather this limitless capacity God has to occupy the murderous place without dying of it. We can "kill" God by eliminating him from our lives, we can rebel against him, throw the worst insults at him, turn back against him all the murderous anger destined for our enemies, make him guilty of all the evils of the world, yet he always rises again, living, in the very place where we thought we had finished with him, in the very place where we thought we had finished with another human being. If he stays at the site of the murder, immortal, indestructible, inalterable, that is because his life is omnipotent. Whatever we may say or do under the influence of anger, God is ready to receive it and to give us in return, hidden behind our tormented faces, the demand for justice that dwells in us. Instead of murder, in both the literal and the figurative senses, God is our demand for justice, even before he is the just God we long for.

The biblical God is not content to receive our sense of injustice, to demand that we name it, to call forth a dialogue that can begin only with incendiary language – even congratulating us afterwards for having dared tell him our complaints to his face, no matter how unjust they may be towards him ("My servant Job has spoken of me what is right"!). Rather, the biblical God seems to be aghast at a situation where we move to take action. "What have you done?" he asks after the murder. It is as if he were formulating a sad truth: my poor Cain, "now you are cursed from the ground ... you shall be a fugitive and a wanderer on the earth" (Gen. 4:10ff). This is precisely our experience: having become prey to our own violence, we are not at peace either with ourselves or with others.

It is then that, for the first time in his life, Cain complains. Yet, it is God whom he reproaches for the situation in which he has put himself: "Today you have driven me away from the soil, and I shall be hidden from your face; I shall be a fugitive and a wanderer on the earth, and anyone who meets me may kill me" (4:14). But before questioning God, he begins by admitting (to himself): "My *fault/punishment* is greater than I can bear." The Hebrew word means both the fault and the direct consequence of that fault – being punished where we have sinned, carrying the weight of what we have done. Thus, since God was at the place of the murder, Cain "killed" him by killing Abel. Cain will live "hidden from the face of God" as if God no longer existed. But he cannot reconcile himself to doing so. This solitude is too heavy, he says, as if in a monologue; I prefer to believe you have driven me away.

And yet, God accepts this, too: whereas others bear the brunt of our counter-violence, and we bitterly regret having let ourselves be caught up in the cycle of violence, when we turn against God and at last call it injustice, the biblical God takes it on, as if he was delighted that at least we are speaking to him. He accepts Cain's fear and responds by coming back once again to the place of the murder: he places a mark (a divine one, according to certain Jewish interpretations) on Cain so that no one who came upon him would strike him (4:15) – or would not "kill him," according to the Targum. This is a symbolic way of saying that he is present, more than ever, invisibly, on the face of Cain as a "place of impossible murder"; no one shall use violence to get the better of God.

And so, confrontation with the OTHER is once again made possible: thus Cain begins to glimpse that there is no life worthy of the name outside this fruitful confrontation with the OTHER. The Targum seems to me to take us in this direction:

... yet from before you it is not possible for me to hide. And Cain shall be an exile and a wanderer on the earth, and anyone who meets him will kill him.[90]

I ... you, Cain, in dialogue with God, is the beginning of a confrontation. Then, suddenly, "Cain shall be ..." in indirect discourse, as if Cain no longer recognized himself in this wanderer without any other person before him than a destructive one. Is it not because he has begun to face up to the true OTHER who gives him life? The Targum of *Pseudo-Jonathan* goes even further:

> Is it possible (for me) to hide from you? And *if* I am a wanderer and an exile upon the earth any *righteous person* who finds me will kill me ... Then the Lord traced on Cain's face a letter of the great and glorious Name, so that anyone who would find him, upon seeing it on him, would not kill him.[91]

Cain experiences that he is more and other than this errant being who is imprisoned in his own violence: he is someone for whom the face-to-face encounter with God is still possible, regardless of the crime with which he has sullied his hands. In other words, he now experiences the fact that "Justice" stands face to face with him: if he says "any just man who comes upon me...," it is because henceforth there is such a thing as Justice in his life. This is because God has manifested himself in this murderous place, which Cain thought he had destroyed once and for all. Cain had complained bitterly to Abel that there was no Justice. Yet God is the first "Just" being he "found" and did not "kill." Therefore, Cain may hope, there may be a Justice that does not meet violence with violence. For when we have eliminated violence through violence, we have not brought about anything new, we do not need another word to express this. The word "justice" adds nothing. Cain is perhaps en route towards a confrontation that is truly *other*, that *does* deserve to be called Justice, for it will not be a symmetrical violence: this alone will bear fruit.[92]

We could say that the biblical God offers himself as a punching bag (to use a colloquial term) to the fury of human beings, in religious terms as a scapegoat, and in prophetic terms as the suffering servant. He is in a position to know just how life can seem unjust to human beings, and seems to do everything possible to advise them to turn their anger first and foremost against him. Paul Claudel writes,

> At the very origin of Cain's act is an idea of vengeance, vengeance for what man considers an injustice towards him. For the first time, we have been shown Someone who pays instead of another. Abel, my brother, who paid with his blood instead of God. God is thus pleased from the very beginning to show himself as being in the debt of one of his children, contracting on his behalf the debt that will be honoured on Calvary.[93]

We could go even further: God was already prepared "to pay instead of" Cain's mother, Eve, the smothering one who claimed to have "had a son with the Lord," as if one could buy a reason for existence in a bazaar of the sacred. God offered himself to Cain so that he might reproach *him* for a life so unjustly deprived of liberty, since he had not yet been able to confront his mother and because his father, Adam, was generally absent: that would have been a good start!

Now more than ever, perhaps, God wishes to be in the debt of the Jewish people, in this age when the temptation to counter-violence has risen to such destructive heights in the Near East. In each generation, in all circumstances, in every personal destiny, God tries to bring down our lightning bolts upon himself, first and before any decision, before any move to action. "Now I am addressing him as someone who has also become to some extent my debtor. This is why I believe I have the right to remonstrate with God ... This is the time when the Almighty turns his face away from his supplicants. God has hidden his face from the world." These were the words of a Jew about to die in the Warsaw Ghetto during the uprising.[94] The hour of revolt against God is here, now more than ever, when the crucifying memories of the Shoah continue to evoke terror and the compulsion of counter-violence. If God seems to "turn his face away from his supplicants," it is because he wishes to see the face of his supplicants outraged against him. When violence is so great that all we can do is pray for peace, the Bible recommends that we cry out first to God our sense of injustice and abandonment, and that we reproach him for doing nothing.

Certainly there is the risk that we will stop there. But the God of the prophets shows himself ready to take this risk, at all times and in all places. And to make sure this does not remain abstract, he places in the midst of our societies "suffering servants" who daily incarnate what he is, in the terms in which Isaiah 52–53 spoke of him: present in each suffering servant, and in danger of remaining misunderstood for good (in other words, "we held him of no account"). He is willing to "bear/carry" not only our "infirmities and diseases" but also our "transgressions" and our "revolts." In short, he wants to pay for us, for the "wicked," for those engaging in counter-violence, if only the murderous violence and the contempt that kills the soul might stop on earth.

It is in this way that, being "just" himself, he "renders justice" to the "many" around him: in our sense of injustice and in our revolt, someone hears us. Someone stands at our side and aspires likewise to justice for all; everyone, including the "wicked," is thus at the service of a "non-violence" that goes hand in hand with a "non-lie." A suffering servant like Martin Luther King, or Gandhi, or so many others, is concretely this OTHER who stands at the scene of the murder, offering every human being the choice between killing himself by killing, or of crying out to Someone our demand for justice by naming injustice. History shows that such suffering servants, by choosing to occupy the scene of murder, allow the OTHER to give peoples and individuals an inviolable space where the demand for justice, both human and divine, remains indestructible. It is this very act that heals us of the injustice we have suffered and of the temptation to be unjust ourselves.

We could say, then, that if we have the privilege, at the moment of anger, to find ourselves face to face with this OTHER who is great enough to endure any challenge, no matter how unjust, we begin to see our violence from another perspective: human anger and divine resistance become not only compatible but complementary. Because you are You and I am me, because there is a right to exist and room for both of us, life on earth (once again) becomes possible. There is indeed a third way, other than "mimetic submission" or counter-violence. We can glimpse, through rereading the book of

Job, the act of trust that hides beneath our anger: if we no longer believed that justice is possible, we would stop getting angry. Job, for his part, gradually realizes that he has no other recourse against God than God himself. But when he begs God to stop turning against him and to remember that He alone can bring about justice, Job is becoming aware of an OTHER within himself – an OTHER who finally rises up from the depths of his wounded humanity. Two brief passages seem to open up this path, where Job comes to know:

> … my witness who vouches for me,
> a judge for a man [in his dispute] with Eloah [= God]

as between a man and his neighbour (16:19ff, based on J. Lévêque's translation)

> … and, a bit further on, with
> my living defender [who] at last
> rises/shall rise upon the dust
> [and that] my eyes shall behold, and not another (19:25, 27)[95]

Yet this third way, which one hardly dares hope for, suddenly opens before Job's eyes immediately after the verses where he was vehemently denouncing the extreme violence of God towards him. Anger and whimpers, the violence of unhappiness and verbal counter-violence… and, finally, when all has been reduced to dust, it is "upon the dust" of his life that Job sees the OTHER "rise up and continue to rise" as if from within himself. Someone inside him begins to stand up for him, to be at his side to confront the adversary and adversity. It is with this Job that God will speak at the end of the book. He will speak to him directly, as to the patriarchs, to Moses and the prophets, because Job will confront him as a true partner who has had reason to reproach him but has never given up calling upon his sense of justice, standing up to him even when deathly afraid. But it will not be until chapter 38, once, it is true, God can no longer make himself heard in our brains, which are held hostage by these imaginary representations of an Omnipotence that is arbitrarily violent.

From chapter 19 onwards, Job thus had a premonition that he would have to get to the bottom of this imaginary invalid so that one day, "at last," when he will have emptied out his reservoir of fantasies, he might stand upright, taking the side, before God, of the human who has been treated unjustly.[96] It is "out of the whirlwind" in which he struggles that Job finally hears God answer him (38:1; 40:6), as if God had been standing at Job's side the whole time in the midst of the storm, trying to make him hear an OTHER voice whose message is now being expressed clearly: you and I against unjust evil, it is the same struggle! It comes down to validating all the complaints of human beings concerning the harshness of life. But for Job, it is at the same time the sudden awareness of the solidity of a God who is OTHER, a God who has been at odds with evil and injustice from the very beginning. You do not know everything, says God, and *my* combat escapes you: do you know that before creating anything at all in this world, I began by putting boundaries on ... the sea? At first reading, we might be dazzled and impressed by the sumptuous evocation of the divine act of creation, but as a result the first verses might go unnoticed. And indeed, as soon as the earth had been created, God describes how he contained the sea (38:8-11):

> Who shut in the sea with two gates,
> when, in its torrent, it burst out from the womb,
> when I made the cloud its garment
> and thick fog its swaddling band?
> *I broke it with my law and set a lock and gates for it.*[97]
> And said "Thus far shall you come, and no farther,
> and here shall your proud waves be stopped![98]

Yet the sea was, for the Hebrews, a symbol of evil, and further on we will see God tame the monsters of the sea. Job's struggle against injustice was thus preceded for all eternity by God's own combat: to place limits, seal off, master, forbid the flood, make the waters that claimed to rule evaporate into clouds ... so many images to say that God is God in that he alone can accomplish this in our own personal storms as well. This, then, is the original counter-violence, of which God alone holds the secret and which he alone has mastered, and which helps us not to yield to the floods of our own counter-violence. It is God who does this within us, for he has been doing so since the very beginning. It is at the point when

Job is no longer blinded by his own anger, when he has managed somehow to pen it in, that he becomes aware of the wrath of God against the sea – the unjust evil whose "pride" or invasion has been stopped short by a boundary since the earth began.

Is it a coincidence that, in the verses that follow, there is talk of the "wicked" from whom light is withheld, and of the "uplifted arm that is broken"? It is important that Job now learns that he was right to believe in a God of justice: there is anOTHER justice, which puts an end to, an enclosure around, a lock on the injustice suffered. This is the justice that rehabilitates our complaint and our anger by making us see God – in hindsight – at our side in the midst of our storms. God renders justice to us as soon as we hear him say that we were right to cry injustice. However, just how far God will go in his confrontation with evil remains a mystery to Job: he experiences the "uplifted arm that is broken" and the fact that he is out of danger, but he now sees as well that the total annihilation of injustice is not to be his. For that, he would have to know all the ins and outs of what he had gone through, understand why a particular person had done him harm, know who had previously done harm to this person. When all is said and done, if he bows before the complete knowledge that God alone has of the distant origins of what he endured, this is because it was enough for him to have been rehabilitated and freed. He willingly agrees to allow God to struggle against evil in his own way, one that is necessarily radical:

> Have you entered into the springs of the sea
> or walked in the recesses of the deep? (38:16)

No, Job would reply, I do not know everything about the unjust evil I endured, but I know that you know, and that is enough for me, for I trust you. You will go to the very end of your struggle for justice, as surely as I went to the very end of my anger. I took up my own defence, since no one else would do so, and finally saw you rise up from the depths of my being, "at last" – when I hardly believed any longer – to come to my defence.

This, no doubt, is why Job is willing to renounce being judge in God's stead. He would not personally eliminate anyone, physically or morally: neither his friends, nor his enemies, nor God, nor even himself. We might say that on hearing God speak to him, he sees that he is alive despite his verbal aggression, which, in the eyes of his friends, was blasphemous. Now it is up to God to defy them: with these airs of a judge that you have assumed, will you decide what is Just, who is Just and who Unjust, in absolute terms, fully aware of all the circumstances? Do you have what it takes? Do you believe you can take my place, to evaluate in each person the degree of suffering and the degree of harm for which he is responsible? Can you even do so for yourself? Has the unjust misery that has struck you removed all responsibility for the evil you may have inflicted upon others?

> Will you even put me in the wrong? Will you condemn me *that you may be justified*? (40:8)

For such is the perverse nature of our thirst for justice: accusing God, implicating him, reproaching him, yes, this is necessary and beneficial to channel our counter-violence and to address ourselves to Someone. But if we take advantage of it to establish ourselves as the judges of others, we deify our own sense of justice and "deny the justice" of God, since we seek to administer it in God's place. At that point it is no longer to soothe our own pain and burning anger that we "condemn" him, but in order "that *we* may be justified" ourselves, to render justice to ourselves by doing without him. How can we recognize that "the just one" that is at work in our anger is indeed the OTHER? This happens when, even while crying out in revolt against him for allowing us to suffer so much injustice, we are sincere enough to recognize that we do not have a monopoly on justice. We see that we, too, are steeped in injustice when we demonize another in order to defend ourselves, that we truly no longer see anything but the beam in the enemy's eye and that therefore our own vision of justice is very partial, deformed by our woundedness and our counter-violence.

Sometimes the reproaches we direct towards God are so severe that we no longer have any reason to believe in him, and all that remains

of the relationship is a sort of childlike trust: I do not understand
you, I am dying of not understanding you, but I nevertheless trust
you. This is my challenge, my protest, my resistance: I continue to
believe in you, even if you have abandoned me. The "Testament
in the Furnace" constitutes a shocking testimony to such an attitude. Written in April 1943, it is attributed to Jossel Rachower,
an Austrian Jew who perished in the burning Warsaw Ghetto after
his wife and their six children died:

> And now my hour has come … Until my death I wish to speak
> live to my God, like a simple man, alive, who has the great but
> fatal privilege of being a Jew. I believe in the God of Israel, even
> if he has done everything to shatter my faith in him … I believe
> in his laws, even if I challenge the justification for his actions; I
> bow before his grandeur but I will not kiss the stick that beats me.
> I love him, but I love his law even more. I love his justice even
> more, Job and countless others would say today. And even if I
> were wrong about him, I would continue to adore his law. God
> signifies religion, but his law signifies the wisdom of life. You say
> we have sinned. Obviously we have sinned. That we should be
> punished for this, I accept as well. I would nevertheless like you
> to tell me if there is a sin on earth that deserves such a punish-
> ment as this. I tell you all this, my God, because I believe in you,
> because I believe more than ever in you, because I know now
> that you are my God, and not the God of those whose actions
> are the horrible fruit of their militant impiety. I cannot praise you
> for the acts that you tolerate, but I bless you and praise you for
> your majesty, which inspires awe. Your majesty must be really
> immense for all that is happening now not to make an impres-
> sion on you … I am dying peacefully, but not satisfied; as a man
> who has been laid low, but not in despair; as a believer but not
> as a supplicant; loving God, but not a blind mumbler of Amen. I
> have followed God, even when he has pushed me far away from
> himself. I have fulfilled his commandment, even when in return
> for this observance he struck me. I have loved him. I was and am
> still taken with him, even when he has lowered me down to the
> ground, has tortured me unto death, has reduced me to shame and
> derision. You can torture me to death but I will always believe in
> you: I will love you always, even in spite of yourself. And these
> are my final words, my God of anger: you will not succeed [in

making me deny you]. You have done everything so that I should no longer believe in you, so that I might fall into doubt. But I die as I have lived, with an unshakeable faith in you.[99]

# II   The human meets his match

## Genesis 32:22-32

22  The same night [Jacob] got up and took his two wives, his two maids, and his eleven children, and crossed the ford of the Jabbok.

23  He took them and sent them across the stream, and likewise everything that he had.

24  Jacob was left alone; and a man *is dusty*[1] with him [or got him in a body-hold] until daybreak.

25  When the man saw that he did not prevail against Jacob,
he struck him on the hip socket; and Jacob's hip was put out of joint as he wrestled with him
[*or* as he held him in a body-hold].

26  Then he said, "Let me go, for the day is breaking."
But Jacob said, "I will not let you go, unless you bless me."

27  So he said to him, "What is your name [shēm]?"
And he said, "Jacob."

28  Then the man said, "Your name [shēm] shall no longer be Jacob, but Israel,
for YOU HAVE STRIVEN[2]-with-God and with-humans,[3]
and have prevailed."

29  Then Jacob asked him,
"Please tell me your name [shēm]."

But he said, "Why is it that you ask my name [shēm]?"
And there he blessed him [shām].

30  So Jacob called the name [shēm] of the place Peny'el,
saying, "For I have seen God face to face, and yet my being/
my life is preserved."

31  The sun rose upon him as HE PASSED Penu'el,
limping because of his hip.

32  Therefore to this day the Israelites
do not eat the thigh muscle *naśeh* that is on the hip socket,
because he STRUCK Jacob on the hip socket at the thigh muscle
*nāsheh*.

## A Few Signposts in Space and Time

> A strange adventure, mysterious from beginning to end, breath-
> takingly beautiful, intense to the point of making one doubt
> one's senses. Who has not been fascinated by it? Philosophers,
> poets, rabbis and storytellers, all have yearned to shed light on
> the enigmatic event that took place that night, a few steps from
> the river Jabbok.[4]

The primitive form of the text dates from the eighth or ninth
century BCE, but is itself the final stage of a thousand-year process
during which oral traditions were passed on from generation to
generation. The history of these traditions is difficult to reconstruct.
Probably dating from before the Israelite era, it goes back to the time
of the patriarchs when what would become Israel was still on the
margins of contemporary civilizations, such as the Mesopotamian,
Amorite and Hurrite.[5] After a meticulous investigation of the vari-
ous hypotheses that have been advanced, H. Cazelles proposes the
following:

> Around the end of the Egyptian Middle Empire and the Amorite
> era ... a certain Abram ... entered Canaan, continued to Sichem,
> and then settled in the South ... It was in the South that he became
> Abraham and that his son Isaac was born, from whom would
> come Jacob, who in turn would go up towards Bethel ...  This
> patriarchal movement seems to have been on the whole a peaceful
> infiltration, and from the second generation (Isaac) onwards, the

Patriarchs became sedentary farmers. Although they reached the
borders of Egypt, this played no role ... The eighteenth century
was a propitious time for this temporary settlement by the patriarchs, and the name of Jacob[6] can be used to designate this era
... But although the genealogies of these semi-nomadic tribes
begin with historical figures, they then go on to create a series
of fictitious bonds of kinship among eponymous heroes ... To
the blood descendants of Abraham, Isaac and Israel-Jacob, other
groups of shepherds came to be added ... It was these groups of
whom later, in the days of Deuteronomy, the Israelite could say
"my father was a wandering Aramean" ... The age of El Amarna
(between 1400 and 1200) may correspond to this second, more
Aramean, wave, which would be added to the first, more Semitic,
Amorite wave ... What makes the interpretation of the patriarchal
traditions in Genesis more complicated is the complexity of the
history of the tribes that preserved and transmitted the traditions
... It was around the God of Abraham, Isaac and Israel-Jacob that
they came to be united, but before this unification there was a
whole history ... Everything is based on actual, historical facts,
but during the seven centuries that we think separate Abraham
and the definitive unification under David, a great many things
happened, including the Exodus under the leadership of Moses
the Levite, and the conquest under that of the Ephraimite Joshua.
These events could not fail to leave marks on the transmission
of ancient traditions.[7]

All this is to say that the story of Jacob speak of a time long before
the existence of the nation Israel, and was set down in writing by
one writer (or several) who lived long afterwards. Moreover, it is
an attempt to give an account of the human and divine action that
brought about the existence of Israel.[8] As for our text, its compi-
lation or definitive version could have been taken place after the
exile (587–538). This would explain, according to H.A. McKay,[9]
the vagueness and the geographical impossibilities that we find in
the story:[10] the prospect of a return from exile, from the North all
the way to Canaan, provoked tensions in the deported community,
for the journey appeared dangerous and risky, and people wondered
how to gain the acceptance of the current inhabitants of the land.

> Just beneath the surface of the narrative, we can sense the conflicts
> and the doubts of the believing community in Babylon: what
> could God's plan really be? Would they truly prosper in the land
> of Canaan if they believed the oracles of Deutero-Isaiah and set
> off for the South? … A group of second-generation Jews living
> in Babylon would have had only a vague knowledge of the ge-
> ography of Canaan, even if they may have become familiar with
> the names of the traditional centres of culture.

Scholars today seem to be unanimous on a number of points: for
instance, the existence of the patriarchs and of a "clan of nomadic
shepherds who claimed to descend from a certain 'Jacob' and who
considered themselves to be the heirs to the promise that – according to their own tradition – had been given to their ancestor by the
God of Bethel."[11] The patriarchs did not live off animal husbandry
alone; they also practised agriculture from the time of Abraham
onwards, and Jacob received an agrarian blessing. The sedentary
farmer was opposed by Esau the hunter; despised, hunters were on
the lowest rung of the social ladder, excluded by the Bible from
the promises of the land.[12] Moreover, it was in the region of the
Jabbok that the traditions regarding Jacob seemed the richest and
most deeply rooted.

It is likewise agreed that the stories about the patriarchs do not claim
to rest upon the testimony of eyewitnesses, but that the reality of the
events that are interpreted theologically by the authors is essentially
beyond doubt. The patriarchs were actual people, not divinities nor
characters of folkloric origin. The author of our text is generally
considered to be the Yahwist, and it is most certainly an "extract
of a story of migration, since it illustrates the theme of an obstacle
to be overcome"; "an element that intrudes upon the account of
the confrontation between Jacob and Esau," it seems to interrupt it
for theological reasons that will need to be identified.[13] If, in spite
of the convergence of numerous archaeological and ethnological
data, we remain very cautious about the historicity of the dates,
places and circumstances, it becomes clear that the essence consists
of the *promises received*, principally regarding the possession of the
land. The prophets and later Judaism continue to refer to it. "It is
Isaiah [40–55] who insists the most on this filiation, which makes

the people heirs to the promises made to the patriarchs," writes H. Cazelles.[14]

As the first heir to these promises, Jacob is both an individual and the people whom God has chosen: "You, Israel my servant, Jacob whom I have chosen, race of Abraham, my friend" (Is. 41:8) – a double value that we find among the pre-exilic prophets as well, since "according to the Hebrew mentality in general, the individual and the collective are never opposed." Whence the interchangeable use of the names "Jacob" and "Israel" in the biblical texts, as if since the crossing of the ford that night, Jacob had become the paradigm of an entire people, the illustration of a new way of living with oneself and with others. "Less frequently than the name of Israel, the name of Jacob appears constantly in the prophetic oracles and in most cases designates the people."[15]

What sort of narrative are we dealing with in Genesis 32:22-32? It is the literary genre known as the saga, where deeds count more than the psychology of the characters. Indeed, no state of mind is ever mentioned in these verses. We find similar sagas in Icelandic, German, Anglo-Saxon and Lithuanian tales. R. Martin-Achard notes,

> It is probable that a *saga* of this sort existed in a pre-Israelite stage. When the Israelites occupied the region, they made this tradition their own by turning their ancestor Jacob into the hero of the struggle at the ford of the Jabbok ... This legend, known in oral form, would have served to exalt the patriarch; it boasted of his cunning, which Genesis frequently evokes ... and his strength.[16]

Structural analysis allows us to conclude, according to Roland Barthes, that the struggle with the Angel is a "true fairy tale" that tells of the difficult crossing of a ford guarded by a hostile genie. It exhibits the same structure as in all fairy tales, namely a chain of "narrative acts" that we find here as in all popular stories, if we are to believe the author of *Morphology of the Folk Tale*, Vladimir Propp.

Contrary to appearances, our story is not intended to explain the origin of the dietary prohibitions mentioned at the end, nor the

origin of the name of the place, nor even the origin of the change
in name from "Jacob" to "Israel." It seems that the primary motif
of the story is the confrontation with the OTHER. Staying close to
the Hebrew text, R. Martin-Achard[17] translates v. 28 this way: "For
you have struggled with Elohim and with men and you have held
out."[18] "The name that Jacob was given refers therefore first of all
to the difficulties he had already faced ... The unknown narrator
celebrates the resistance of the patriarch, the fact that he had held
out all night long." A struggle of this nature is part of the intimate
relationship that the patriarch enjoys with a God who knows his
whole being and his actions. Abraham had already struggled with
God to obtain justice in Sodom, in a prayer that pushed the limits
of his capacity to confront God.

Well before this story, from the time he was an infant at his mother's
breast, the name of Jacob was linked to the theme of conflict, but in
a most particular fashion; it was not conflict as such that interested
the author or authors, but rather it was conflict that put the divine
blessing at risk. After the threats linked to Esau's violence, to exile
and to economic exploitation, the nocturnal struggle once again
led Jacob to question his conviction that he had been blessed by
God. Everything was as if God had withdrawn, whereas like with
other patriarchs God had acted directly. In Jacob's story, he works
through the twisted behaviours and conflictual imbroglios. Thus, as
L. Hicks notes, "When Jacob rises to a height of blasphemy unprecedented in patriarchal history and declares to his blind father that
he has found game so quickly 'because the Lord your God granted
me success' (Gen. 27:20),[19] he also utters the most profoundly true
explanation of his career."[20]

It seems surprising that this story is so rarely cited in the Bible; it is
referred to only in Wisdom 10:12 and in Hosea 12:4ff (for purely
polemical reasons), despite the fact that it gives the origin of the
name of Israel, a name that appears there for the first time. This is
the first of the shadowy zones that surround this text. Could one
not sense that there was something different there, which could
both be told and yet not told? The reason is that at the dawn of its
existence, a people in the person of Jacob had a wish-fulfillment

dream: to be the "prince" of God, for, according to the rabbis, "Israel" contains the words [śar], the "prince," and ['el], "God."[21] Similarly, at the dawn of the history of this people, God dreams of struggling with them, provoking them, opposing them. For, since the classic etymology derives Israel from [śarah], "to struggle,"[22] we can understand "God fights" as referring to equals. It is a double wish-fulfillment dream, then, that will determine reality: Israel will indeed become the people of God. By playing on the "el" of the word "elite," R. Couffignal succeeds in joining all these meanings together:

> You will be elite ... Isra-ël, does its name not henceforth bear the *mark* of divinity: El? What is more, to say that it will prevail over Élohim and over man, that it *shall be elite* – as the translation tries to show by a wordplay that is analogous to that of the Hebrew text, to say this is to say that he "ascends the throne."[23]

Everyone who writes about the struggle of Jacob highlights its deliberately ambiguous style, the chiaroscuro of the expression, the discontinuities, the absence of logical articulations. There are a score of literary works on the struggle of Jacob, of which more than half were written in the twentieth century. Several, of which the most famous is perhaps *The Story of Satan* by Georges Bernanos, see in this mysterious night a story that is located at the border between dream and reality. "Does not the symbolic explosion of the text," writes Roland Barthes with reference to another logic to the work – that of the unconscious – sooner or later set us on the path of an interpretation of the text in the light of dreams? How to speak of a combat the result of which would be good for both adversaries? How to evoke this unique combat, one hundred per cent fruitful, that is the combat with the OTHER? Would not the best language be that of the dream?

# 1   The signs of a dream: "And Jacob was alone..."

... tonight, I wish to dig around
In the mountains of ash piled on top of me.
A single spark in the darkness will suffice
Smouldering for so many vain years under the slag heap
For a burning bush to rise up to meet me,
God upon my face. I know Who I am facing here
I want to see Him face to face at last and go to Him

... Abyss of Jacob rushing at Jacob!
From all eternity God could no longer abide this absence:
Without humanity, what can any world mean to Him? And
what heavens
Can be as high as the thought of a human being in God?

... Love of God for humankind, accomplished by a man
A gulf of being that is unbridgeable and yet incarnate!
The glory of Jacob is to feel this abyss
This storm of love against him takes shape:
With all his heart God desires to limit Himself. Power
Of Jacob who receives limitation by resisting!
Through the pain of a gaping resemblance
The soul listens to God becoming a beating heart

... If Love gives a new name to the one he loves
It is to show that he alone is the master of meaning.
If he wills, he changes blasphemy into baptism
In his worst enemy he hears the voice of a son
... You shall never be able to escape from yourself
No hope of having done with this Other within you.
Face, abyss: you fall in but you love it.
There the unfathomable Love that has captured you blesses
you![24]

In one of the testimonies of Hasidic Jews in the World War II
death camps, Yaffa Eliach tells how three people in similar circumstances survived thanks to a dream. In Bergen-Belsen, a woman
had daily repeated a prayer that seemed to have been written for
the circumstances, "a prayer from the valley of death that kept
the soul alive." She eventually forgot the words of the prayer, but
"in the vacuum left by the prayer, I distinctly heard my mother's
voice. 'We are all God's children. He can do with us whatever he
pleases.'" Encouraged by her mother's voice, she walked out of the
camp and reached her hometown on the Sabbath; her mother fed
her and told her with conviction that she would recover and soon
be liberated. The woman did indeed survive typhoid, attesting to
the power of a "very special prayer and a dream, a dream in which
reality overshadows dreams, and dreams overpower reality."[25]

Another woman suffering from typhus at Bergen-Belsen was equally
determined to live. Left for dead by her companions, she dragged
herself to a "hill" which suddenly became for her a symbol of life, so
sure was she that if she reached it she would survive. Once she got
to the summit of the mound, she called her father and suddenly felt
on her forehead the hand of her father blessing her and foretelling
her imminent liberation. She later learned that he had been buried
with thousands of others, there under that mound, but she was
unaware of this when she called out to him. She, too, survived.

Finally, in a camp in Hungary, a man who kept repeating "I want
to live" was also struck down by typhus. Confined to the barracks
for the dying, he no longer had the strength even to move his lips
and utter the confession of the dying. He thought the prayer and

fell into a deep sleep. He dreamed of returning to his family in the middle of the Sabbath. His parents gave him some Sabbath cake and wine; his father assured him that he would live. He awoke absolutely certain that this was the truth, and with a feeling of enormous strength. He survived as well.

In all three cases, then, the desire to live gave rise to a dream or vision of desire that would shape reality in a spectacular fashion. The psychology of religion today takes into account these "dream experiences of such intensity that the next day we wonder with astonishment whether we had been dreaming or undergoing something real"; A. Vergote adds that the borderline between vision and dream is blurred: "Of course, visionaries are not in a state of sleep. The experience of dreaming, nevertheless, confronts us with the same type of psychological phenomenon."[26] The biblical authors, however, had already understood this, according to several Jewish writers. According to J. Eisenberg, "in the Bible, dream and reality are often confused. More specifically, a single 'vision' itself can be a source of visions."[27] E. Fleg, for his part, entitles his poem on the struggle at the Jabbok "The Vision of Jacob," and concludes it with these words: "And the Enemy left. And Jacob fell asleep."[28] There follows the famous dream of the ladder between earth and heaven – an inversion of the biblical text that stresses the proximity, at the experiential level, between vision, sleep and dreams.[29]

For the Ancients,[30] visions and dreams were of supernatural origin and allowed human beings to receive signs from on high without having produced them themselves. The research done by A.L. Oppenheim on the interpretation of dreams in the ancient Near East[31] shows that there are symbolic dreams and message dreams, although the boundary between the two is far from clear. There are, however, a few constant features in message dreams that seem to me to be remarkably present in the story of Jacob's struggle:

–   The message is always proclaimed by a divine figure: "Your name shall no longer be Jacob but Israel ..."

–   The appearance of the divine figure is sudden and surprising, which is one of the most remarkable of the constant elements in these dreams: Jacob falls violently to the ground, without warning, in the middle of a verse.

- Very often, the divinity stands at the head of the sleeper – thus, at ground level, which is true in the case of Jacob, who fights in the dust.

- After the message (sometimes communicated in a dialogue), the dreamer wakes up with a start, noticing that he has been dreaming: in v. 30, without any transition, Jacob "shouts the name of the place."

- The vision of the divinity is a constitutive element of the dream-message. Jacob immediately says he has seen "God face to face," though it was in the dark of night.

- The divine figure sometimes reinforces his words with a gesture: Jacob is touched on the thigh.

- Dream-messages end in the command to perform some ritual action or in a divine promise that will affect the destiny of the dreamer or his people: here we have both – the ritual prohibition and the new name, which tells what this people will become: "You shall be Israel."

It is above all the conclusion of this study that is to be noted, for it converges remarkably with the experience of survivors as recounted by Y. Eliach: "The function of the majority of these elements is to stress the 'reality' of the vision ... The transition between the state of dreaming and that of being awake was often poorly marked, given that for ancient narrators both states belonged to 'reality.'"[32]

As for the Jewish interpretations of our text, in the Midrash we find an image that recalls our expression "to fall into the arms of Morpheus," meaning a deep sleep: "They [Jacob and his adversary] fell [plunged] into each other."[33] Further on, to explain the passage "Leave me for the dawn is here," a rabbi cited Lamentations 3:23, where God says that he his mercies are "new every morning." God is faithful enough to revive us from death in this way; for, as we read in the note, "Sleep is regarded as a minor death."[34] The

Midrash thus implies that Jacob was sleeping. Finally, some of the earliest Jewish commentators, such as Maimonides, have suggested that the experience of Jacob at the Jabbok may have been one of his dreams.[35]

If we turn to authors with a psychoanalytic background, W.G. Niederland speaks of this story in terms of a nightmare,[36] and A. Vergote stresses the richness of the Freudian interpretation of dreams for understanding visions and dreams of a religious nature. The three elements of the Freudian theory of dreams can reinforce the conviction that on that night, Jacob was up against his unconscious, that he heard the Other and understood himself at a much deeper and more authentic level than during the day, where his conscious mind exercised judgment. Are we not surprised at what we are capable of dreaming, and thus of producing and hearing in the most hidden parts of our being, both in terms of "good" and of "evil"? A murderous anger, completely hidden before others and even ourselves, may rise up in a dream to our great astonishment. Will we at last own this violence that is ours? It is *I* who dreamt this, and thus it dwells in me. Or an unhoped-for outcome can open up in a dream, when everything in reality is blocked; will we at last allow ourselves the conviction that we have the solution within ourselves, and that our unconscious already believes in our healing or liberation? If it is I who dreamed of the light at the end of the tunnel, this must mean that I am capable of reaching it. And in this mysterious passage from the unconscious to the conscious mind, is it not the Other who is continuing his work of creation? What was but chaos yesterday becomes, in the early morn, a clear vision, face to face, of reality.

The first element, according to Freud, is that the dream expresses ideas with a strong affective charge (desire, anguish) that are inscribed in the memory. And indeed, the day before, Jacob had been in a deep state of anguish, which was being fed by the memory of the hostility of Esau twenty years before: the problem has thus remained intact and, given that the unconscious is atemporal, the fear of being killed is permanently inscribed in Jacob's memory.

The second element, in Freud's view, is that these strong affects appear in the dream in the form of images drawn from the perceptions of the day before; we "choose" the perceptions that most closely resemble our unconscious affects. Thus, Jacob had heard that Esau was approaching with four hundred men; his anguish, both very present and yet ancient, led him to conceive of a bitter struggle. In the practice of analysis, both words and images need therefore to be decoded. There is something of the present that triggers the dream, but the affects that accompany the dream reveal to us our forgotten experiences. Something happens in his dream that will inform Jacob of what he had forgotten; it has to do with the *image of the thigh*, linked to a strong affect of impotency.

The third element in Freudian theory is that affects tend to irrupt into the conscious because they are bearers of a desire. Thus, what finally pushes a dreamer to relive, and thus take ownership of, the terror inscribed in his or her memory is the desire for a life of freedom that is at work beneath this affect. The dreamer notices this when he begins to dream that he has escaped from extreme danger; he lives under a sort of propulsion towards the future, a future that already inhabits him for the simple reason that underneath his terror or distress lies is a strong, vital force that is seeking accomplishment and satisfaction by all possible means. Hence the "sense of a reality that is truly being lived": according to A. Vergote, "*What we perceive is what is real and realized.*"[37] I would add: whether we are dealing with a past injury (in which case we would say the dream is a reliving) or a happy outcome (as in the case of the prisoners in the death camps). Whether Jacob was dreaming or had a vision,[38] I would say that in any case he experienced a reality that is even more true than reality, or that he perceived the real to the second degree, whereas in normal circumstances he would have remained at the level of appearances.

---

Which elements in the text itself might point to a dream?

**a)** Jacob is alone at night. The text repeatedly emphasizes the fact that it is night-time: in v. 13, "He spent that night there"; in v. 21,

"He himself spent that night in the camp"; in v. 22, "The same night, he got up." The story ends with daybreak. Yet from v. 24 we learn that a man got covered in dust with him *until daybreak.* Why not wait until the end of the story, respecting the passage of time? Is this not an example of that contraction of time so typical of dreams, which makes the dreamer think that the dream had been very long, whereas in reality, as one can demonstrate scientifically, all dreams last only a short time? Moreover, the temporal indication given at the beginning of our text seems illogical. For v. 21 – "he himself spent that night in the camp" – seems to end the day. Why, then, the need for this detail if the whole camp was moving that very night?

Certainly it will be argued that two traditions (the Yahwist and the Elohist) are intersecting here. But why is it that during the final redaction this contradiction was not noticed? The contradiction disappears if we take the hypothesis of the dream: the camp did not in fact cross the stream until the next day. What is more, whereas Jacob had called this place *Peny'el* ("turn *yourself* towards God!"), the text ends, in v. 31, with "the sun rose upon him as he passed *Pe-nu'-el*" ("turn *yourselves* towards God!"), as if Jacob were inviting all those close to him to take the same step as he had just done.

In the same vein, we may note that all the verbs, with the exception of three, are in the imperfect mode,[39] as if the action had not yet taken place, and as if it were speaking of an exemplary time, open to the future, of a process that one would continue to make one's own. The imperfect tense of the dream leads, in v. 31ff, to two verbs in the perfect tense: "he passed" and "he touched," which attest to the fact that something has happened in reality – it took place and continues to exist. As for the third verb in the perfect tense, it is situated at the very centre of the text, in v. 28, indicating that the dream has begun to be anchored in reality: "You have struggled and you are still struggling"... you are in the process of learning what a fruitful confrontation might be.

**b)** "And he, Jacob, was left alone" (v. 24). If this were not a dream, why would Jacob go back across, only to find himself alone on the other side? Does it make sense to seek solitude if the place is sinister[40] and one is terrified at the prospect of confronting the next day a hostile brother accompanied by four hundred men? The verb, moreover, is in the passive voice, as if to suggest the absence of a deliberate choice. What could have compelled Jacob to remain alone, if not sleep? And, conversely, is not insomnia often a sign of our fear of "remaining alone," vulnerable before the messages that our unconscious seeks to send us by means of dreams and night-mares? Elie Wiesel makes the same suggestion:

> Man must be alone to listen, to feel and even to fight God, for God engages only those who, paradoxically, are both threatened and protected by solitude. God, traditionally, elects to speak to His chosen in their sleep because that is when they are truly alone, removed from all alien presence to distract them.[41]

Moreover, citing verses 22ff. – "The present [gift] paraded before Jacob, and he remained at the station that night. He rose during the night, etc." – Rashi agrees with the Midrash, which "here gives the word *face* [the gift ran across, literally, his face] the sense of *anger*: Jacob was irritated at having to do all this." If we assume it was a dream, then having reviewed all the gifts, he fell asleep in anger … and all his repressed violence expressed itself freely in a dream.

Another indication is the statement "he rose" in v. 22, which sug-gests that he had been lying down. Why would he have been lying down if his day was not yet over, if he still had to bring the whole group across the stream? J. Skinner remarks, moreover, that such an operation would have been necessary only in case of an attack by Esau; the latter, however, was approaching from the south, whereas Jacob was hurrying to bring his entire camp over to *the side of the river* from which Esau was coming. "Either the narrative is defective on this point, or it is written without a clear concep-tion of the actual circumstances."[42] A third hypothesis, which is the one I hold, is that the dangerous operation in question was taking place in Jacob's dream … for he was left alone, up against the wall of his own anguish.

**c)** Let us suppose, then, that v. 22ff. evokes a *falling asleep*, as, on the night before a trip or a very busy day, before going to sleep we review all that we have to do. Our thoughts end up going around in circles. Thus Jacob might have said to himself, "Tomorrow I *will take* my two wives, my two maidservants, my eleven boys,[43]

> I will ford the ford of the Jabbok [repetition]
> I will take them [repetition]
> I will take them across the torrent
> And will take over [repetition] what belongs to me.

At this stage of sinking into sleep, the associations of words and thoughts begin. "He will take them across *the torrent* and take across *what belongs to him.*" Yet to "torrent" [na*h*al] corresponds the verb [na*h*al], signifying "to take possession": taking possession … what belongs to him. We shall see how Jacob will take possession of himself that night!

**d)** Another element, the imprecise nature of the subjects, is very striking between verses 24 and 28, that is, as soon as Jacob "is left alone," until he receives his true identity: first, "a man," then a succession of seven times "he," and finally, the identification of the unknown person by Jacob who has become fully himself ("I have seen *God*"). There is no angel in the text, even if the prophet Hosea notes a tradition that saw in Jacob's assailant an "angel" or "messenger." "Having reached a mature age, he struggled with God. He fought with an angel and triumphed. He cried and beseeched him. At Bethel he found him and it was there that God spoke to us" (Hos 12:3b-4). Who cried? Who beseeched? Who found?

The imprecision continues. It extends, at a literary level, the very experience of Jacob. It is common in dreams to feel as if split in two, as if we were speaking, moving, struggling with a part of ourselves – at once oneself and an OTHER whom we are unable to identify clearly. If this OTHER haunts our nights much more than it makes itself felt in the fabric of our days, is it not from pure discretion, in order not to startle us, but also to take advantage of those precious moments where we at last let ourselves go?

Given such imprecision, anything can be imagined and everything has been. For instance, it is said that it was Jacob who asked to be let go (having been injured in the hip) and it was the adversary who

asked for the blessing, in the hope of withdrawing from Jacob his
usurped blessing and thus subjecting him to what he had once done
to Esau.[44] The hypothesis is not far-fetched at all if we acknowledge
that our dreams allow us to give free rein to our most negative
images of God: if Jacob had lived up to this point with repressed
guilt, he could dream of a divine punishment of the same nature as
the injustice he once committed; and since he had heard his father
appear somewhat short of blessings,[45] he might have failed to believe in an unlimited divine generosity: give me back the blessing
that you stole!

**e)** At first reading, we may have the impression that it is a harmless
struggle: "He sees that he can do nothing to him" (v. 25). It would
appear to be the sense of powerlessness that we sometimes feel in
a dream where we strike out with all our might against something
or someone, without any result, as if we were surrounded by cot-
ton wool. But at the same time – in the same verse – a minimal
gesture, a simple touch[46] provokes a veritable "dislocation." We are
sometimes uninterested in the truth that our dreams may contain
because of certain features such as this disproportion between cause
and effect: it's too absurd, we say to ourselves. But if we make up our
minds that everything in a dream has significance, we let ourselves
be alerted by this disproportion. What does the thigh represent in
Jacob's life, for the slightest contact with the memories connected
to this part of the body to provoke such a major dysfunction?

It can happen in real life as well that a simple touch on a part of the
body can unleash a flood of affects and memories. Certain therapies
today thus allow us to reconnect with entire chapters of our personal
history. In the end, it matters little whether Jacob was dreaming
or whether he was physically touched by the adversary in a spot
charged with meaning. The truth of the story lies elsewhere: that
night, Jacob allowed himself to be touched in the deepest part of
himself, in a zone within himself which he could not and did not
want to touch until then. The dream favours this act because it offers the sleeper a battlefield that is perfectly "secure," as we would
say today: our own violence can be unleashed without anyone
dying as a result, and thus we can, sometimes for the first time, be

truly ourselves, with all our combativeness but also *with what we had always had to hide (from ourselves)*.

**f)** "And a man *covered himself in dust* with him" (v. 25). The verb ['avaq] means first of all to flee, which immediately reminds us of Jacob's habitual reflex, to flee rather than risk confrontation. The second meaning, however, does not appear anywhere else in the Bible. We can translate it by "covered with dust" because of the noun that corresponds to it: ['avaq], dust. A word that is used only once (a *hapax*) is undoubtedly, at a literary level, the best translation of an indescribable affect. A way of saying that there is something exceptional going on, a dream that will go so deep that we cannot find the right words to express it. We need in a sense to create words for it in order to avoid betraying the dream by telling it.

The irruption of the unknown in Jacob inspires him first to flee, and this is perhaps the nightmarish side of the dream. In these two senses of the verb we would see the concentration of two elements in a single image, which is characteristic of dreams: the flight is nipped in the bud; the dreamer has no time to find an escape route. He is literally "in the dust with him," with this passive voice in the Hebrew, which in the Bible discreetly indicates God while preserving the mystery of the attacker.

If we take into account the fact that dreams visually present images by using a part to signify the whole, we can think of multiple meanings evoked by the term "dust": to bite the dust, grovel, return to dust, the dust and ashes of a life that turns to dust, to be pulled out of the dust. Why is the idea of a hand-to-hand combat seen as second to that of "being in the dust," since the two concepts are perfectly compatible in any case? Does this not point to the very nature of a dream? For the dust, as a visual image, means that the dreamer cannot distance himself from the scene to see the two bodies struggling and identify the adversary. The only thing he *sees* is the dust in which he is brutally rolled without knowing against whom he is fighting. In the commentary of Rashi we can identify the work of interpretation that is grafted onto the raw material of the dream and the text:

[The grammarian] Menachem (ben Saruk) explains: "A man covered himself with dust" *taking the verb as connected* in sense with "dust." *It would mean* that they were raising the dust with their feet through their movements. I, however, am of opinion that it means "He fastened himself on." ... It denotes "intertwining," for such is the manner of two people who make strong efforts to throw each other – one clasps the other and twines himself around him with his arms.[47]

**g)** A play on words frames the text ("v" and "b" being the same letter in Hebrew): Ya'aqov (Jacob) ... ye' aveq ... Yabboq ...

R. Couffignal tries to express this linguistic proximity by translating it "Jacob boxes on the Jabbok."[48] Word plays are typical of oneiric activity, in which one word calls up another with similar sonority, depending on the preoccupations of the dreamer. For Jacob's dream, this would mean: I, Ya'aqov, I will cross the Jabbok to confront [ye'aveq] my brother Esau, to be covered in dust with him, and I feel like running away!

It is possible that the expression "you became powerful" in v. 28 conveys the principal affect resulting from the dream: namely, one of force and of self-affirmation, since the verb is used in the absolute. This may be the result of the unconscious activity of the dreamer. In reality, v. 28 – "What is your name? Jacob!" – seems to give prominence to the effect of the dream, which gives the part for the whole and willingly transforms thought into images: the image here is the heel, since Ya'aqov comes from the verb ['aqav], "to grab the heel, deceive," which gives us ['aqev], "the heel." By pronouncing its name in a dream, Jacob may be seeing a heel, which would give rise to the statement that is absurd in appearance only: "What is your name? 'Heel!'"

But only a little later, in v. 28, he visualizes something quite different that he is told in the dream: a *forehead*. You shall be a con*fro*nter, a fighter with God, as E. Fleg translates it: "Your name shall no longer be Jacob, but Israel, *confront-God*. For you confronted God and men and you prevailed."[49]

To speak of the forehead is to speak of the face, whence the verbal expression by Jacob of what happened to him: he saw himself as a heel (always ready to turn on his heels) and then saw himself and was seen as a forehead, capable of "seeing God face to face." Behind these visual images (the heel, the forehead/face), we can thus discern the thought underlying the dream:[50] I am a deceiver, I want to be a legitimate "prince," empowered to come face to face.

h) In reality, we know whether we are dealing with a friend or a foe. Here, by contrast, we never escape the ambiguity between a struggle with or a struggle against. In v. 25, the Septuagint (Greek translation of the Hebrew Bible made in the second century BCE) says that Jacob fought *with* the unknown one. For some, it is *against* an adversary that he fought, but *with* the help of the angel, for the book of Hosea says of Jacob: "He was strong *against* God [pros] *with* an angel [meta]" (12:4ff., Septuagint). We find the same ambiguity in v. 28: "You have struggled with God" is translated, in the Septuagint, by the verb [enischuô], measuring one's force *against* ... but is followed by "with" [meta], which gives the reading "you have measured your strength–against with God."

The affect of the dreamer is cruelly lacking: only Jacob could say whether his adversary was friend or foe. The only indication is that he himself extends his dream in v. 26. If it were a question of reality, how would he have had the upper hand at the very moment when he was injured, and afterwards, how can it be that he wishes to hold on to his adversary? In fact, he does not have the upper hand, because there is no physical combat. This explains why it is impossible for the dreamer, the author and the readers to decide between *with* and *against*. If it is a dream, v. 26 appears to be the sign that Jacob does not want to wake up, but is resolved to hold onto his dream: let me go, release me, I am only a dream, it's time to wake up. "Leave me for the dawn is breaking!" No, Jacob appears to reply, "I will not let you go until you have blessed me"; I will not wake up until everything is clear.

We have the impression that the ambiguity of the real events persists. In fact, Jacob lay down without knowing whether Esau was coming as a brother or as an enemy; according to the Targum, he "was coming and with him four hundred men on foot"[51] or with "four hundred warriors."[52] The Targum considers that the ambiguity continues through the encounter of the two brothers in the next chapter. Esau apparently came not to kiss his brother [nashāq] but to bite [nashāk] him – an interpretation already proposed by the Midrash – but Jacob's neck turned into marble, and Esau's teeth were loosened:

> Esau ran to meet him and embraced him and inclined upon his neck and bit him; and they wept. Esau wept because of the pain of his teeth that were loosened; and Jacob wept because of the pain of his neck.[53]

Underneath the story's fairy-tale, vaudeville nature, with a magic spell-like dream, is revealed a truth that we do not easily address in reality: the inextricable mixture of hatred and love, opposition and aspiration to harmony, resentment and forgiveness that so often takes the place of relationship. The development of the Targum marvellously evokes those desires to bite and those fears of being bitten that lurk at times behind our conventional embraces.

If we adopt the hypothesis of the dream, the request for a blessing in v. 26b can be understood as a request for clarity. A benediction is to "speak well" to someone. Tell me what is going on: I want to understand my dream, Jacob is asking. We are familiar with the efforts, in our dreams, to understand something that appears incomprehensible. And as dreams bring a sequence of images, Jacob too needs an image here. A little earlier, the dust allowed him to visualize the struggle, and now it is the *gesture of blessing* that turns his deepest aspiration into visual form: speak well to me, talk to me so that it might do me good, speak well of me and for me! Another way of visualizing is given in Calvin's commentary. With one hand God fights Jacob, with the other he blesses him by "teaching" – that is, by explaining to him what is happening during a "night vision" which, according to Calvin, is not a "mere dream," since Jacob would limp thereafter, preserving in his flesh the mark of the struggle:

For we do not fight against him, except by his own power, and with his own weapons; for he, having challenged us to this contest, at the same time furnishes us with means of resistance, so that he both fights against us and for us ... He fights against us with his left hand, and for us with his right hand ... The reason which the angel assigns, namely, that the day breaketh, is to this effect, that Jacob may know that he has been divinely taught by the nocturnal vision.[54]

**i)** How can we move beyond the apparent absurdity of the sequence of events that follows? The request for a blessing leads to a discussion about names. It is often difficult, at first glance, to see the connection between two consecutive dreams. And yet, as we know, there is often a cohesion, a single concern. "Jacob asks. He says: 'Explain your name!'" (v. 29). Let us suppose that this is one of those inversions typical of oneiric activity: the unconscious is always centred on itself and all dialogue turns around the name of Jacob. Perhaps there is still a doubt in the dreamer's mind: is it really about *me*? Tell me more about who I really am, a heel or a forehead? Explain it to me, tell me,[55] give me proof that what you say is true! "Your name" would thus be the result of a work of inversion that operates so often in dreams: explain to me, tell me the name you said, *explain to me (the story of) your name*!

Is this hypothesis far-fetched? Not if one considers the following elements:

–   In v. 26, Jacob had asked to be blessed without worrying in the least about the identity of the adversary; why would he be interested in it now?

–   Thus the contradiction with v. 30 disappears: although the adversary refused to let himself be known, Jacob will say that he "saw God face to face." For it is true: if Jacob had asked questions about his own name, one would understand that it was at the very heart of his discovery of his identity that he encountered God face to face.

–   The gesture of blessing, then, would not signify a concession (I will not reply to you but I will bless you nevertheless). It would signify *in itself the response*, the response to the doubt that lingered in Jacob's mind. This gesture would be the equivalent of a response: your name suits you; you are indeed who you want to be and dream of being; there is nothing to add to this "speaking well," to this "bene-diction."

**j)** Without a transition, "Jacob called the name of the place" (v. 30), and that resembled a brusque awakening and an immediate awareness of what he had just dreamed: "For I saw God face to face and my being/my life is/will be redeemed." It is a pleasant, strong affect, the feeling of being profoundly free, as happens when one awakens in a good mood, inhabited by a significant dream. The verb is in the imperfect mode, suggesting an enduring deliverance. Such a feeling of liberation is well known to anyone who has been able to draw out the meaning of a nightmare and, through this torment, become liberated from something.

"To call out the name of …" in Hebrew means to make someone or something exist by naming it. It is thus that the human was associated with the work of the Creator in Genesis: God had all the animals come towards the man "to see what he would call them; and whatever the man called each living creature, that was its name" (Gen 2:19). Jacob had only just become convinced of being blessed and welcomed in his authentic identity when he became capable in his turn of naming a place, as if God was coming to incarnate in his life. Of course, the OTHER always remains unnameable, hidden by the dark of night and the fleeting nature of the dream and safe from being captured and schematized. But the space Jacob occupied on the earth at that moment became a space inhabited by God's presence: Peny'el, "turn towards El [God]" *right there where you are.*

From now on Jacob will have his own place: he who, condemned by his agreement with Laban not to turn back towards the place of his exile, thought he was forbidden to have access to the land of his youth because of Esau's hostility. The feeling of deliverance is so intense that he is immediately able to name his own place, that place that no one can take from him because it is already occupied by God, the one that he will bring with him everywhere he goes, for *Turn towards God* will always be his refuge. Yet nothing has really changed in objective terms. The confrontation with Esau has not yet taken place, but everything is proceeding as if Jacob's prayer were already answered. Thus it happens that a dream functions like the lamp a miner wears on his forehead as he goes deep into the pit; his feet move forward in the dark but the lamp reveals his possible paths. Those dreams are precious: they anticipate what is to come but that we already carry within ourselves, just as the lamp is part of the miner's body.

---

We can decipher a biblical text through a number of perspectives: Jewish, historico-critical, structuralist, psychological, narrative, semiotic, etc. To interpret a dream, we can have recourse to psychoanalysis (Freudian or other schools), to the science of archetypes and universal symbols, to religious understandings of the reception of divine messages, to poetical intuition, to philosophical reflection, etc. It is therefore impossible to block the question "What does this text or that dream mean?" Any interpretation remains temporary, and the most authoritative commentators on our text always end up hitting a hard to understand kernel that eludes all analysis. According to G. von Rad,

> It is because of the flaws and patches [that one finds in the tale] that it has acquired that interior literary breadth; the relaxed character of the internal relationships between the phrases leaves room for all kinds of thoughts ... What exegete will not come up against a remnant in the story that defies interpretation?[56]

The initial intention of a biblical author cannot be teased out with certainty. As for the person who dreams, he or she interprets the dream differently at different times in his or her life. In both cases, one can see the trace of the unconscious in the ongoing lack of clarity, especially when the biblical text recounts a dream or a vision.

If it is already difficult to interpret someone else's dream, how can anyone claim to interpret Jacob's dream thousands of years after the fact, and, what's more, when it is a dream that is told to us by others? It is the biblical text itself that authorizes us to do so; criss-crossed with interpretations that come out of the unconscious and conscious activity of the authors, it calls forth *our* conscious and unconscious interpretation. In each generation and in each individual's history, it waits for us to appropriate it. From then on, we cannot say that a given interpretation is correct because a particular exegete or psychoanalyst or authority has been conclusively convincing, but because it touches something in me as well, and causes a change, an unexpected shift. Recall the strange gesture of Jacob's adversary, putting his finger on something in Jacob and causing a shift that is so remarkable it can be noticed the next day.

We can choose not to remain outside Jacob's dream. We can engage in an act of interpretation that is not simply an intellectual exercise, a mind game. Just like any exegete, psychoanalyst, rabbi, or poet worthy of the name, we can desire an encounter of our own unconscious with the unconscious of another by means of that person's dream or a biblical text. Such was no doubt the approach of the final redactor of our text, even if he was unable to explain it in the terms that we use. Indeed, there are three indications that suggest linkages between the two unconsciouses. They are the "white spaces" of the text, those things that await explanation, that attest to a discontinuity in the thought of the dream. Those blank spaces are found in the three *hapax* of the story that describes the dream. The indecisive literary expression signals to us the places where the affect of the dreamer has remained in flux. When we are not too sure what we are feeling or what has been happening in the dream, we have trouble finding the right words to express it, and therefore the words we use are rare words; one may even invent words. This happens in three places in the story – at the beginning, in the middle, and at the very end:

> In v. 24: "he was covered with dust"
> In v. 28: "you have struggled/held on/been a prince"
> In v. 32: "the nerve [nāsheh]."

Because they are hard to translate, these three *hapax* appear like hazy areas that invite us to use our full interpretive abilities. The first is found at the surface of the human condition; to be covered with dust is to tackle the problem, to grab hold of it, to get busy kneading the (human) dough. We even say that such or such an event floored us. In the blurriness of the text, anyone grappling with an urgent personal problem can slip in; it is up to each person to "translate" what is really happening at ground level. The second zone concerns the face-to-face encounter, the manner of resisting, of confronting, of getting on one's feet: confront, become a prince, vanquish ... Anyone who is experiencing deliverance at the end of their night can fit into this haziness; it is up to each one to translate what his or her own victory could or does consist of. The third area is by far the most opaque. It is found at the level of the wound, of what hurts, of what one does not dare touch: the nerve [nãsheh] that makes walking difficult. We begin with the idea that the harm has already been done; if there is something in me and my life that limps, is it not the result of a blow that was experienced long ago and that is lodged in my body and in my whole being? What does the dysfunctionality of my body tell me? In the haziness of the text, I can come in contact with the desire to know more about who I am, who I was and who I am capable of becoming. It is up to me to get myself moving, even if I am limping, towards the old wound that is mine, rather than blocking myself from seeing my handicap!

It doesn't matter, in the end, if the text gives the impression that there is no affect. We are not told what Jacob is feeling, about "what that did to him" while he was living it. And it is often the same when awakening from a dream, as if any affect was in a hurry to disappear from the dreamer's conscious mind at daybreak. More significant than the description of affects are their placement in the text. These are points of collision of the conscious into the unconscious, and they are large enough for each reader to be able to transpose them in his or her own life.

In such a work of interpretation, nevertheless, there is a great risk of projecting one's own affects or theories onto the text. Echoing the theories of of Lévi-Strauss and Freud, some see the combat of Jacob as an anxiety dream of sexual origin in which Jacob, seeing his own image, is attacked by Esau and then by the divinity, which generally symbolizes the father, who wants to kill him, to wound his reproductive power: in other words, to castrate him. In the end, the devil becomes a beneficent god: that is, Jacob's projection of his idealized father.[57] This reduction of the adversary to the simple superego, persecutor and divinized by turns, is perplexing. In spite of the element of truth it contains, such an interpretation does not seem to me to do justice to either the dream or the text. It is based on Jacob's statement "My life has been saved," which one must understand to mean "I almost died."

But if we stay as close as possible to the text, we read, "My being/my life is/will be delivered," as if it had been taken prisoner. We have seen how Jacob, according to the Midrash and Rashi, had gone to sleep angry and not distressed, as in v. 7. Meanwhile, he had put in place his strategy to mollify Esau, and the irritation of having to do all that had doubtless put him in touch with his own fighting spirit. If our text were recounting a fit of anguish, it is hard to see where Jacob would have got the energy to fight all night long. Anyone who has lived through mortal anguish, like Jacob in v. 7, knows how it destroys the capacity to act. The least we can say is that at the moment of the scene on the bank of the Jabbok, Jacob is no longer paralyzed by anguish. The only indication he gives about what he had just lived through leads rather towards a feeling of total powerlessness, gradually converted to the possibility of life. "He did not prevail against Jacob" (v. 25), and, after a struggle, as the night ended, "You have prevailed" (you are rendered powerful) (v. 28). Upon waking, Jacob says that he has been "delivered," freed certainly from a great dread, but above all from the burden that was his life of submission, of his cumbersome past, his assumed identity.

The dream hypothesis has allowed us to see Jacob get to the authentic Jacob. Dream, vision or reality, when all is said and done what counts is that he is given the opportunity to see himself as he is and as God sees him. In his 1941 play *Jacob eo Anjo*, José Regio constantly and deliberately mixed the dream and the real together. "If you had understood [the struggle], you would have known that I did not come in the confusion of your dreams, but at a moment where the dream had freed your intelligence from the lies that were smothering it."[58] The important thing is that something happened, that one hear what one has not heard, that one see what one has not seen, and that one believe it. We will see that Jacob himself believes so strongly in what happened to him that his confidence is contagious. In v. 31 Peny'el will become Penu'el, "turn *yourselves* towards God!" Luther, speaking of an "event" (both the ladder and the struggle at the Jabbok), includes dream, vision and reality. For him, confidence or faith is nothing other than a real dream, in which one can see what one does not otherwise notice.[59]

# 2   The Unusual Detail

> Out of everything that happened in that night when the name
> of Israel was given to Jacob, it is the patriarch's wound that has
> become the subject of scrupulous commemoration. [Two traces
> remain in the narrator's time], in the name of Peniel and in the
> practice concerning the ligament of the hip in sacrificial offerings.
> Unanimity rests on this point: the story goes back to the most
> distant times: in this case, well before the Israelite era.[60]

The people of Israel were asked to memorialize the wound that
was at the origin of their existence. From a distant prehistory that
was largely inaccessible, Israel recalled that there is no authentic
power without acceptance of the wound. How many centuries
will it take to verify such an intuition? In our time it is the human
sciences, especially psychology, that explain this point to us. Of
course, anyone who speaks of science is speaking of universally
valid reality. Why would biblical texts be disconnected from the
universally valid? And if they are not, why not use the results of
other scientific approaches than history in a case where history does
not yield sure truths?

In brief, the historico-critical quest regarding our story is pretty
disappointing. An exegete such as J. Skinner shows its limits very

well: we do not know if the nerve [nāsheh] of v. 32 is actually a nerve, an artery, a tendon or a muscle, even if the first seems the most probable. The site of Peny'el is unknown and we know nothing at all about the worship at Peny'el; we do not know if the authors of the story really believed that the combat was meant to be taken literally. To these writers, the main interest lies in the origin of the name "Israel," and the blessing bestowed on the nation in the person of its ancestor. So how can Skinner decide that it is a question of neither a dream nor a vision like Jacob's dream at Bethel, but of a "real physical encounter ... against a divine antagonist" and that "we have to do with a legend, originating at a low level of religion"? In spite of a total ignorance regarding worship at Peny'el, how can he agree with the other exegetes to affirm that Jacob's limp refers to a ritual dance practised in this place?[61]

In the face of so many unknowns on the level of history, and in order to avoid falling into inconsistency, it is in our interests to concentrate on what Jacob could have experienced on that forever mysterious night – without dissociating that experience from the strong emotions of the preceding day. The explanations of B. Cyrulnik seem enlightening to me if we accept the hypothesis of the dream:

> REM sleep, which corresponds to the time of the most fantastical dreams, increases on the very night that follows the confrontation of a problem ... When the day was upsetting, the increase of REM sleep the following night allows one to incorporate the event in the traces of the memory. An emotional alarm during the day leads to an oneiric alarm that night.[62]

Jacob went to sleep fully conscious of his dread. It must have awakened in him a long-ago terror, as if the two frights belonged to the same underground stream.

What element of the dream is going to alert Jacob to something other than his omnipresent dread? What detail of the text shows that the dream follows its own logic, which is not necessarily that of the dreamer in the conscious state, nor that of the author of the story, nor of the readers? Does there exist in the text anything that is intriguing, unexpected, absurd, that can indicate the irruption of the OTHER in Jacob's mental world? Wouldn't his dream be centred otherwise than on the thoughts regarding the dream that are at work behind the scenes in the unfolding of the tale?

In fact, this detail does exist: on first reading, we have a tendency to disregard the last verse because it seems so superfluous, insignificant, apparently stripped of meaning, for abstaining from eating the nerve of a kind of meat does not cause a great deal of frustration. This is not the very reflex we often have in the face of the absurdity of a detail in a dream when we wake up. "That has nothing to do with anything," we think, and we rush to forget it. But experience shows that if, rather, we take that strange detail very seriously, sooner or later it will put us on the path of something unknown in ourselves, whose existence we did not suspect. In this way the most incomprehensible dreams are often the richest in meaning; the same is true for biblical texts. We shall therefore take the opposite way from the *Jerome Biblical Commentary*, where E.H. Maly says of the touching of the thigh (v. 25ff.) and of the story of the nerve (v. 31ff.) that this seems to be an addition and "disturbs the order of the account."[63] On the contrary, to me such details seem to provide a key for interpreting the story.

It is often said that v. 32 is etiological, for it gives the reason, it justifies the existence of a dietary practice by means of its religious origin. That interpretation minimizes the scope of this verse. It is a question of a taboo that is no doubt ancient but not mentioned anywhere else in the Hebrew Bible – which shows that it was no longer observed, even if it is recalled in the Talmud of Babylon[64] – that permits us to see much more therein, in the context of the story of Jacob. What, then, does v. 32 suggest to us? Is it not, ultimately, a story of thighs – of buttocks! – of sexuality? Indeed, as we have seen, a certain type of psychoanalytic reading tries to reduce our story to one of father-son aggression and to see in the detail in question a symbol of castration.[65] For the "hollow of the thigh" is often interpreted (including by the French Traduction œcuménique de la Bible), as a place near the male sexual organs, and thus as the site of procreation. This is in line with Genesis 42:26 and Exodus 1:5, where we find the expression "come from the thigh of …"; likewise, St. Augustine says, "For the breadth of the thigh is the multitude of the family."[66] With this to support his claim, R. Martin-Achard cites biblical passages relating to the genital area, where it is recalled that the life force does not belong to man.[67]

However, it is difficult to see in what sense the virility of Jacob could be a problem, since he already has twelve children and his descendants – God has promised him – will be as numerous as the "dust of the earth … spread abroad." It is likely that in the dream Jacob had something like castration anxiety, that fantasy of a father who prevents him from becoming autonomous and living his male sexuality. But there is much more in the text, and that is what directs us to the real knot in Jacob's past. The Midrash sets us on course, not tarrying over Jacob's virility but suggesting that the place is symbolic of something factual. It comments on v. 25 in two lines: "He touched [wounded] the righteous ones who would be his descendants: the generation of the destruction [which would be persecuted and destroyed]."[68]

The Midrash says, in effect, something is going to happen. Jacob is not only a link in the reproduction of the species; there is something even more important than his biological lineage. It is his spiritual lineage: how will his descendants behave as "righteous ones" among persecutors? The Midrash does not say, but it suggests that it was necessary for something in Jacob to be touched in order that he should have spiritual descendants, thirsty for righteousness, so that another way of responding to destructive violence, other than flight or counter-violence, would be born in and transmitted to his descendants.

"He touched him in the hollow of his thigh" evokes the expression "to touch something deep." What will happen that is just in the generations that follow is only possible through a return to what has already happened and which asks to be awakened in Jacob. What happened in his history that meant that at the simple touch of the adversary, Jacob's thigh was dislocated and the place became taboo? What can the word [ierek] mean? The Koehler-Baumgartner Hebrew dictionary gives a range of meanings:

– it is the fleshy part of the thigh;
– it is the place of wounding, of procreation and of decay;
hence, in Numbers 5:20-26, a matter of an oath provokes a
curse ("and her thigh [ = her breast] shall waste away");
– it is the place where the hand is placed for taking an oath;
– it is where one wears a sword, where one is struck and
where one strikes oneself as a sign of shame or pain (Jer. 31:19;
Ezek. 21:17).

On the one hand, it is thus a place that symbolizes what is best in the
human being (the transmission of life), what is worst (violence that
is experienced and reproduced, and the decay of death), and what
is lame (compromise with others and with our own conscience).
On the other hand, it is the place of the oath, of giving one's word.
Indeed, one put one's hand under the thigh of the person to whom
one swore an oath.

It is a highly symbolic region of the body, which thus has to do with
trust, assured or destroyed. Now, we have seen that the dream puts
thought into images. In his dream Jacob visualizes that by touching
that place, his adversary causes a displacement, a dislocation. At the
beginning of that same v. 25 the text says, literally, "He sees that he
can do nothing for him." Why not, if not because Jacob does not
lay himself open? His system of self-defence works so well that the
adversary cannot communicate with him. No verbal exchange is
possible between them until something in Jacob shifts. Up to that
point, the word seems lost in the depths of him, shut away …

Let us recall that according to Rashi, following the Midrash, Jacob
went to sleep irritated at the thought of all these gifts – a trigger
for aggression, a refusal of dependency, a sign of vitality that the
dream is going to prolong and increase. All the adversary has to do
is touch him for Jacob to lose his temper (come unhinged) and be
beside himself. Just as the dream images put it, it is his hip or his
thigh that dislocates, comes unhinged, is "torn away from the place
where it was attached," according to Rashi. That makes us think
of an affect that is at once violent and painful: the story will finish
with the mention of the nerve, which one supposes is the sciatic
nerve,[69] the source of a lot of pain. The text itself evokes a painful

stripping, by using the verb [iaqa'], to crack, to dislocate, to expose (a dead body, for example), to tell what happened to Jacob in an area of himself that was as if "dead." The adversary seems to have touched a nerve, opened an old wound that still hurts and that Jacob did not suspect he had. Ordinarily, a dream reveals thoughts that are unknown to the dreamer and that are disagreeable to him or her. If the last word of the text does not refer to the hollow of the thigh but to the nerve, this is the sign that Jacob has been liberated from something painful in allowing it to enter his consciousness.

In the story of Jacob, no doubt that was the moment to touch it. It is not by chance that the verb that is used is equivocal: [naga'] is both *touch* and *wound*. It would have sufficed for the author, notes S.A. Geller, to have chosen another, more straightforward verb, for the Jewish nation not to have been implicated. "What prevents an angel from simply appearing to Jacob, touching his thigh and blessing him, in the same way as an angelic touch gives mouths a mission to prophecy?"[70] Here the issue is not only the vocation, but the deep identity. Israel recognizes, in the history of its ancestor Jacob, the formidable hand of this God who is so alive that he cannot touch a human without wounding him or her, or rather without putting a finger on what in him or her has already been wounded.

It is the same for Job. The *satan* – the adversary, the one who opposes and incites the human to face and state clearly who he is – therefore obtains God's permission to touch the possessions and even the person of Job. "But stretch out your hand now, and touch all that he has, and he will curse you to your face … But stretch out your hand now and touch his bone and his flesh, and he will curse you to your face" (Job 1:11, 2:5). There we have the same ambiguous verb as for Jacob, [naga']. For Job, the moment has come in which we touch on his relationship with God, with others and with himself. We do not know his story before the avalanche of misfortunes, other than that he brought his ten children to be purified after each series of those feasts that they organized. He offered a sacrifice for each one, saying to himself, "It may be that my children have sinned, and cursed God in their hearts" (Job 1:4-5).

This is astonishingly symbiotic behaviour, hardly conducive to the individuation of each one before his or her God. Did Job believe he could save his children by his own righteousness? The adversary, with God's permission, is going to touch him right in the heart of his illusion of power. Job, like Jacob, has yet to confront God bare-handed, without seeking to please or cajole Him. One day Job, like Jacob, having nothing left to lose, will let himself be touched at the very root of his dysfunctionality, where the old wound had been covered over by conduct dictated by fear. The true power of Job and Jacob has to be cleansed of all servility, of all the will to power that is hidden by servility. God touches and strips away that which does us harm until we consent to the power that is not of ourselves and we cry with Job:

> But I would speak to the Almighty [ = Shadday],
> and I desire to argue my case with God [ = El]. (13:3)

Nowadays we would say that Jacob lived the whole time of his exile in denial, never making the least allusion to his familial past. It is a protective denial, "avoidant of confrontation" with painful reality, a beneficent attitude in the short term since it prevents re-examination. B. Cyrulnik notes,

> Denial leads to a too-good adaptation, an astonishing absence of conflictuality, since the subject denies the danger and the pain of his or her experience ... He or she does not forget what has happened. This works well (like an airplane that flies with only one engine), until the day when reality raises an event that *touches the wounded one in the hidden part of his or her personality* [and then it is like the explosion of a] time bomb.[71]

For Jacob, it is the adversary who brutally throws him to the ground, without warning, when he least expects it.

What in Jacob's past is the place where it hurts when someone touches him there, if not the lie in which he was caught? The lie is first and foremost that of his mother, Rebecca. She was the one who taught Jacob the destruction of trust and put in place the deceit that would permit Jacob to wrest from his father the blessing that was meant for his elder brother. "Now therefore, my son, obey

my word as I command you" (Gen. 27:8). In the face of Jacob's
objections, she repeats, "Only obey my word, and go, get them
for me" (Gen. 27:13). She was the one who prepares the dish
requested by her husband and who dresses Jacob in goatskins. She
was the one who lies to Isaac, making him believe that she cannot
stand the idea of seeing Jacob marry a woman of the land, as Esau
has done. She thus conceals the real reason for Jacob's exile: fear
of Esau's revenge. She manages to fool Esau, who starts to think
that his Canaanite wives are displeasing to his father and hurries to
marry an Ishmaelite descended from Abraham. In all this, Rebecca
is the worthy sister of Laban, who will not cease to betray Jacob
throughout his long exile.

As for Isaac, what kind of a father is he for preferring "Esau, because
he was fond of game" (25:28)?[72] By loving his children according
to what they brought him, he was betraying them in his own way.
His inner dark night is remarkably illustrated by his blindness.
Incapable of identifying the manipulations of which he is the object,
he could only submit, "seized by an extremely violent trembling"
or "shuddering with great strong shudders" (Gen. 27:33, in vari-
ous translations). He gives no support to Esau and raises no protest
towards Jacob, no more than he had raised a protest when his own
father had held the knife to him. The two sons grew up with fragile
parents, caught in their own fears, incapable of clearly confronting
others, in the habit of using their children rather than considering
them as different beings from themselves who were responsible
for their actions. Jacob no doubt carried into exile an inner sense
of division due to the conflicted loyalties in which he was caught,
even if the fear of Esau would override everything else.

The hollow of the thigh, as we have seen, designates among other
things the place where the hand is placed for swearing an oath.[73]
One might think that the symbolic gesture of the adversary, in the
dream, reminds Jacob of incidents in his past. On a mental level,
had he not made this gesture mentally when his father asked him
three times if he were really Esau (Gen. 27:18, 21, 24)? Certainly
his father had felt him without asking him to swear that he really
was Esau. But does it not boil down to the same thing for Jacob?

We know that in every dream there is a visual arrangement of psychic material, by means of symbolism. We also know that this happens thanks to childhood impressions, where events were lived without the visual and the thought content being dissociated. We may thus suppose that the oath and the gesture that accompanies it, not dissociated in the head of the young Jacob, remained so until that night when the traumatic memories resurfaced. As a child, he must have seen it done to his father, at the time of the alliance with Abimelech where they "exchanged oaths" (Gen. 26:31). As a young man, he must have done this with Esau when Esau gave up his birthright for a plate of lentils: "Swear to me first," Jacob had said (Gen. 25:33). Esau had probably made this habitual gesture, which is equivalent to our "spitting on the earth" or saying "hold up your hand and repeat after me: 'I swear by what is most precious to me.'" One would say in some way, "I swear it under your thigh," and that would symbolize as well the most precious thing because in that time, the most valued thing was fertility.

Having perceived the subterfuge, Isaac said to Esau, "Your brother came *in* disguise and he has taken away your blessing" (Gen. 27:35). That night, at the Jabbok, we see Jacob "*in* the dust." Disguise is a way to betray the trust of another, as indicated by the etymology of [ramah]: to abandon, to trick, to betray. In tricking his father, Jacob had not only betrayed his trust, he had also "abandoned" something: the possibility of being recognized (blessed) in his identity as Jacob. It was not only a blow to his moral values, it was also an alienation of his identity: having been taken for another, Jacob was alienated for a long time. But, just as the adversary at the Jabbok will be *in the dust with Jacob*, we may think that Isaac was also *in on the deceit with his son*. In preferring Esau because Jacob did not bring him anything, he had "abandoned" Jacob to maternal domination. He had betrayed the trust of his son in not placing himself before him in his identity as his father. And if afterwards Jacob had scorned his father for letting himself be taken in, he had thereby developed scorn for himself, without knowing that he had fled from a father whom he did not at all wish to resemble, and without being able to establish himself, in the certainty of his difference, free from the fear of resembling him.

That is why the beginning and the end of v. 26 are not contradictory. By the simple touch of the adversary, Jacob's thigh became dislocated because, symbolically, that spot was already wounded. He dreams of really confronting his father as an equal, as Jacob, without an assumed identity. He dreams that that confrontation takes place in truth, in the dust of a body-to-body struggle and not in deceit. The symbolic place of the oath, even if it is wounded, is going to be inhabited anew and a real benediction is going to become possible.[74] Jacob will prolong his dream and will be able to write his own story.

At the break of day, he will believe that he struggled with God himself ... even though he had just called for God's help (Gen. 32:9-12). No doubt it took nothing less than a betrayal by God himself to awaken in Jacob the old pain. This is often the way in our experience: when we trust God the most, turning back to him as we did when we were children, He seems to choose that moment to betray and destroy us. But then we notice that we needed this to get in touch with an old betrayal of trust that we had hidden away. The more trusting we had been, the more we fell from on high. And if God is the only one whom we still trust, he must also let go of us in order for the old, infected wound to be brought to light. A. de Pury writes,

> If God permits the realization of the promise in sparing Jacob the confrontation with vengeance, he acquiesces in the fraud committed by Jacob; but if, on the other hand, he prevents the realization of the promise by abandoning Jacob into the hands of Esau, he renders himself unfaithful to himself. It is in this sense that the insertion of the story of Penuel takes on its entire meaning: when Jacob feared the vengeance of Esau (and thought he had God on his side), he was attacked by God in person, the very night on which he had spoken his prayer ... and at a place where he was not expecting it. While with regard to Esau, Jacob seemed to fear only for his goods and his family, that is, for the fruit of the blessing, at Penuel it is his very life that is at stake.[75]

This is an incomprehensible betrayal of the bond of trust by a God traditionally considered the protector of all that lives. The *Mishna* compares this dislocation or straining of Jacob's hip to a brood of chicks that one snatches away or a root that one pulls up.[76]

It is the question of victory that rests once again on Jacob at the Jabbok. Is it possible for him to emerge victorious from his history, integrating it and transforming it into life energy? As B. Cyrulnik recalls,

> It is not the traumatizing event that is dreamed of, it is the impression that it triggers ... The astonishing capacity [of dreams] to bring to life in the present time of the night an intense representation awakens the traces of emotions provoked at the time of the real past. And the dream, a representation of images, awakens those strong emotions ... But as the dream is also a learning process which clears some new neural pathways, it incorporates in the memory what we have thought about unusual events. If our entourage presents that trial to us as a victory, we experience pride, but if it tells us that that same experience is a humiliation, we will dream the metaphor of someone who paraded nude among elegant guests at a fancy reception ... What the event evokes is the meaning that it takes on in the history of the subject.[77]

Jacob was not congratulated by his mother, and even less by his father and his brother. He left like a thief, full of fear. The blessing took on the colour of a curse. Rebecca, the sole witness of the real facts, did not present them to Jacob as a "victory," and what Jacob held onto from his history was that he had been impotent all along: unable to defend himself against an abusive mother, unable to face up to Esau and to take responsibility for his actions, unable to be recognized by his father and appreciated for himself ... only capable of obeying the members of his family to *their* hearts' content.

Among those whom I've read, S.A. Geller is the only exegete to ascribe to the hollow of the thigh the meaning of "place of swearing." But he does not pursue it, for he sees there only an allusion to the oath of God, to God's promise of blessing on all the descendants of the patriarchs. For Geller, the story "lacks coherence," for the same touch cannot at one and the same time "inspire Jacob and make him limp."[78] Everything becomes clear, on the other hand, if we adopt the hypothesis of the dream: in exposing what was making Jacob limp, the adversary permitted the Spirit to blow in his "cryptic zones," which would inspire all the people descended from him without the process of that victory ever being explained. "Although it is night," St. John of the Cross would say.

# 3  From Jacob-Heel to Jacob the Confronter

More than anyone, Jacob wanted, with every fibre of his being, to be chosen. He had wanted this from the time he was in the womb. He worked unceasingly at it. If Esau had wanted it more, he would have returned earlier from hunting … To be chosen is to want to be chosen … The better we understand human desire, the more the priority of God is rendered invisible, *as is proper.* While from the highest heaven we receive an image of it, the depth of the torrents hides the place where God himself gives humans the desire that he wants to fulfill. For where did Jacob get this desire?[79]

The very name of Jacob is code: it is built on ['aqav], "to seize by the heel, to supplant," or ['aqev], "heel." We find this etymology in Genesis 25:26, with the story of his birth: "Afterwards his brother came out, with his hand gripping Esau's heel; so he was named Jacob." In Genesis 27:36, "Esau said, 'Is he not rightly named Jacob? For he has supplanted me these two times." The idea is taken up again in Hosea 12:3 ("In the womb he tried to supplant his brother"). "For the ancients … in a name, there was always something that contained the very nature of its bearer … Jacob's

name marked him as a deceiver," notes G. von Rad.[80] The image
of the heel leads us towards the way in which Jacob lived that out.
It evokes the well-known feeling of not being able to fill another's
shoes. This is a sign of an identity crisis: "I have such-and-such a
title or socio-professional status, but I am not up to it and, what's
worse, I don't even know who I am."

Born "the last of the litter," and thus without rights, Jacob could
have considered himself the weaker (compared to his brother the
hunter). Being more affected by the unspoken history of Isaac, he
experienced his life as if he were atoning for it, according to Elie
Wiesel, who presents Jacob as the first dreamer in biblical history:

> Who was Jacob? The son of a survivor ... Isaac never spoke of
> the past. Yet Jacob wanted to know ... He was jealous of his grief,
> his memories ... he tried to live dangerously, in his own way ...
> [But] next to his father's life, his own seemed flat and bland.[81]

For the rabbis, Jacob had a real inferiority complex towards Esau.[82]
The Zohar specifies that Jacob felt guilty for prospering in exile
while Esau looked after their parents.

On his way home, Jacob admits to God that he has scarcely changed:
"I am [too] *small* for the favours and all the truth/faithfulness you
have shown your servant" (Gen. 32:10). The adjective that is
sometimes translated as "unworthy" also means, according to A. de
Pury, "not having the right."[83] We could say that Jacob has never
known how to accept the good things that came to him. This is
how it is for many people who have the feeling of having usurped
what does not belong to them, of taking a place that is not theirs
by right, of living as impostors: "If people only knew how mistaken
they are about me!" As an adult, Jacob continued to feel like this:
threatened, exiled, a victim of Laban, never rising to the height of
his personal aspirations and even now incapable of taking his place
before Esau, who seems to occupy the entire ground with his four
hundred men.

With J.G. Janzen, we can nevertheless suppose that Jacob had to
fight from the time he nursed at his mother's breast against the
fatality of his name, in order for his authentic self to come to light.

"Insofar as his parents named him after something that was indeed the case about him, but was not the deepest truth in him, they misnamed him."[84] Jacob therefore began living out the parental "script." At birth, he displaced Esau by taking hold of his heel. Near the stream, he was displaced, or rather his false self was, so that he could no longer displace others.

We may be astounded by this portrait when we remember the "gigantic power" of Jacob, to use G. von Rad's term. "It seems that the biblical tradition knew, as well as a gentle Jacob, sticking close to his mother in the tents (Gen 25:27f), a Jacob who was capable of extraordinary physical exploits ... with the ways of a giant, of whom the ancient version of Gen 32:23ff tells of another feat of prowess."[85] The prospect of confronting Esau the day after his night by the Jabbok no doubt causes in his dream the confrontation that he could never have with his father. Perhaps the dream was induced by conscious effort; he had accepted to return to the place of his youth; he looked squarely at himself and became conscious of his past as a "heel," always "too small" for everything that happened to him. He is ready to behave differently. The body-to-body struggle would also be a manner of visualizing hard inner work, as is the case with those dreams that leave us exhausted in the morning. The confrontation with Esau becomes, by the miracle of the dream, a confrontation with his own history and his alienated identity. This time, he does not want to crawl in the dust like a snake that is content to bite humans in the heel (according to the image of Gen. 3:15). It is as if the name of the ford, the Jabbok, challenges Jacob regarding his identity. At last his own desire emerges from the depths of his unconscious: to become a wrestler, no longer to lie nor to lie to himself, no longer to hold back from confrontation, but to live freely.

Still today many of us find ourselves resonating with Jacob's evolution. Because of difficult circumstances in our past, we may have developed the persistent impression of "never getting there." It is as if others always know better than us, even in those areas where people consider us competent. There is a compulsion in us to submit, a sort of ban on affirming ourselves, on taking our place, on succeeding where others fail. With the years, the gap widens between the image that others have of us (you are so gifted, you are lucky, you have a strong personality), and the image that we have of ourselves (if they only knew … all I'm doing is fooling them). That is why Jacob could feel that he was "too small," incapable of confronting life alone, even as he was possessed of enormous power. The more others consider us invulnerable, the more they envy us and the more they want to crush us.

It takes time and thought to understand that the vengefulness of others is directly proportional to our capacity to resist, to oppose, to affirm ourselves. The aggressiveness of others increases tenfold because the fragility that we think afflicts us hides a strength of character, without our knowing it. It is in this sense that we may consider the hostility of others as revealing what we carry within us that is invincible. Proof of its own fragility, the hostility of others gives us the chance, one day, for the first time, to hold our head high and discover the extraordinary resistance that we carry within. We would never have believed ourselves to have such a strong power of refusal. It only has to happen once; now, it is finished, I can no longer continue to function this way. I will no longer tolerate a lack of respect and I will say so; even if the situation does not change, I will have lifted my head, and this act is irreversible. To our amazement, many things change from that moment.

"Where did Jacob get this desire?" asks P. Beauchamp in the quotation that opens this chapter. Why do some people begin to affirm themselves while others remain Jacob-heels all their lives? It seems to me it is a question of hearing. Some, more than others, hear the desire of *others,* and that desire awakens their own. For Jacob, it was the day when he heard the OTHER say to him, I want you to return to your country; I believe you can do it; I will help you throughout the journey. We might object that at no time have we heard God express such a desire. But can anyone state that he or she has never, not even once in their life, heard another human say, "Don't let yourself be pushed around. I want you to react. I need you to be yourself; I need you to take your place"? Even in Jacob's history we find this need for human support when the desire to resist is awakened, the desire to say no, to return to the place of his authentic identity. Jacob heard the desire of God; something in that desire awakened in him. He called his wives ... and they too begin to affirm themselves, blaming their father, Laban, for robbing them, and encouraging Jacob in his own path: "All the property that God has taken away from our father belongs to us and to our children; now then, do whatever God has said to you" (Gen. 31:16).

Will it be servile submission to God from now on for Jacob? In listening to God, is Jacob really listening to the voice of his own desire? Yes, if one reflects further on the etymology of his name. According to the *Interpreter's Dictionary of the Bible*, Jacob is not only a biblical name, but is also found among Arab personal names and in the Near Eastern onomastic. As a common noun, ['aqav], it is used in Hebrew, Aramaic, Syriac, Arabic, Ugaritic, and Akkadian, and it means "healing." As for the meanings of the corresponding verb, they are not clear and "the biblical etymologies may even constitute a deliberate desire to obscure a more ancient meaning which might be 'to protect,' 'to watch over' ... In all probability, the name Jacob was originally theophorous"; it contains the word "God" (El), which it later lost, which leads to the hypothesis that a primary meaning is something like "may God protect!"[86] The least we can say is that Jacob's identity, linked to his name, is far from being reducible to a "heel" without self-will. His name may express implicitly his desire "to heal" from something and his desire to be protected by a God who will accompany him on this path. From the outset, he would have refused an existence as a "heel" that was largely programmed by his parents at an age where he was not conscious of his identity.

---

The question by Jacob's adversary, in v. 27, may seem superfluous: doesn't he know whom he's dealing with? "What is your name?" On the contrary, it is of primary importance for Jacob to admit the dysfunctionality that, up to now, has taken the place of his identity. "He said 'Jacob-heel-usurper.'" In popular Hebrew, the verbal root of his name means twist, seize by the heel, usurp, mislead, ambush, trick.

From birth, Jacob was crafty. To affirm himself before Esau, he used crooked means. However, he was a fundamentally straight man; we will see how scrupulously he served, for twenty years, his father-in-law Laban, even though he used ruses to preserve his rights. Everything that happens suggests that for the first half of his life, Jacob could not escape from the fatality of the ruse, up to the day when, after the combat with the angel, he took the name of Israel. If Jacob means scheming, one of the roots of the word Israel is YACHAR, uprightness.[87]

Dysfunctionality is not limited to Jacob in that family. We have seen how Esau, in speaking to his father, compared the episode of the dish of lentils as being, on Jacob's part, a trick of the same type as the blessing: "Is he not rightly named Jacob? For he has supplanted me these two times. He took away my birthright; and look, now he has taken away my blessing" (Gen. 27:36). This is wrong: "The deal was completed properly."[88] Moreover, the episode of the dish of lentils has "no effect on that of the blessing"; Jacob never mentions it. He could have taken advantage of having acquired the birthright to receive the blessing destined for the eldest. You would think that he does not give himself the right to have rights. One might detect behind this totally useless deal the pathetic attempt of a young person, very unsure of himself, to be recognized and valued by his father.

The episode of the struggle at the Jabbok takes on a deeper meaning if we stop trying to assess Jacob's morality, and therefore trying to see in it only the spectacular transformation of a twisted person into a "morally straight"[89] person. It is as if we stop seeing Jacob's limp as a punishment or a tacit judgment on his limited morality.[90] In fact, in the Hebrew Bible itself, Jacob's improved status is ambiguous. In the stories in Genesis, the predominant view is positive, but in the prophets, it is fairly critical. In the Jewish writings of the Hellenic-Roman period, Jacob is unilaterally idealized. Rabbinic literature generally validates Jacob, despite some critical remarks.[91]

Genesis 25:27 tells us that Jacob was "a quiet man," with an adjective [tam] that is also attributed to Job, and which means complete, whole, straight, peaceful. J. Eisenberg raises the point that Jacob did not steal anything from Laban: "The biblical text insists on this; he carries away what he has legitimately 'acquired' (twice in 31:18)."[92] At last we learn, from R. Michaud, that the Elohist redactor had undoubtably reworked the texts about the patriarchs in order to rid them of any error and to present them "as divine intermediaries, models of fidelity to the God of the covenant and to the demands of morality," for he was reworking the patriarchal traditions in the eighth century, when the monarchy was threatened and it was necessary to fight against corruption and paganism.[93]

We can therefore forget about both the defenders of a perfectly virtuous Jacob and his detractors once and for all, leaving within the mystery of God that which should always remain there: namely, the ultimate value of a human being whose behaviour is secondary to the life force that he communicates to us. Noting that the Greek translation for the adjective [tam] to describe Jacob's integrity is the adjective [aplatos], "without guile, simple, faultless," St. Augustine takes us beyond moral categories:

> In the receiving of that blessing what is the guile of the man with-
> out guile? What is the guile of the simple, what the fiction of the
> man who does not lie, but a profound mystery of the truth?[94]

The question of the OTHER is not an innocent one. It can only awaken in Jacob the question of his father when he touched him and asked, "Who are you, my son?" That night, Jacob wished to be himself, to see himself as he really was, to be seen for who he was, with his dysfunctions and with his spiritual being, his authentic self. The hour of truth had come, because Jacob declared himself to want at any price, again, to be recognized, validated, blessed. "I will not let you go, unless you bless me" – that very desire being my deepest identity, which I will never renounce. At that instant Jacob steps into his deepest being, his unique identity, and he is thereby distanced from that Jacob-usurper whose name he bears. Immediately, that name comes to his lips like a confession and a conversion: I no longer want to be reduced to that Jacob. For F.C. Holmgren, the blessing does not depend on any repentance. Jacob is not criticized either in the Pentateuch or in the New Testament or in the story of the struggle. The Israelites admired in his craftiness the wisdom of a survivor putting an all-out effort, as Esau had done, in fact, into finding a way out of a threatening situation. The Jewish tradition is negative towards Esau and the Christian commentators condemn Jacob, but "does there have to be a villain in this story?" No, replies F.C. Holmgren, if we admit that "both Jacob and Esau live in us."[95]

At the exact moment when Jacob is in touch with his desire to be blessed, he recognizes himself as Heel-usurper, and suddenly his readiness to fight seems beneficial. It is revealing to him his most authentic identity (v. 29). The Midrash and Rashi, as we have seen, do not doubt his fighting spirit, but up to now it has gotten lost amidst ruses and lies. He could distrust himself, fearing that it could crush others, in particular fragile relatives. He had never before seemed violent, by contrast with the violence of the bloody fight that went on all night long in the dust. Had he been able to confront his father, he would no doubt have learned that his combativeness was a blessing for him, the source of a life of freedom once it had forced him to come up against the limit that is the OTHER, and thereby get in touch with his own limits. Only thus would he have been able to stop dreading his combativeness.

It took nothing less than God to liberate Jacob from his compulsion to usurp others; because God is not "usurpable," it was with God that Jacob was provoked to fight face to face, to discover that neither he nor the other would die from it. Strengthened by the experience, he was able to counter any human from then on. The combat revealed to him a conscience, in himself and in each OTHER, that remains "un-supplantable" no matter how violent the confrontation. For the first time in his life, he will learn that he is just like any OTHER – a living being incapable of usurping another living being. Rupert de Deutz wrote: "Your name will no longer be 'usurper' but 'prince with God.' Just as I am Prince, you will be called prince, you who have been able to struggle with me; and if you have been able to pin me down, I who am God or an angel of God, how much more will you will be able to combat humans, that is, Esau! Therefore, do not fear it!"[96]

Many commentators accord a theological significance to the crossing of the Jabbok, making of the combat and the crossing one single event. Thus, according to H.A. McKay, the episode functions as a rite of passage that permits Jacob to become fully adult.[97] We may think that displaying his combativeness, recognizing his dysfunction, discovering his hidden wound and his truth constitute a single step, one that is indispensable to become a human worthy of the name. In those societies that practise rites of passage, a trial is imposed on a youth, who does not escape being wounded and being stripped naked in the face of his limits and weaknesses, but who calls forth and awakens all the combativeness of which he is capable. His accession to the society of OTHERs will depend on his capacity to mobilize his potential for combat.

Something similar happens in individual therapy, even if that means using the term "combativeness" in a very broad sense. To begin a healing journey is in itself to become combative: I refuse to go on like this; I have had enough of suffering, of dysfunction, of not understanding myself; I want to tackle the heavy burden I am carrying. Already we are confronting the OTHER. We prepare ourselves to tackle dysfunction and wounds about which we as yet know nothing, or very little. To want to "come out of it" is to fight with the OTHER, the adversary, the still ungraspable unknown.

That is why it is said of Jacob, in v. 29, "You have striven with *humans*," although up to that time he had opposed only one human: Laban. Some manuscripts add a future action: "You have wrestled-with-God and you will-wrestle-with humans." In fact, it was with humans from his past that Jacob was confronted all through his therapeutic night. Little by little his dysfunctions and his wounds showed themselves with their faces uncovered. He refused the ex-propriation that he had been a victim of before: he fought with his mother, who had not only guided him from afar but had also had taken from him the responsibility for his actions. If the trickery is discovered, Rebecca had told him, "Let your curse be on me, my son" (Gen. 27:13). He stood up and faced the OTHER in the truth: I am called Heel-usurper.

> Jacob, the nonviolent, the timorous, Jacob the weak, the resigned,
> the coward who always succeeded in avoiding confrontations,
> particularly violent ones, suddenly resisted the aggressor, plunged
> into the fight and returned blow for blow ... Was this what Jacob
> had needed in order to become aware of his own strength, his
> own truth, and the hopes he personified? Had he really needed an
> adversary, a dangerous adversary, in order to become Israel?[98]

Yes, he needed "the OTHER" and he needed adverse circumstances
and a situation that appeared inextricable from a human standpoint
to do some soul-searching. Many people do not want to know anything of their dysfunctions, and even less of their wounds. Jacob had
forgotten his. In fact, it is significant that the *hapax* designating the
famous nerve [*nāsheh*] is derived from or is from the root [nāshāh],
which means only one thing: *forget*, or from the root [nāshā'], which
means, among other things, *to mislead*. Unknown in the rest of the
Bible, this nerve could therefore be at one and the same time the
nerve of forgetting, the nerve that misleads, and the nerve of the
war with Esau. Jacob believed he had no wound; he misled himself,
he had forgotten it. It is through his fight to get past his fear and lies
that he discovers that forgotten wound. When he confronts Esau
he will be limping. That is to say, he will be fully conscious of his
wound; he will never be able to forget it.

Studies show that seriously traumatized persons begin by having
dreams in which the affect of fear is totally absent. Threatening
images parade by without causing feelings during the dream. It is
as if the feelings are paralyzed. That night, Jacob therefore went
to sleep fearing the idea of confronting Esau, and it is well known
that the first thing fear does is paralyze. The Greek translation of
the Bible, the Septuagint, renders v. 26 thus: instead of "the hollow of the thigh of Jacob was dislocated," the hollow of the thigh
of Jacob "was numb or paralyzed," from the verb [narkaô], which
has given us "narcotic." It is thus possible that the text is describing
two different facts: "He touched the hollow of his thigh," and then
we have, amazingly, "the hollow of Jacob's thigh was paralyzed."
In other words, Jacob noticed that the hollow of his thigh was
paralyzed.

The "hollow of the thigh" seems to be uselessly repeated in this verse (two mentions, one after another). The precision "of Jacob" also appears superfluous. "He touched him in the hollow of his thigh. The hollow of the thigh of Jacob dislocated ..." The repetition confirms that the two facts are not related in terms of cause and effect, for how could a simple touch cause paralysis? It was said from the beginning that Jacob wrestled with a "man" and not with an angel or a demon with supernatural powers. We know today that some areas of the body that had at one time been traumatized may become insensitive to any feeling and that certain repressions in the unconscious cause actual physical paralysis. An entire part of Jacob's personality has remained "forgotten," as if anesthetized or paralyzed.

According to Rashi, if Jacob was limping when the sun rose, it is because of another etymology of the nerve in question: if we think in terms of the verb [nāshāh], "to jump," it is the nerve that "*is removed* from its place and *rises up*." And Rashi notes a relationship with Gen. 41:51: "God has made me forget [*removed*] all my hardship." If we follow Rashi, the nerve in question becomes even richer in meaning. It is not only the nerve of forgetting, of treachery and war, it is also the nerve that hurts when *it is removed*, to be taken up, supported, raised, forgiven, according to all the senses of this verb [nāshāh] that we encountered in the story of Cain. God had said to Cain that he had the choice between not doing well and "doing well *in order to* accept, carry, support, lift [the face], raise, forgive" (Gen. 4:7). "The sun shines-*for Jacob*" once he has withdrawn the forgotten wound from his history, once he has taken responsibility for it, supported it, raised[99] it and forgiven it." Here, Rashi cites the Midrash, which sees the sun "healing Jacob of his dislocation," as well as the prophet Malachi, who speaks of a "sun of love: healing is in its rays" (3:20).

The issue of power seems absent from our story. It is about strength. Jacob discovers he is strong to the extent that he takes ownership of his resistance and his combativeness. We have seen the challenges that translators and commentators have faced through the centuries as they opt for a "struggle with" or a "struggle against." But what if there was neither a winner nor a loser? Indeed, v. 25 points to a lack of strength on the adversary's part ("he could do nothing for him") and, for Jacob, to a strength evoked by a verb in the absolute in v. 28 ("You can. You have become strong"). The risk is projecting onto the text something that is not there, seeking at all costs for a victory and a defeat and ending up translating falsely, "He could do nothing *against* him."

Such is human logic, in extreme circumstances: kill or be killed. The Midrash does not envisage any other alternative in Jacob's mind. It is a logic that leads nowhere as long as nothing of the OTHER irrupts: "of the OTHER" whom one can trust, from whom to keep your distance, from whom to understand a different approach to the situation – in short, of the OTHER-mirror who brings us to the essence of what we are, were and can become in a time of great distress. That is what the adversary does: touching the identity of Jacob is going to allow him to see himself as other than a poor "little one," maddened with repressed rage, confined to the option "dominate or be dominated," which constitutes the hell of power. Jacob the confronter begins to see the dawn of the day where, in the words of Elie Wiesel, "It would be possible to obtain a pure victory – pure of death, pure of guilt – a victory that would not imply the opponent's defeat or humiliation. A victory over himself."[100]

The passage of Hosea that alludes to Jacob's combat puts it like this: "In his manhood he strove with God. He strove with the angel and prevailed, he wept and sought his favour; he met him at Bethel, and there he spoke with us – 'The Lord, the God of hosts, the Lord', it is thus that he must be invoked" (Hos. 12:3b-5). It is rather strange, one reads in a note in the Traduction œcuménique de la Bible, that Jacob, the victor in the struggle, is the one who weeps and implores. The tradition of Hosea, in contrast to that of Genesis, would therefore have mentioned Jacob's *defeat*. If this lack of clarity is found in the biblical texts, is it not because it is a faithful reflection of experience? We sometimes pass through episodes of conflict from which we emerge peaceful and fortified, not needing to determine who won and who lost. It is as if we were beyond that. At the time, we could have done without the confrontation, but in the end we note that our adversaries were useful to us. They gave us the opportunity to discover and own a power of refusal, of resistance, of affirmation of ourselves that was hidden in us, "paralyzed" by a fear linked to old wounds.

What of that unknown strength, deeply hidden within us? The Midrash puts us on the path: "He saw that he would not carry it with him and he saw the *Shekinah*," that is, the (divine) Presence. And such was Jacob's success: he saw that God was present right in the heart of his wound, in the forgotten root of the violent conflict in which he was caught up. Such was the power of Jacob: he had not vanquished anyone; he had simply become conscious of the living Presence "there" (v. 29), there where he was not really dead. "You are made powerful. You can!" says the OTHER, without having to kill men or be killed. Life is generous enough for there to be enough room for me and for you at the same time. "Power has shifted between God and humankind," comments W. Brueggemann. "Something of the power of God has been entrusted to Israel. Unlike every other such relation in which God rules and humankind obeys, Israel is a newness which has prevailed with God … Israel is not formed by success or shrewdness or land, but by an assault from God."[101]

The very mystery of God seems to surround that "you can." It is striking that Hosea concludes thus his evocation of the struggle at the Jabbok; literally, "The Lord, God of combats/of combatants, the Lord its memory" (Hos. 12:6). What memory is this, if not Jacob's? Following their ancestor, a whole people will keep the memory of a God who has spoken "with us" (v. 4) through a combat, through a confrontation, thanks to a struggle. It will be necessary to remember, always and still to this day, a God *of* the powers, literally of combats and combatants, that is, of a God who does not keep his power for himself alone – not an Almighty God, but a God of all power, the God of the powerful ones that all of us are when He speaks to us and we hear him. It is a shared power that will inhabit Jacob's memory, and that will even structure it: "[That Lord], his memory."[102] From where does it come that from now on Jacob "can"? We might as well ask how God is God. On the other hand, what lets us see that God is God? We can see this in the metamorphosis of a person who, one day, consciously integrates his or her combativeness, finds himself or herself to be inhabited by a powerful Presence and takes his or her place among others. "It is in a relationship of strength that Jacob stands before God," says A. Abécassis. "He needed God to be powerful and he also needed to prove his own power." "If God is called "the Powerful one *of Jacob*," adds J. Eisenberg, it is obviously because Jacob – exiled, persecuted – strongly felt the divine protection. That power protected him from numerous enemies who threatened him with death – Esau, Laban, the inhabitants of Sichem. But one might also think that Jacob had a personal relationship with the power.[103]

From Jacob-heel to Jacob the confronter, the road travelled is one of incarnation. Jacob came out of his night by seeing little by little that the other – the unknown adversary – was invested by God with powers just as he himself was, although he had never realized it. He will see Esau in the same way. He will say to him, "For I have seen thy face, as though I had seen the face *of a god-like being*," according to Rashi's translation of Genesis 33:10 – the face *of God*, in Hebrew. "It is as dear to me as the sight of the angel, for I have seen your heavenly prince."[104] I have seen on your face that God of all power who assailed me all night long and who, by saying to me, "You can," made me admit that you, too, "you can." Once Jacob had forded the stream, saying, "I have seen God face to face"; now it is Esau whom he says he has seen face to face. We can thus confront the OTHER without dying … because we recognize in him or her, *as in ourselves*, the sign of the God of all power.

# 4  Who is the OTHER?

Too long I have kept silent towards You. Against your silence, I reinforced my silence. I stifled my want; I muzzled my inner depths. Right under your eyes I pretended to be without You; I pretended that I exist and You do not. I have struggled from the time I was at my mother's breast: that long, dead time that I call my life has been an endless dispute against You. That impatience that devours itself, that life that can never catch its breath, that blindness, that obstinate sleepwalking. Labour in the hope of being somebody, of being everybody ...

It is You who compells me to evict that God whose carcass is blasphemy ... You interrupt the gestation of the tomb. These words that I still spit in Your face, your breath alone can eradicate them. Blessed are You for making me curse You: I have flushed out my dead foetus.

I would have struggled through my entire human night to rip Your name away from You: now the prize of my ambiguous victory is not Your name that is beyond my grasp, but a new name that You give me.

This name that is Your hold on me is also my hold on You: it contains and does not contain the Ineffable, it claims it and recognizes it as transcendent. Who is the vanquisher, who the

vanquished? Is there neither victor nor vanquished? As I left
Peniel I felt how I limped from the hip. You, You carry like the
sign of Your glory the bruises of the crucified one.

You have taken upon Yourself the one who is obsessed with
God, the one whose life is a crater that he falls into, God bound
like a stone around his neck. Your cross hoists me out of this
bottomless pit that I am to myself. I am in the world! I am in the
world! This cry is an echo of Your name.

I am in the world where every visible thing is a gesture of Your
blessing. I will wash myself in the water of the ford, I will re-
fresh myself after the struggle. I will sit on the bank with my feet
hanging down.

Listening to the water utter Your name. Your grace on the other
bank has the smile of your servant Rachel: on a day that begins
like any other, to breathe is to praise You![105]

Who is Jacob's adversary? Every scholar seems to have a theory,
based on his or her imagination or inspiration. In the original form
of the story, it is one of the demons opposing the hero's passage,
says A. de Pury. "In the night, the divine antagonist tends to take
on the features of others with whom we struggle in the day," remarks W. Brueggemann. "This is no ordinary man. And certainly
no ordinary God! Clearly, this is no ordinary story."[106] According to
R. Couffignal, the Jews, wanting to preserve the transcendence of
God, saw the assailant as an angel. The most complete transformation
is found in E. Fleg. He followed "a tradition of late Judaism that
recognizes in Jacob's aggressor the enemy of humankind: Samael,
an evil angel, another Satan:[107]

> Now as he prayed, a strange form
> Came out of the night. And that form was an angel
> Black, advancing on him ...
> Thus their mute bodies wrestled
> Until dawn. Then with a sure hand,
> The man of light
> Made the dark angel
> Fall into the dust.
> And the Enemy

Took flight. And Jacob slept ...
... Samael, the Archangel of Death ...
... Did you not defeat Samael that night,
O my son, O Jacob whom I name Israel?[108]

In most of the rabbinic tales and in the Aramaic translations, the adversary is an angel, the guardian angel of Esau, or, according to Elie Wiesel's preference, Jacob's own guardian angel; he fought against "the side of him that harbored doubts about his mission, his future, his *raison d'être*."[109] The angel thus permits the Jewish exegetical tradition not to have to claim that a human could triumph over God. As for the Greek and Latin translations, they see in the adversary the "human beings" whom Jacob would have defeated.[110]

For G. Bernanos, it is a question of a decisive battle with Satan himself, who ends up being confused with Jacob's double. "And yet when, with sacrilegious mockery, the obscene lips pressed down over his, cutting short his breath, so intense was his terror that the very life in him was suspended." Later, "Still humble in his triumph which every moment became more certain and complete, the priest of Campagne was in no doubt that victory over such an enemy is always precarious, fragile, temporary." When he looked into Satan's eyes for the first time, "his most cogent thought was a dull kind of defiance." To the "monster" who tells him to make the most of his power, he replies, "This strength doesn't come from me, and you know it ... It is God who sends me this strength which you cannot break." And "suddenly he saw before him his twin, such a perfect, subtle likeness ..."[111]

The midrashic commentaries free us from the need to identify Jacob's adversary. The only thing that counts is what Jacob makes of the combat. The identity of the assailant is of little matter, but his function is important: to make Jacob lose his temper. In the first midrashic interpretation, the angel is disguised as a shepherd. Jacob and he help each other across the Jabbok, then the shepherd attacks without warning. In the second interpretation, the angel is disguised as a robber. The same deal based on reciprocity is reached, and then Jacob is tricked; he will never finish helping the other get his flocks across to the other side. Knowing Jacob's past in exile, we can see him, in his dream, facing this reality with more and more insight. First, he hopes that the OTHER is a conscientious shepherd, as he himself always was for Laban. Then he perceives that the OTHER is swindling him, as Laban had always swindled Jacob – he had never managed to earn the right to get married despite all his labour, and he had never finished trying to please Laban by his acts of submission. Thanks to the dream, which lifts the sanction, Jacob lashes out at the OTHER, says the Midrash, and smothers him with a piece of wool, crying out, "You are a sorcerer! You are a sorcerer! The magicians will not succeed this night!"

In the end, the angel decides to make himself known. He puts a finger on the soil and fire bursts forth from it, which enrages Jacob. "Would you terrify me with that? Why? I am of that species, too!" And the Midrash refers to the biblical verse "The house of Jacob shall be a fire" (Ob. 1:18) – an eloquent symbol of what is forever ungraspable, incorruptible, indestructible in the human. We could say it is the first cry of a Jacob who at last has appropriated that fire of which he is made, and who at the same time recognizes in the OTHER someone made of the same material.

The Midrash puts forward a third interpretation which, to my mind, goes even deeper into Jacob's unconscious. There God recreates and restores in the most mysterious way, as in those beacon dreams that are so hard to recount, where an unimaginable outcome leaves the dreamer with the impression of receiving a generous gift that is meant for him or her alone. This time the assailant is Esau's guardian prince (angel); Jacob is an athlete who struggles with a prince of royal blood. As he recognizes his adversary and prostrates himself before him, he sees that he "can do nothing against him" for it is the *Shekinah* – the Divine presence in person.

What is striking in this interpretation, where the "he"s are reversed and the "for him" is changed to "against him" (Jacob trying to defeat Esau), is the transformation of the OTHER-Esau into an OTHER-God. Jacob understands that he is dealing with the spiritual being of Esau: that is, with God himself. Whatever the conflicts we find ourselves in, that which is "of God" in the other human being is as invincible as God himself. Such is Jacob's dream experience. His rage hurls itself against a limit – the spiritual being of his worst enemy. He no longer has to fear his own violence. He does not run the risk of killing Esau; the other human is made of the same material as he is: fire. The Midrash thus leads us deep into an understanding of the link between anger and identity.

It has to "heat up" between us and the OTHER so that, in a fit of temper, we can access the indestructible fire in ourselves and perceive that it burns in the other human as well. For Jacob, as for Cain, it is first the divine OTHER who makes himself an outlet for the human's anger. The grandeur, the majesty and the power that the biblical authors attribute to God are based above all on his capacity to resist the reproaches, attacks and revolts of humans. For many people, God is the only one they know who can handle their violence without being annihilated and without responding with even greater violence. Until the last breath, he remains He who agrees to occupy that place, that "place of murder." Thus, when Bernanos was dying he asked his friends to withdraw and he was heard to murmur, "Now it's just the two of us."[112]

## The OTHER: The One Who Refuses

Before the drama happens – before Esau sacrifices Jacob to his own idea of justice, or Jacob sacrifices Esau to his blind obedience to the God of his emotions – the OTHER throws himself into battle to prevent any sacrificial violence, so that Jacob might kill Him rather than killing Esau, or that Cain might kill Him rather than killing Abel. It seems that the Midrash confers on the murder of Abel the same function and meaning as the sacrifice: Cain would like to make atonement because his sacrifice has been rejected. Abel would be the scapegoat whose sacrifice would serve to let Cain be forgiven and discharge the violence.[113] The story of the near-sacrifice of Isaac, with other biblical passages, shows us that God refuses to accept the very idea of human sacrifice. "The single victim mechanism is a purely human abomination," writes R. Girard. "The one God ... reproaches humans for their violence and has compassion on their victims. Yahweh substitutes the sacrifice of animals for the firstborn sons and later objects even to animal sacrifices."[114]

God is thus the one who rejects humans' enslavement to the idea that one should kill to have the right to live, even if it means "killing" oneself, for "killing" the OTHER (human or divine) means killing the relationship that alone brings life. God never demands that we sacrifice a relationship, and certainly not that we sacrifice it to Him. We might wonder: had Jacob inherited from his father, Isaac, from the unconscious to the unconscious, that deep-seated fantasy that he had never put into words: God could at any time demand of me a sacrifice that would put me as well as others to death? Should I obey? I do not feel I have the right to exist in revolt and opposition. I have the choice of dying because I disobeyed him, or dying in obedience to him. There is an interpretation of the passage at Hosea 12:4 that I think is a replay by Jacob of the drama of his father bound on the altar of sacrifice. It would be enough to admit that the original Hebrew word designating Jacob's adversary is not [maleak], the angel, but [malak], that is, the god Malak (or Molok), the god of death and the underworld who demands human sacrifices.

When Hosea recounts that "he wept and sought his favour" and that "he met him at Bethel, and there he spoke with us," this could be taken to mean that Jacob lost the battle not against the angel but against the god Malak, that he cried and sought the help of the God (of) Beth-el, and was saved by Him from the god Malak.[115] It seems to me that this reading sheds extra light on the combat of Jacob. In spite of all his efforts (his legendary strength) he could not *by himself alone* have done with the god of Sacrifice. He nevertheless fought as much as he could, and his combativeness kept him in contact with his hope to come to the end of this deified fantasy. To cry, to supplicate and to persevere through an entire night indicates that one is not giving up. Hosea does not mention the "dislocation" at the hollow of the thigh, but he does recount the dislocation of Jacob to Bethel, where his dialogue with God takes place.

This is, from another point of view, the same idea as the notion that we do not "find" the OTHER unless we change location. When, with all of our conscious resources, we have struggled to get rid of a God hungry for sacrifice (simply an extension, often, of abusive parents or teachers), the admission of defeat makes us let go of the pressure and brings us back to ourselves. If sacrifice has given structure to our life, it is because we have been sacrificed, without our consent, obviously. That experience programmed us for so long that an inner voice still orders us to sacrifice ourselves, even if that enrages us. Such is our dysfunction, which thrusts its roots into inaccessible wounds. Only One breaks down our resistance, for all that we have done the preliminary work.

Tears and supplications would remain futile if Jacob had not welcomed with friendship that image of himself that he detested: someone weak whom others abuse because he always needs to sacrifice himself. By consenting to that reality that is his, he sacrifices the only thing that God asked him to sacrifice: the idealized image of himself as a free, independent Jacob. Having done that, he recognizes himself to be un-dislocatable[116] and without any transition finds himself in Bethel, "found" by that OTHER who, "speaking with us," has refused since the time of Abel all sacrificial violence against any human being.

The fantastical idea that God would require violent sacrifice resurfaced after the death of Christ. Let us remember, however, that the sacrificial reading of the Passion is far from being the most common one presented in the gospels.[117] At the birth of the people of Israel, we find, in what can be called the story of the vocation of Jacob at the Jabbok, a combative God who calls forth the combativeness of the human without either of them having to sacrifice the self. We could say that Christ fought in another way at God's side, but without sacrificing anything of his freedom and his identity as a son of the house, a worthy descendent of Jacob the son of Bethel, the house of God.

Moving to a new place, or rather accepting being moved, consists essentially of renouncing a neutrality in which one stagnates. The OTHER induces Jacob during that extraordinary night to make an unceasing affirmation of himself. The hour is come to declare war on the icy peace that takes the place of relationships for him. Jacob could consider himself non-violent, without an active share in the conflicts of his family. He took no part therein, neither before nor during nor after his exile. His father continued to be deceived, Rebecca having tricked him about the reason for Jacob's exile; his brother held onto his hostility and bitterness; Leah and Rachel remained disinherited (Gen. 31:14f); Laban himself acted unjustly for twenty years. All this because Jacob did not clearly take his place in the society of humans where he took full responsibility. Through wanting to be nice and wanting not to contradict anyone, we often end up contributing to the worst injustices. R. Girard describes that subtle passage from unconsciousness of oneself to actual participation in persecution.

> The Holy Spirit gives the disciples the strength to stand out from the crowd and to contradict it … To know the scapegoat requires a kind of conversion because it means also knowing oneself as the persecutor … The victim is not guilty, and therefore no longer has the power to absorb violence.[118]

On that night, there were no more good guys and bad guys. In Jacob's past, each in his turn had been the victim or scapegoat of others. Fruitful combat — combat that mirrors who we have been and who we are capable of becoming — begins by showing us in what circumstances we have been victims and in what circumstances we have been persecutors. It will no longer be enough for us to be victims to believe ourselves incapable of violence. Either we continue to absorb the violence of others, claiming to remain neutral — and we persecute without even realizing it, by other means — or we take a stand on who we really are and we staunchly defend our territory, in such a way that others are led to defend theirs without encroaching on ours or other people's. When Jacob rolls in the dust, his image of himself arises with the same brutality as the assailant. The nice Jacob no longer exists. If he does not stand up for himself aggressively, he risks leaving behind a lot more than "the hollow of his thigh." The OTHER is God, by the effect he produces; who else could cause such a metamorphosis?

In Jacob's personality, there is from the outset a refusal to "know his place," to quote an expression that is often used to keep someone from affirming himself or herself by taking their proper place. Jacob does not want to be confined to the mould that his tradition offers him, to be nothing more than a younger, inferior son. God refuses to accept the cultural favouritism of the time that gave all the rights to the elder son. At the Jabbok, the OTHER is the one who rejects the conformity of humans to the place and role that their culture assigns. Whether one is born the younger or the last of siblings, Black, Aboriginal, or female, one can count on the OTHER for encouragement not to conform – with his blessing. It is He who takes over that inner demand, in Jacob, to leave the artificial framework that confines him. On that night, Jacob receives in his flesh the certainty that his identity is not reducible to his role in society.

> Jacob having made his mark in his struggle with God, one could say that in a sense [God] is the substitute for the elder brother, who is beaten once again by the younger. The conflict with Esau is *dislocated* (every symbol is a *dislocation*; if the "struggle with the Angel" is symbolic, it is because it has dislocated something) … In this universe [of brothers who are enemies in the Bible], God puts his stamp on the younger ones, acting against nature. His (structural) function is to constitute a counter-marker.[119]

Jacob had paid dearly, by a long exile, for his refusal to do what was expected of him. That is the source of his tendency, at Laban's house, to do what his uncle and his own wives wanted. He saw himself as the ideal shepherd during his exile, far beyond his legal obligation[120] (Gen 31:38ff). It is certainly not by chance that, for the Midrash, the OTHER begins by disguising himself as a shepherd who is perfectly respectful of the contract, only to let loose all of a sudden for no apparent reason. We have seen how much, in the commentaries, the OTHER takes on the characteristics of Jacob himself. It reminds us of what people say after someone goes on a violent rampage. How could this happen? He was such a kind father. She was a respected woman. That person was well brought up – and so forth. There comes a time when the person reaches the boiling point, as we also say, and it is better for Jacob that God is there when he boils over, and better for him that it is God who makes him boil over, without witnesses. At that moment the inner need to conform comes to an end once and for all, and even if the impulse arises from time to time, the process is nevertheless irreversible.

Also the aggression of God is a grace. Often God will be aggressive without one recognizing Him, in an apparently incomprehensible and unexpected way, as with Jacob. He "falls" on us. His aggression is judgment. He destroys all false hope and security ... To accept that life may challenge us without our recognizing Him, we do it spontaneously, like the humans that we are. To recognize the Attacker – and he lets himself be recognized by anyone who is attentive – and to thank Him, that is our task.[121]

We can speak of "grace" at that unprecedented moment where what we gain has more impact than what we lose. This is the moment of grace where we willingly let go, as if they were just old rags, of flattering images of ourselves that prevent us from seeing ourselves as servile and as doing evil "behind the scenes." It is better to suddenly *be ourselves* – recognizing our behaviours as Jacob-heels – because Someone has made the mask fall away and we gain thereby the right to show our opposition openly. The OTHER is the One before whom our objections crumble like clay, especially the ongoing need to prove ourselves, but also the reflex of defiance and the compulsion to defend ourselves from others or the obsession to get revenge.

However, the same movement that causes those objections to crumble rallies our resistance to the OTHER, and the feeling of having won a hundredfold is born. For at last our identity as a full human being, capable of baring our teeth, meets an image of ourselves that we no longer have to worry about. It is the struggle to reach the real self that occupies our body, soul and mind, and it is there, we now realize, that the OTHER wanted to come from the beginning, doing everything possible to break us. For the apostle Peter, it took the arrest of his Master and friend, the triple denial, the cock's crowing and the divine sweetness in the eyes of Jesus. "Thus was Peter flooded with pain and joy when the look on Jesus' face dealt him the final blow – the *coup de grace*, in fact – the blow that put an end once and for all to a certain resistance," writes M.-D. Molinié, who also says of Jacob, "Jacob was defeated, and as a result, Jacob becomes a victor."[122]

The OTHER would be He alone who waits and desires that we take
him on, for then we would be ourselves as much as we can be in
earthly life, without subterfuge, without leaving things unsaid, without hypocrisy. "There is a dispute with God from which no one
will be exempted because God wants the dispute to take place."[123]
When Christ recommends going to reproach someone who has
sinned against us (Matt. 18:15), we resist for fear of being further
wounded or from fear of unduly tormenting the offender. The
ambivalence of the OTHER at the Jabbok is useful to us here. The
Hebrew text speaks of a man; the tradition speaks of an angel; the
commentators swing constantly between the human and the divine.
The thing is, we need a *human* adversary to stop us from clinging
to the illusion that we have been freed from fear and resentment,
an adversary that we can dare to look in the eye without putting
our own truth under a bushel. But it is also necessary for God to
be part of the confrontation for us to dare to plumb the depths of
our anger, without censoring any of what we are.

"No one will be spared" confronting the human as one confronts
God himself, with fear in the belly or rage in the heart, at the risk
of always being in the role of the under-son, which Jacob refused
to be. To believe we are above such a step would be to flee once
again into a beautiful and illusory image of ourselves, as if Jacob had
refused the combat and preferred to take refuge in his fantasy of the
kind, non-violent Jacob. Reaching our full human stature, standing face to face with the OTHER (human and divine), can happen
only through a confrontation. The occasion for such a confrontation will arise sooner or later as long as we have not smothered in
ourselves for good the desire to believe in our consistency or our
resistance.

An adversary in human form, the title of this part of this book, is
the human whom we dare to oppose, transgressing the unwritten
commandment that has kept us muzzled to that point. But there
is also, implicitly, behind the human the God who, in every case,
will welcome with benevolence our counter-violence and who
will rejoice in it as one rejoices in the birth of a baby in spite of the
blood and the pain. That confrontation, which takes place at night,

in the solitude of prayer and dreams, is of an unusual violence and avoids putting the human adversary in danger. It incarnates God's dream of partnership with humans, as if God continually took the form and appearance of a human adversary so that at last we would stand up to Him and really be partners with him. "Truly, he appreciates it when you do violence to him, he wants you to lose your temper with him," writes Guerric d'Igny.[124] "Even when he is irritated and holds out an arm to strike, he is seeking … a human like Moses who knows how to resist him." It is thus scarcely surprising that God, at the Jabbok, agrees to let himself be persuaded by Jacob's violence.[125]

## The OTHER: The One Who Compromises

In reading many biblical texts, we may wonder if the God to whom they bear witness goes out of his way to make himself misunderstood. But how could he prevent himself from being caricatured, when the authors have such trouble moving beyond humankind imprisoned by its representations of the divine? One might say, therefore, that the OTHER is he who lets himself be taken for who he is not, all the while struggling to be identified. Such is his way of "breaking out of the mould" in which humans think they have captured him, with each new style of ready-to-believe. The OTHER gives the example by refusing to conform to our ideas, our expectations, our biblical knowledge. The God of the Bible assumes a certain ambivalence in the eyes of humans. As he has Isaiah say, "I form light and create darkness, I make weal and *create woe*"[126] (Is. 45:7). In Deuteronomy we read, "I kill and I make alive; I wound and I heal" (Deut. 32:39). And the redactor of Exodus 4:24ff has God attack Moses, whom He has just called. There are many passages in the Psalms and Job where God is described as hostile to believers, being aggressive towards them for no reason.

"It is not necessary," comments F.C. Holmgren, "to protect God from taking responsibility for ambiguous actions. As Israel sees it, whatever happens in life, good or evil, is intimately related to God's actions in the world. In pre-Christian Jewish literature and in Christian literature the figure of Satan (the devil) becomes respon-

sible for many 'dark events' in the world, but Israelite writers, for
the most part, know nothing of such a figure and therefore address
themselves to God,"[127] to criticize him and to fight him. One might
say that they prefer to see God as "the creator of evil," responsible
for wounds and death in order that humans would have recourse
to no one else. These declarations were not to be taken as absolute,
but to highlight the fact that God is the One who claims to be the
only partner of humans when they confront evil – the One who
wants to take responsibility for human reality so that they stop going after each other to the point of killing each other.

If God himself shocks us by his behaviour, eluding our ideas of good
and of justice, we can see dimly that he is perhaps OTHER precisely
by and through all that escapes us of him, and we can suspend our
judgment, giving him the benefit of the doubt. Our violence di-
minishes to the extent that the space of not-knowing between him
and us grows. The adversary, human or divine, has a malevolent
and hostile air, but perhaps that is an optical illusion and, in our
uncertainty, we suspend judgment. The irreparable gesture towards
the human is put off until later. Meanwhile, we can blame God
who, by his silence and rigidity, seems to justify our adversary and
thereby makes our anger and desire for vengeance come to light.
As René Girard puts it, "God Himself reuses, at his own expense,
the sacrifice of the scapegoat in order to sabotage it."[128] Since the
sacrifice of the scapegoat is not practised in our societies, God offers
himself to our counter-violence so that in no circumstances is the
human adversary killed.

The OTHER is thus He who gets involved with violence, meeting
with the human where he or she is, to free him or her from it.
But it took centuries for the Hebrews to discern behind the de-
monic appearance of Jacob's aggressor the God of the covenant,
from whom life must be fought for and won. It would have taken
years for Jacob on his own to have the experience at the level of
his body. No one is exempt, it seems, from combat with his or her
own caricatural representations of the OTHER, human and divine.
In this sense the nomadic world of the era of the patriarchs is not
so far from our own. Originally, our text carried traces of the threat

that demons held over the nomads during their migrations, says A. de Pury, and later Jacob will thank God, at Sichem, for having delivered him from the "demon of Penuel."[129]

In the toughest combats there is often a sort of fog that prevents us from knowing which side God is on, and even which side humans are on. It is because those nearest to us, whom we wish to be the most unconditionally caring, flay us as much as or even more than our worst adversaries. Who is the OTHER in the battle where we no longer know whom we can count on? We will learn who it is only at the break of day. For the moment, all that exists is the violence of the struggle. We are fighting with an OTHER, an adversity by which we refuse to let ourselves be crushed, a human adversary who is clearly identified but behind whom is silhouetted a strange and foreign God – a God who is linked with both injustice and justice, with destruction and life, a God whom we suspect does not want "to keep his hands clean," in the shelter of his heaven.

> To wrestle with Elohim can mean to fight against God, but also to fight with God, or simply – since Elohim also refers to the divinities – to fight the *divine powers*. That is the translation adopted by many exegetes. The combats Jacob will have – and which Israel will have – will always be marked with duality; to confront humans in daily life, but also to confront the forces of evil, of annihilation, which are god-like, radical.[130]

The OTHER is, in the end, He who gets involved in the intricacies of the individual unconscious. If our text does a good job of relating Jacob's dream, we should see how the transcendent is rooted in the psychic material of that dream. God is mentioned only in v. 28, when Jacob receives the name of "Isra-el" for having "wrestled-with-God and with-men" – a change of name that offers a new understanding of God. Let us come back to the root of the name of Jacob, for we have not yet exhausted all its meanings. There is the verb ['aqav], to grasp by the heel, to betray, to stay. There is the noun ['aqev], meaning heel, footprint, rear-guard, and another noun ['aqev], which means "to the end," "result" or "recompense."

Perhaps this is a dream-name (one that is actually dreamt) that expresses the ambivalence of God in the eyes of humans. In this particular context, taking account of the polysemy of the root, it could wonderfully evoke a God who grasps by the heel and does not let go, a God who "abides," going "to the very end," a God who keeps "the rear-guard" no matter what happens, and at the same time a God who "betrays," who in effect does not seem to keep his promises (Gen. 32:9-12), responding to the prayer of distress by initiating a merciless combat, as if Jacob needed a sleepless night on the eve of his confrontation with Esau! The feeling of being betrayed is well known to those who, in response to their cry for help, receive from the OTHER an extra blow.

There is probably no good reason to attribute to the OTHER the character of Samael, the enemy of humankind, as many of the Jewish commentators have done. If we stop making God conform to our definition of goodness, we will one day come to recognize that God has the freedom to take on the appearance of our adversaries and the adversity that does us harm. This time, we are beside ourselves and we want to know more about him: Who are you? What do you want from me? "Tell me your name" (Gen. 32:29). We said earlier that Jacob wanted to know more about himself. "So explain *the history of* your name." But in the interpretation-laden version that has come to us, v. 30 shows that Jacob's request also concerned the name of God. He says he saw God face to face, when in fact he had obtained no response about the identity of the adversary. The history of his own name seems inseparable from the story of his perception of God. Something has just changed in his experience of God. The OTHER "follows on his heel" to one day "confront" humans face to face and make himself known as the God whose Life will always take them back, no matter what they may have destroyed. Whence the name of [Peny'el], "turn towards God": face him instead of running hot on other people's heels, turn to-wards the One who follows at your heel to cause that face-to-face encounter in truth where your life will take place – or where your life as a wanderer will find a place.

But, one might object, Jacob did not see God, first because it was pitch black and because it was a dream, and also because it was considered impossible to see God and live. His enthusiasm, never-

theless, is eloquent. He has been given new eyes to see. What did
he see of the OTHER? Who did he look at in a new way? Before
that night, he prayed thus: "Yet you have said, '*I will surely do you
good*, and make your offspring as the sand of the sea" (Gen. 32:12).
A. de Pury indicates that this utterance is not found in any of the
patriarchal promises, where it is only a question of the gift of the
earth, of offspring and of flocks.[131] However, the verb in question
[ya*t*av] is the one used by God to invite Cain not to give in to
murderous violence: "Is it not true that if you *do well* [it is] to raise
[your countenance], and if you *do not do well* ..." (Gen. 4:7).

Jacob had not killed anyone. But had he "done well," he who
had never been himself, having survived only by betrayal, ruse
and flight without ever facing the OTHER in any form whatsoever?
Clearly not, since once again he found himself in the situation of
kill-or-be-killed. That night, an OTHER suddenly appeared to "do
well *with him*." He did not arrive at this point on his own. Certainly
he was less lost than Cain, but he had wandered in search of his
identity, imprisoned by that which was unspoken in his past. In the
morning, a third way opened within and before him. Abandoning
the alternative of death (kill or be killed), he met in the OTHER a
"kind" opponent, someone who helped him by driving him back
to fight *with him* for his freedom. If "God alone has the right to attack Israel" in that way and the "power to bless Israel,"[132] is it not
for the same reason? Jesus will later say, by its fruits will we know
the tree. If Jacob looks back and sees the hand of God in what happened to him, it is because he feels freed and blessed – "to do well,
the OTHER having done well with him." He deduces from this that
he was dealing with the God who made promises to his ancestors
and the God of his innermost prayers, and he admits that God was
right to provoke him and roll in the dust with him. But he sees this
after the fact, and that connects not only with his experience but
with ours. In this sense, the Bible is right to recall that one does
not see God "directly." "Surely the Lord is in this place – and I did
not know it!" Jacob had exclaimed on awaking from the dream of
the ladder (Gen. 28:16).

## The OTHER: The One Who Lets Me Decide
## Whether He Is Friend or Enemy

In accordance with numerous interpretations, N.M. Sarna speaks
of a "deliberate ambiguity": "To 'see the face' may describe an experience of either cordiality or hostility. 'Face to face,' used only of
divine-human encounters, may be an adversary confrontation or an
experience of extraordinary intimacy."[133] But what exactly is meant
by the word "face," which occurs 2100 times in the Hebrew Bible?
And as for the face of God that we are supposed to adore in spirit
without making any "graven image" thereof, why is it so important
that the biblical authors refer to it so often? We sometimes describe
a face as inscrutable. But modern observations show rather that a
strange osmosis occurs between two people who face each other.
"When people view a smiling or angry face, their own faces show
evidence of that same mood through slight changes in the facial
muscles. The changes are evident through electronic sensors but
are typically not visible to the naked eye."[134]

To show one's face is to expose oneself to communicating, without
realizing it, one's emotions and deep thoughts, and it risks being
misunderstood, another risk to which the God of Jacob consents.
When His anger threatens to destroy everything, the Bible says
that He hides his face. But in so doing he deprives humans of his
presence and resigns himself to being deprived of theirs. The face-
to-face encounter says something else: when the OTHER assails Jacob
at the ford of the Jabbok, he is not moved by anger and does not
exercise punitive violence. There would exist – and once more it
is God who gives the example – an attack without hostility that
forces the other, in some way, to lift up his head and show his
face. But it is impossible for him to know whether he is dealing
with someone who wishes him well as long as he has not lifted
his head and risked discovery. Up to then, the ambivalence of the
OTHER remains impassable for him: friend or enemy? He oscillates
constantly, at the whim of his fears.

It is up to the reader to settle it. In terms of the original form of the
episode, the most important question remains open: that of "knowing if the adversary of the patriarch is an *enemy* god (or a demon) or

if it is the god *El*, the *protector* God of the patriarch."[135] Jacob settled it on the basis of his experience at waking, and the author of the story does his best to bring us to see in the OTHER the God of all blessing. As if preparing the ground, he preceded Jacob's crisis of anguish with the following story: "Jacob went on his way and the angels of God met him; and when Jacob saw them he said, 'This is God's camp!' So he called that place Mahanaim [two camps]" (Gen. 32:1-2). According to the author, this is rather reassuring, but that does not seem to be enough to reassure Jacob. From up close, the "friend or enemy?" problem is already present, and he will have the whole night to deal with it. Any encounter with the OTHER – human, angel, God – is uncertain from the outset. Will he show himself as benevolent or hostile? Is he really benevolent? Is his hostility only for show? Is he going to change "camps" suddenly and become aggressive? Is Jacob sure that he is dealing with the camp of God? If so, why does he call it "Two Camps," as if he already saw some ambivalence in the OTHER?

The Hebrew text itself reveals the ambivalence. According to J. Skinner, the verb that is used – "angels of God *met* him" – usually means "to oppose." This expression, as well as the word "camp," which is close to the idea of divine armies and the Host of heaven, "suggest a warlike encounter."[136] The Targum clearly expresses Jacob's doubts:

> And Jacob said when he saw them, "Perhaps they are messengers from Laban, my mother's brother, who has returned to pursue after me; or the hosts of Esau, my brother, who comes to meet me, or hosts of angels from before the Lord come to deliver me from the hands of both of them."[137]

The OTHER leaves us free to judge: will we decide to trust him, counting on his store of blessing? Or will we seek to know more about him, will we keep waiting for proof of his benevolence before we risk facing him?

Waiting is in vain, as Jacob experiences on that critical night. His search for an explanation will not come to an end. One cannot "explain" to others that one is benevolent. Either they believe it or they don't.

> Then Jacob asked him, "Please tell me your name." But he said, "Why is it that you ask my name?" And there he blessed him. (Gen. 32:29)

Is it a friend name or an enemy name? Or, as in the hypothesis that Jacob wants an explanation of his own identity – explain (the story of) your name, that I may know whether or not I can trust myself! Is this new name (Israel the confronter, the powerful) a friend name or an enemy name? Can I adopt it with serenity? Is it threatening for me or for others? Should I be wary of it? If the question is unanswerable, it is because the identity does not refer to either the knowledge of self or the knowledge of the other. One does not explain an identity; one is who one is and if others feel threatened, that is their problem, as we say nowadays. To demonstrate that one is not threatening, in no way hostile nor desirous of crushing anything, does not serve much of a purpose. At each new encounter with others and with God, Jacob will have to rely on himself – to take himself for what he is with friendship and benevolence – in order to welcome the OTHER as he is, hostile or friendly in appearance, simply because it is his OTHER and he wants the relationship.

In fact, there are more important things about others than their proportions of hostility and benevolence, which are impossible to establish with certainty. There is his or her face. That is what Jacob will cry out in the very next verse: I could not know anything, he did not explain anything to me, but I saw him face to face. His identity is his face and not his intentions. My identity is my face and not the failures of my past or my fear of introducing myself with my new name. At the same time as he agreed to know nothing of the value of the OTHER's identity, Jacob received the blessing that he had begun by asking for, and he ordered himself, "Turn towards God!" This is, as we have seen, the meaning of Peny'el, the name Jacob gives to this place of revelation. For, he says, "I saw God face to face and my being is and will be freed." By showing my face to the OTHER, by exposing myself to him and running the risk of being taken for what I am not, I have welcomed the face of the

OTHER like a similar gift. He lets me decide for myself if he is friend or enemy, if I am going to turn inward or show myself to him as I am, regardless of what it may cost me.

Let's look once again at the initial question: where is the grounding, the anchoring, for the transcendence at the level of the dream? How can God speak with us through a dream? The spiritual interpretation is clear at the level of the story in its final form. One can discover it in the ending of the dream, as if, at the point of awakening, Jacob already understood that he had dreamed of God. But what about during the activity of dreaming? The answer is perhaps to be found in the three *hapax* used by the author. They show that if God is present in the dream, it is in dotted lines. Behind those strange words, unknown in the rest of the Bible, there was something vacant, a mysteriously free place so that the dreamer writes with the OTHER a story that he had already exhausted himself in writing alone.

The *hapax* can help us in some way to trace the OTHER. The first, in v. 24, is written in a kind of solidarity: "He rolled in the dust *with him.*" It is someone like him, a man ['ish] who espouses his human condition in space (in the dust) and in time (for an entire night). To speak of struggle is already overly precise: Jacob lived a body-to-body encounter in the thick of night and in total silence. They were two, but we don't know what really happened between them on the ground.[138] How would the divine transcendence make even the least sense for us if it had no point of contact with the human condition? One might think that God does not cease to incarnate in humans who lay hold of others to urge them to take their place on earth.

Jesus was the first to "roll in the dust with" his fellows, without being preoccupied with convincing them of his benevolent intentions (of his divine identity, says the tradition). He was therefore accused of acting in the name of Beelzebub, the chief of the devils. His response did no more to dispel the ambivalence than that of Jacob's adversary did. It is up to you to decide whether I am friend or enemy, but know that "But if it is by the Spirit of God that I cast out demons [he had just cured a man who was blind and mute], then the kingdom of God has come to you" (Matt. 12:28). Doubtless for God the best way to face humans is to incarnate as a human and to let the dust cover everything, to the point where one can no longer clearly distinguish what is of God and what is human.

Then, the body-to-body encounter with the OTHER gives power (v. 28b) and life (v. 30b). But the *hapax* here evokes the impossibility of rendering an account of the how of that victory: "For you have struggled-with-God and with-men." However, the hyphen offers an interesting precision, still in the sense of solidarity: an OTHER "rolled in the dust" *with* him in such a way that Jacob became an integral part of humanity without fearing to be killed by or to kill them. You have struggled-*with* or being part of God and *with* or being part of humans (plural of ['ish], the human being in the masculine), so you are wholly a man.

It is still up to Jacob to decide if the power of the OTHER is beneficial for him. He has perceived that his adversary is not all-powerful over his life. "He saw that he did not prevail against Jacob" (v. 25). It is Jacob who can prevail, but because he has been "rendered powerful." How? The only power of the OTHER was to be there where Jacob suffered – once again, solidarity. We have seen that the Midrash understands, according to one of its interpretations, that "the *Shekinah*, the Presence, was there, at the hollow of the thigh." Is this not God's mooring in the dream? In the gesture of blessing of the OTHER "there," at the very place of Jacob's wound? "He blessed him there," concludes v. 29, as if in that wound was inscribed the possibility for Jacob of hearing the OTHER "speak well" of him and for him, according to the etymology of bene-diction. Only an OTHER of this scope could make Jacob hear that he was a fighter and that he had the right to be who he was deep down.

It is an inexplicable communication between God and the human at the most unconscious level, right in the heart of the dream. A visitation of the secret wound: Jacob had never felt blessed. In the past he had basically blessed himself, and his whole life he had worn himself out claiming the right to exist by his own efforts. That night, he asserted himself once again, but that was not enough for him anymore. He could no longer "get out of it" on his own. He wanted, for the first time in his life, to feel himself truly blessed by a strong and powerful OTHER, someone capable of standing up to him and facing him, a credible OTHER, so that he would no longer have to wash himself in the truncated blessing of his past: "I will not let you go, unless you bless me."

The OTHER put a finger on his sensitive spot. If Jacob keeps the OTHER there, he does so because he, too, from now on would be in touch with his old wound. I will not let you go until you *speak well* about what is wrong in me. The OTHER did not ask for more: "He spoke well of him *there*." The Midrash, intrigued, had sought to understand this word "there." The adversary could have begged Jacob to wait, for he would bless him later, elsewhere, and Jacob could have refused. But what if this "there" was not a geographic place? Jacob could have asked for and received his blessing at the very site of his wound, at that spot of his identity, of his simplistic and ridiculous surname.

At first glance, the story of the thigh seems to have nothing to do with the request for a blessing. But if it is true that often, to connect two thoughts in a dream that seem unrelated, the dreamer creates an intermediate thought that finds itself in both of the ideas in the form of a pun, then the connection becomes clear:

| the thigh/the wound<br>the place of the swearing<br>"there" [sham] | discussion on the<br>"name" [shem] | the thigh/the<br>wound/the place of<br>the blessing "there" [sham] |
|---|---|---|

The "name" [shem] would be the intermediate thought that, as a play on words with [sham], "there," links the two thoughts that seem unrelated: the wound on the thigh and the blessing. In light of this, we can say that God has no better ally than our unconscious to help us reach our own truth, in making Himself known as the unconditional ally of our real identity.

To confirm the foundation of transcendence in the psychic material of the dream, we need to check in the text if Jacob's dream has really changed his reality. We could also admit that God sometimes uses dreams to push humans to grow. The text says at v. 31, "He passed, limping because of *his* hip," with a verb in the perfect tense.

It could be the onset of a case of sciatica, just as we can have a stiff neck the day after a dream where we wanted to wring someone's neck, or a dislocation of vertebrae during a time when we are carrying a heavy load. In any case, Jacob really limps, which means something has visibly changed in him; he was in the grip of something important.

But our third *hapax*, at v. 32, would lose the richness of its meaning if we were to translate it as "the sciatic nerve." Let us rather look to see what light that *hapax* throws on the dietary restriction. The site of a wound that God has visited (wherever it may be), where one has found to be deeply rooted something of one's own identity, where one has received the most intimate blessing that can be, that place has to be protected, permanently OTHER. No one can take on the suffering of others, their search for identity, their blessing. Each life, each confrontation with God or others, is itself a *hapax*: "Therefore to this day the Israelites do not eat the thigh muscle (the nerve [nāsheh) that is on the hip socket." Not to eat from the part that symbolizes the oath and the promise is to abstain from consuming or appropriating the word of another and his or her witness. A promise is not edible; it is a word to be believed. A promise exists only in the space between the person and the OTHER, and thus with the constant risk of being destroyed. In this dietary practice can be seen the trace of an OTHER who cannot be consumed. The reality of Jacob and of his people has thus extended and confirmed his dream.

The taboo, as we have seen, is not mentioned anywhere else in the Bible. Is that because the "children of Israel," thus of Jacob, took it at face value? Peny'el (turn [yourself] to God) became in a later verse Penu'el (turn [yourselves] to God). When someone's dream transforms their reality, it affects people around him or her. Jacob from now on has a word that the others believe without consuming it, that is, without destroying it. His descendants will believe what happened to him. In v. 31, "The sun rose upon him." It is a symbolic sun, to express that Jacob's identity has come fully to light. The truth of his dream will take shape through his encounter with Esau. The sun will shine for Esau as well, and that is perhaps the meaning of Penu'el: "Turn [yourselves] towards God! Do the same!" For St. Ambrose, it depended first on Jacob letting go of his possessions, remaining alone, and fighting with God, thus advancing on the path of his inner realization. "For whoever forsakes worldly things comes nearer to the image and likeness of God. What is it to wrestle with God, other than to enter upon the struggle for virtue, to contend with one who is stronger and to become a better imitator of God than the others are?"[139]

It seems that at the time of the redaction of our text, they had not yet decided on a benevolent adversary. Jacob, it was thought, had "wrestled to his advantage with an evil genie who tried to stop the realization of the promises of a land and numerous descendants."[140] The final redactor succeeded in making Jacob's assailant the God of Israel, faithful to his promise of a good life, all the while safeguarding the ambivalence of the OTHER in Jacob's experience. For it is not a question of a dogmatic truth on the nature of God. The OTHER is only benevolent and beneficent as far as the human believes it. Overcoming the ambivalence is the result of a struggle.

That is perhaps why we do not find anywhere else in the Hebrew Bible a blessing that is obtained by means of a struggle.[141] The understanding of what blessing is deepens. It is no longer an external good that is transmitted from father to son. It demands an investment of body and soul on the part of the one who fights with the OTHER to receive it. And it is received at the moment when the human recognizes himself or herself to be "of the same material" as the OTHER, to use the expression found in the Midrash. It is only then that ambivalence is surpassed, in the face-to-face encounter of two faces that have equal dignity.[142]

## A Possible Reconstruction of Jacob's Dream

A man in the dust with me.
He does not prevail against me.
He touches the hollow of my thigh.
The hollow of my thigh becomes dislocated/is paralyzed in the dust
with him.
(Him): Let go of me (no, I will not wake up).
(Me): I will let go of you if you speak/do well for me.
(Him): What is your name [shēm]?
(Me): Heel!
(Him): Your name [shēm] is no longer "heel" but "con-fronter of all"
(Me): Please, say your "name" [shēm] again!
(Him): Why my "name" [shēm] again?
He spoke/did well for me there [shēm].

# III  For the sword to pass ...

# 1  "Do not think that I have come to bring peace!"

Who ought to be, or who are more friendly than those who live in the same family? And yet who can rely even upon this friendship, seeing that secret treachery has often broken it up, and produced enmity as bitter as the amity was sweet, or seemed sweet by the most perfect dissimulation? It is on this account that the words of Cicero so move the heart of every one, and provoke a sigh: "There are no snares more dangerous than those which lurk under the guise of duty or the name of relationship. For the man who is your declared foe you can easily baffle by precaution; but this hidden, intestine, and domestic danger not merely exists, but overwhelms you before you can foresee and examine it." (*In Verrem*, 2:1, 15) ... In our present wretched condition we frequently mistake a friend for an enemy, and an enemy for a friend.[1]

Such is the difficulty with human relationships: we often feel caught in the ambivalence of the OTHER – humans and God – as if we are stuck in a honeypot. The sweetness of a bond of affection, and inextricable entanglements in situations that trap us, to the point where we no longer know who we are or what we want. The result is separation, or rather a clear distinction between beings, whether

they are friendly or hostile. But the issue is knowing if we can really get past the ambivalence that surrounds us: the more we need
to know who and what we can trust, the greater the odds that we
have already experienced the destruction of trust that has plunged
us into mortal confusion. So many people who seemed nice have
led us into disaster! How much happiness have we turned our backs
on, for fear of being had?

It is generally thought that the last verse of the story of Adam and
Eve, following the mention of their exile far from the garden of
Eden, is simply a retelling of the same event but in mythological
terms: "He drove out the man; and at the east of the garden of
Eden he placed the cherubim, and a sword flaming and turning
to guard the way to the tree of life" (3:24). Sometimes the truth
to be communicated is so unfathomable that the author resorts to
symbolic language. In fact, the "sword flaming and turning" has
no parallel in the Hebrew Bible: it was necessary to evoke the rift
of the separation, as well as the never-blunt edge of a divine sword
that never stops "turning." But it was necessary to eliminate any
gratuitous hostility that might have heightened the fear of God in
the humans' imagination. The invisible God behind the cherubim
does not wield the sword out of malevolence; far from it, since his
only desire is to "guard the way of the tree of life."

In his fear (expressed in v. 22) of seeing humans appropriate for
themselves the origins of life (and thus the power of life and death),
and in his care to mitigate the exile in which they were leading
themselves astray, far from Him, God made sure that the path to
the tree of life would not be lost. He keeps a record of the route
himself, so that humans could borrow it at any time and enjoy
a face-to-face encounter with the master of life and death. We
have, therefore, from the opening lines of the Bible, the image of
an ambivalent sword. The reality described is painful (thorns and
brambles, the sufferings of childbirth and relationships of domination, wandering far from God, and, thus, insecurity). The sword
prevents any confusion. God is God; he alone is master of life and
death. When the human believes he can replace God in claiming
to know good and evil – symbolized by a tree that grows as if by

chance "in the middle of the garden," precisely where the tree of life is growing – then no other can be OTHER; everyone believes he can "eat" everyone else and death is on the prowl …

Thus we see that the sword, if it adds to the pain of the human condition, represents that alone that gives access to both the feeling of being alive and to life in society. The sword wounds but at the same time it guarantees the inviolable space of the OTHER: when we respect the life of another human being to the point of not killing him (without saying it and probably even without knowing it), we bow before an OTHER; we stop assuming that we have the right to master life, to the benefit of someone or something OTHER who alone holds this right. We are not giving in to the illusion of "knowing Good and Evil" in this other human; we admit that we are incapable of knowing for sure if he is our personal enemy, an enemy of society, an enemy of God.

We leave to the OTHER, whatever name we give him, the just knowledge of the *living being* that is that human who is so mean and so evil-spirited, to judge by his behaviour. Because an OTHER is the guarantor of the indestructible life of that human, the one who we do not know is friend or enemy, we leave to Him the right and the power to put a limit on his ambivalence Himself. Freed of the need to "know" good and evil in those closest to us since we leave that to God, we can focus on the rocky road which, because it is ours, with each step brings us closer to the tree of life, the symbol of the divine presence. Our basic condition is that of Adam, Eve, Cain and Abel: calamity or injustice from the very dawn of life, rebounding back on ourselves and preventing us from lifting our heads or daring to have a face-to-face encounter with the OTHER; dysfunctionality and confusion in our relationships; verbal and physical violence that reproduce and perpetuate the misfortune and injustice of our origins.

Ambivalence endures through each episode of the family drama of Genesis. The misdrashic commentaries are unable to resolve this ambivalence. Thus the "sign" placed on Cain before his exile far from the face of God (Gen. 4:15). It is a manifestly positive sign in the Hebrew text: "The Lord put a mark on Cain, so that no one who

came upon him would kill him." There are about ten interpretations of this sign in Judaism, including five in the Midrash *Rabbah*,
in which the rabbis go endlessly back and forth between seeing it
as a positive sign and as a negative sign. For one, it is a question of
a sun that God causes to shine for Cain. Impossible, says another;
it is leprosy that he caused to break out on this evil individual.

It is not a sign of shame, comments A. Abécassis, since the light
must permit Cain to perceive his enemies from afar. The sun appears miraculously, states J. Eisenberg; God abruptly stops the night,
which is an ideal opportunity for crime.[2] But, we could object, if
the sun is a protection for Cain, helping him to prepare to confront
an other whose intentions he perceives to be hostile, we may say
as well that the sun exposes him: he will be seen just as he sees, he
will not have recourse to the cover of night to attack by surprise,
he will have to face the other as an equal and the light of day will
not be an advantage for him.

Here, there is perhaps a convergence of meaning with the ending of
the story of Jacob's struggle: "The sun rose upon him as he passed"
(32:31). For Jacob also, the confrontation with Esau will take place
in the light of a true meeting of equals. From this point onward
he is assured that the sun shines *for him*, but it is rather in the sense
of shining *for him also* than in the sense of shining *for him and not
for Esau*. On the one hand, Jacob is in the process of healing from
his inferiority complex towards Esau and from his position as the
younger son: from this night onward he is also a fighter, capable
of facing the OTHER, human and divine. On the other hand, when
in the Bible it is a question of authentic encounters, one no longer
finds oneself in value judgments that are linked to favouritism. God
makes his sun rise on the evil and on the good, and sends rain on
the righteous and on the unrighteous (Matt. 5:45).

Other Jewish commentaries, including the Zohar, see in the sign of
Cain a letter of the alphabet that is meant to protect him.[3] But the
ambivalence reappears, as if it were impossible for humans, even
when inspired, to extricate themselves from it: some commentaries
put forward the *tav*, the last letter of the alphabet, which in Jewish
symbolism is the sign of death. Thus, is it a promise of life or the

announcement of a reprieve for a man destined to die? Is God showing himself to be a friend, or must one expect the worst with him? For the Midrash, God's ambivalence seems to embrace that of humans, and the question remains firmly open. The sign would be Cain himself, because for one rabbi he is a sign for assassins and for another a sign for penitents. "The character of Cain remains ambivalent," concludes J. Eisenberg. "If he is, in the universal consciousness, the prototype of the assassin, if he witnesses to the violence of man, he also witnesses to the divine leniency."[4]

If other people are at the same time both beneficial and harmful, how does modern psychology recommend that we separate from them? Would Cain have been able to extricate himself from the enmeshment with his mother without killing anyone? How could the OTHER (human and divine) suddenly exist opposite Cain, to the point of arousing in him the awareness that he was on the point of killing someone? Who could have showed him that he was sinking into the honeypot with his mother, if God himself had not done so? Must one always plead that it is up to the other person to begin the work of awareness? The story of Genesis 4 clearly says "no": God addresses Cain because someone needs to initiate this process, especially since he is now in greater danger than his mother, about to be engulfed by his counter-violence. The commentary of M. Balmary explains the psychoanalytic meaning of what is at play between Cain and Eve:

> Eve reveals in the first child what she wants to have. Warned by the god, "Your desire shall be for your husband, and he shall rule over you" [Gen 3:16], she responds, "I have acquired an *ish* – and I rule over him." In the second child, Eve reveals this time what she believes herself to be as a woman, as a subordinate: *Hével*, a breath, that which is vain ... Would Eve in her own eyes be an "addition," as she adds Abel?[5] ... If Abel represents Eve's scorn for herself, this brother added to him is therefore for Cain the nonentity for which Eve wrenched herself from him. Because she was secretly Hével, she wanted to acquire an *ish* with [the LORD]. What son, possessed by his mother because of her own pain, would not want to make the face of that pain that had devoured him disappear? ... He kills Abel as Abel kills

his sheep. Guardian of an inferior man, destined to destruction
by his name. When one kills "vapour," does one realize one has
killed someone?[6]

As for Jacob, a fairly widespread psychoanalytic reading of his
struggle at the Jabbok, as we have seen, evokes castration anxiety
and Jacob's acceptance, during that unprecedented night, of a symbolic castration. Indeed, waterways and rivers often symbolize the
mother and the sister, vengeful river gods standing guard nearby;
but they also symbolize birth.[7] In this respect, the ambivalence
highlighted earlier becomes a very law of life: one does not separate
from one's mother or sister, however painful and anguished that
process may be, without at the same time being born to oneself.
The first separation – birth – is both the first trauma (according to
current observations) and the most unlikely of gifts. The necessity
of separation is associated with the inevitable ambivalence of life
from its first moments.

What is it that holds us captive to the ambivalence of others? At least
three elements: the love for their attractive, fragile and wounded
sides; the fear of possible retaliation from their negative side; our
difficulty in being ourselves, in our own desire, in our otherness.
For René Girard, we become engulfed in violence through our
incapacity to separate or differentiate ourselves from others because
human desire is mimetic: "This human being has no desire of her
own; men are strangers to their desires; children do not know how
to desire and must be taught"; our desire is essentially imitative and
"our unshakable cult of desire prevents us from recognizing this
process of uniformization."[8]

That is where we must seek the reason behind the tenth commandment: "You shall not covet, or, more precisely, you shall not desire
that which belongs to your neighbour" (Ex. 20:17). Since "the
principal source of violence between humans is mimetic rivalry,"
God forbids us first from killing, then from the root of murdering:
desire inspired by what our neighbour has.[9] Girard approaches the
gospels with the same point of view. All human relationships, in his
opinion, can be reduced to one factor: that mimesis that is

the original source of all man's troubles, desires, and rivalries ... the source of all disorder and therefore equally of all order through the mediation of scapegoats. These victims are the spontaneous agents of reconciliation, since, in the final paroxysm of mimeticism, they unite in opposition to themselves those who were organized in opposition to each other by the effects of a previous weaker mimeticism.[10]

I believe that we have to look beyond from violent mimetic behaviours. It is clear that we become human by successive identifications with one human or another whom we wish to resemble. But it is also clear that we discover our unique personality as the desire to be ourselves grows and is affirmed. No one can dictate another person's deepest desire: that hope to be realized that is held within and that has no model to follow. The tragedy is that in many cases, not to say the majority, our desire has been stolen from us since childhood. What we have been forced to undergo has more or less crushed within us the desire to be ourselves. A small child who is respected in his deepest being does not lose the sense of what is truly his – his ideas, his wants, his body, his feelings. Nothing can fill the adult that he will become with more joy than the harmony, unique in the world, between what he *is* and what he *does*. The inverse is equally true: dispossessed of the right to be himself from a young age, the human no longer knows his desire: "I don't even know what I want," people tell their therapists.

The more the child's desire has been destroyed, the more imitation comes into play, as a last resort: unable to appropriate his own desire, he tries either to appropriate others and the fruits of their desires, or to fit the desires of others, which one comes to confuse with his own desire. This gives rise to confusion, in which the person does not find what he or she wants, because the child's moaning, in each person, remains smothered. This also gives rise to an ambivalence that is fatal for relationships and generates the worst violence because the protagonists themselves have long since abandoned the claim to be heard in their specific desires. This is, for me, the question to be asked of René Girard: if human desire is nothing but pure imitation, how is it possible for us to renounce violence without having a scapegoat to blame? On whom should we lean if we are not to give in to mimetic rivalry? On what part of ourselves should we rely in order to refuse being dragged into violence, if what we wholly are is mimetic desire for what others have and are?

For Girard, at the collective level, the only thing that gives us security is the fear of being engulfed in the chaos that existed before the world was made, when God had not yet separated the darkness and light, the oceans and the dry land, and so on. "The great social crises that engender collective persecutions are experienced as a lack of differentiation,"[11] to which we must associate the theme of twins or brothers who are enemies. At one time, twins were killed at birth because of the fear that their great resemblance to each other would cause conflict between them. "It is not difference that dominates everything, it is its elimination by mimetic reciprocity that, itself, is truly universal ... Violence, reciprocal vengeance, always makes perishable cultures redescend into the chaos from which they arose."[12] From this point of view, is it by chance that the Bible tells us so many stories of brothers who are enemies? Differentiation is not a natural given, but the fruit of a conquest, basically in the spiritual realm, if one is to judge by this biblical emphasis.

To what extent can the Bible cause the effort of each culture to rise like yeast in dough? For Girard, culture "consists essentially in an effort to prevent violence from being unleashed by separating and in 'differentiating' all the aspects of public and private life which, if one were to abandon them to their natural reciprocity, would risk being engulfed in violence that cannot be undone."[13] Such a statement appears to me to be compatible with the spirit of the biblical texts taken as a whole, notably because of the emphasis that they all place on the holiness of the OTHER: that is, his non-confusion with that which is not him. Thus, in refusing the offering of Cain, God differentiates himself from both Cain and Eve: His desire is OTHER than that of Eve, to which Cain had always sacrificed his own. Being OTHER, God therefore does not need to do violence to Cain's desire. Cain can at last feel liberated from having to please others in order to exist.

But he will give in to violence because he does not hear God call him for the first time on the road to his own desire. Killing Abel is, for him, a way to try to rediscover that fusion with God that he was used to with his mother, to act as though the OTHER did not exist: neither Abel because he is nothing but the wind, nor God because Cain wants him to be the Same-as-his-mother, without his own desire. He must eliminate as quickly as possible that human brother who risks revealing to him, by the divine blessing on his offering, the existence *in him also* of a specific desire (other than that of his mother) that God could also develop. Such a path towards his authentic being makes him afraid, for, being unknown to himself, he resembles that void that he had always tried to fill. This void leads to the desperate flight ahead, something that is familiar to all humans who have not yet been able to live other than by proxy.

---

There seems to be no way out of the complications: the ambivalence of others cannot be overcome since God persists in not separating good from evil once and for all, and shows himself to be ambivalent. Our personal confusion is aggravated by this, which makes our relationships with others even more ambivalent. How are we to behave when we don't know where we stand? How are we to avoid turning to blind violence when we cannot see clearly around us? It is at this point that we do well not to overlook an essential gospel text, where Christ says:

> Do not think that I have come to bring peace to the earth; I have not come to bring peace, but a sword. For I have come to set a man *against his father, and a daughter against her mother, and a daughter-in-law against her mother-in-law; and one's foes will be members of one's own household.* (Matt. 10:34–36)[14]

For Jesus it is a question of clearing up a misunderstanding. According to our spontaneous way of approaching the biblical message, we are expecting only peace and harmony from the "good God" and the "gentle Jesus." If we are faithful to this image, we think we can avoid all conflict. However, for Matthew, and for Luke who passes on the same words in a different style and according to a parallel tradition (12:49–53), the unwatered-down teaching of Christ makes it possible for us to situate ourselves clearly, to find our way

out of confusion in our relationships with those close to us, to take
a stand for ourselves in grasping the sword that he keeps holding
out to us. This will not necessarily please those we love: when we
break with the dysfunctionality that held us in confusion, we are
following the path to our own desire. The light shines on "what
was hidden" and what prevented us from moving forward – from
following Christ on the path of who we really are.

Do not fear your enemies, Jesus told his disciples as he asked them
to witness to the Truth that lived in them as in him. For "nothing
is covered up that will not be uncovered, and nothing secret that
will not become known" (Matt. 10:26). All the dysfunctions will
one day be recognized for what they are; all the wounds that were
inflicted in the past and long hidden will sooner or later be uncovered; and all that is of the order of the truth of your beings is to be
brought to light, in union with the God of truth to whom you refer:
"What I say to you in the dark, tell in the light; and what you hear
whispered, proclaim from the housetops. Do not fear those who kill
the body but cannot kill the soul [psyche]!" (vv. 27-28). The truth
that breaks out in families and groups can do much harm when it
is long denied. The sword cuts into the core of relationships just as
it does into the deepest being of the person who, having received
it from Christ, has chosen to use it.

That is why He who is *the way, the truth and the life* always provokes
conflicts and dissension even in those families and communities that
seem to be the most united. "The [synoptic gospels – Matthew,
Mark and Luke] have Jesus say that he brings war and not peace,"
notes René Girard. "John shows that everywhere that he intervenes,
Jesus causes dissension. The eruption of the truth destroys the social
harmony founded on the lie of violent unanimity."[15] The violence
of reactions is proportional to the hiding of the truth in interpersonal
relationships: if today I affirm that my truth is not yours, if I do not
"deny" it any more than I do not deny Christ within me,[16] I elude
you from now on and you feel that you can never destroy me.
Suddenly, you are back to your own denial and you can no longer
unburden it on me by means of your dysfunctionality. There is no
compromise possible between my truth and yours, and that is what

shows my exit from confusion. The sword is the clear distinction between my truth and that of others, and it is Christ who wields it in me: "I have come to *set* a man *against* his father," etc. – a verb [dichazein] that appears nowhere else in Matthew. This is saying that the operation is delicate, without antecedent, and impossible to copy from one situation to another. The word means dividing in two, separating two beings or two things.

Luke goes even farther in evoking an approach that is beneficial for everyone: "Do you think that I have come[17] to bring peace to the earth? No, I tell you, but rather *division*! From now on, five in one household *will be divided*, three against two and two against three; they *will be divided*: father against son and son against father, mother against daughter and daughter against mother, mother-in-law against her daughter-in-law and daughter-in-law against mother-in-law" (12:51-53). Now, this is a gift: Jesus has come to "give" us that which is of God alone: the differentiation between humans, or, literally, the setting against or splitting [diamerismon]. "They will set against each other" and "they will be set against each other": the verb, from the same root, is in one instance a way, for it is up to us to want to emerge from confusion, and in one instance in the passive, suggesting the action of God, for He alone can bring such a step to a good end.

Within a household, each person is called to separate and to let himself or herself be separated by the sword of Christ. And if several find themselves on the same side, it is because they will have begun by differentiating themselves from the person they most resemble, the one that they are most in danger of merging with. Little by little, there will be on one side those men and women who allow themselves to be separated, and on the other those who have not yet grasped the sword of life. It is never a question of breaking off relationships; the sword works to render them fruitful.

The cutting word of the Gospel invites us to welcome the times of conflict and crisis not as a calamity but as the painful time of a birth. Agreeing to be separated, differentiated, *split off* from others will allow us to reach the share that belongs to us. This share is not transferable, even to those closest to us; it is a tongue of fire that no one will receive in our place, as Luke recounts on the night of the first Pentecost: "Divided[18] tongues, as of fire, appeared among them, and a tongue rested on each of them" (Acts 2:3). The sword is thus of the order of Pentecost, to give to each human his tongue of fire, which works more than ever as "a sword flaming and turning," which we encountered in the first pages of Genesis.

Is this not the same fire that Jesus affirms himself to be – "I came to bring fire to the earth," just before the sword passage in Luke's version? He Himself, truly human and truly God, was not spared from living the burning of separation, in the positive sense of differentiation. Instead of fleeing from it, he desires it: "How I wish it were already kindled!" He was no doubt sensing the baptism of fire that other humans were going to live at Pentecost; he would be the first to "pass through" it. "I have a baptism with which to be baptized, and what stress I am under until it is completed!" (Lk. 12:49-50) The separation is a costly step but one whose end we ardently wish to see, like the experience of bringing a child into the world. It hurts, but at the same time we desire it. It marks us with the branding iron of separation: soon after birth our infant is taken from us. This being is going to act to "bring to term," like Christ, the process of differentiation which will make of us, mother and child, two distinct beings, alone before God, at last baptized with her or his own unique name.

Immediately after the discourse on the sword, Matthew has Jesus say: "Whoever loves father or mother more than me is not worthy of me; and whoever loves son or daughter more than me is not worthy of me; and whoever does not take up the cross and follow me is not worthy of me. Those who find their life [psyche] will lose it, and those who lose their life for my sake will find it" (10:37-39). We can add today: whoever has done serious work on herself and from it has lost all her reference points and certainties is literally experiencing an irreversible death – the death of that which she believed herself to be – until her authentic self makes itself known to her little by little and is given to her in the fullness of a blossoming that goes beyond her most beautiful dreams. The experience is fundamentally the same for whoever invests body and soul in a public commitment in the name of that OTHER who calls her to differentiate herself from all those that she is not, to follow her own path behind Jesus.

Is this selfishness, insensitivity, scandalous indifference regarding those closest to us? Certainly not, for, let us repeat, the process hurts. We must "take up, accept, receive one's cross";[19] both sides of the sword cause wounds, like birth causes both mother and child to suffer, each in its own way. Besides, the point of all this evolution is to arrive at loving ourselves differently; the word [philein], used here as elsewhere by Matthew in a pejorative manner, indicates that "natural" or "honeypot" love that we spoke of above, particularly between parents and children, where that ambivalence that engenders confusion so often reigns. Jesus seems to want to say this: if you love father and mother, son or daughter "more than me," more than that "me [who am] the way, the truth and the life," therefore more than *your* way, *your* truth and *your* life, if you prefer to remain stuck in relationships of *friend and enemy, unity and rejection, hate and dependence, disgust and fascination* with those closest to you, then you are not yet "worthy of me": that is, also, worthy of that me that you carry within you. You are not yet worthy of that Me who, living in me, Jesus of Nazareth, wants to live in each of you and who, himself, is infinitely lovable because he is free of any fusion and confusion. The word that expresses that love in the New Testament is [agapein]. As long as one speaks of loving more or loving less, one is not yet in that love [agape] that tries to embed itself in the heart of deep-seated family relationships.

Nevertheless, this vocabulary does not resemble the unconditional welcome of Jesus that we are familiar with: should we prove ourselves, to be worthy for him to tolerate our company? "Whoever loves father or mother, son or daughter, more than me, has no value for me," translates A. Chouraqui. On three occasions, it is a question of being not worthy, of not having value. Who is devaluing whom? If I prefer to remain tangled up in my relationship with father, mother, son or daughter, if I refuse to allow the sword to pass through to differentiate me from him or her, isn't that because I am not worth enough *in my own eyes* to take my own path in the company of the I-way-truth-life who is Jesus, or any other human since who invites me to him in the name of All OTHER? It is up to me to decide one day that I am worthy of this Me who wants to live in me, worthy of listening to him, of giving him my word, of spending time with him.

What is it that holds me back? Fear of abandoning that father, this mother, that son, this daughter whose inner misfortune I sense behind the dysfunctionality, whose suffering I sense behind the harm that he or she does to me? It is here that Luke goes further towards the OTHER love. In a passage parallel to Matthew's, he has Jesus say, "Whoever comes to me and does not hate father and mother, wife and children, brothers and sisters, yes, and even life itself, cannot be my disciple" (14:26) – will not manage to be my disciple. How widespread is this incapacity to live one's Christian faith because of family dissension! We are not usually taught that God's blessing is to be found in hatred towards those close to us. But such is the radicality of the Gospel: the sword passes or does not pass; to speak of hatred is not to minimize the pain nor the violence of this step. The meaning is the same in Matthew, according to P. Bonnard, for the verb "to hate" "marks not so much an inner disaffection as a concrete gesture in which one leaves others to themselves, here in order to follow Christ."[20]

What can make us decide to leave that close relative to himself so that he, too, can go to the end of the separation, escape from confusion once and for all and find that I-way-truth-life that is worth the difficulty of being found, in the OTHER and in himself? Luke has Jesus express it in the verses that follow: one must "sit down and estimate the cost" (14:28). This is once again the radicality of the sword, but we can already see the benefits. If I follow through to the end of this step that God himself asks me to perform – like Jesus, who desired to "complete his baptism of fire" – it is not only to "extricate myself," but also to yield to my close relative his freedom to be himself and to follow the I who wants to lead him to life through his own truth. It is *to God* that I abandon him, so that he will be in the best of hands, infinitely.[21]

I perceive then that I will find him again in a new kind of closeness by means of prayer. No longer threatened with being engulfed in relationships of confusion, I let God lead the person on the path of his own differentiation; I attain an OTHER love, made of compassion and blessing; I discover that it was never asked of me to abandon him and that I have never done so. I will remain in solidarity with him, with his indestructible spiritual self, regardless of how our relationship may evolve. I will not be able to, nor should I, "take up his cross" in his place, help him avoid suffering, prevent him from choosing by himself to allow the sword to pass. It is up to me to let myself be differentiated, just as it is up to him to allow himself to be differentiated. And, a few verses further on, in chapter 15, Luke brings us the story of a family wherein the sword did cut: a father and two sons, the death of relationships, crisis, anger, the one who says he is "not worthy," the other who complains he is less loved. Then the father who takes up his cross, accepting to "lose his being" – "my son was dead" – the father who, experiencing joy, "finds his being" and opens his arms to both of his sons.

The sword passes when we agree to lose our being *because of I-way-truth-life*. The tools that psychology and psychoanalysis give us today may make us believe that we have "found our being [psyche]." If we stop there, it is not the symbolic sword of the Bible that has passed but, too often, the sword of war that destroys relationships for good. Yes, I have become me, without fusion or confusion, but the OTHER no longer exists; there is no bond at all. Christ indicates that there is another way to mourn for what we were and for the type of relationships we had: not to take this mourning as an end in itself, not to handle the sword oneself simply to let the sword pass, not to "cut the cord" for the sake of cutting the cord, but to mourn our old being *because of* someone ("for my sake," says Jesus). In other words, to be moved, charged, motivated by this self that is way-truth-life not only in ourselves but also in those close to us from whom we painfully separate. At issue is not the sword but the being [psyche] that we are going to "find." The time will come to appropriate what is ours, but we will receive it from the hands of this I-way-truth-life – from that OTHER who is so intimately bound up with our story. We will not give ourselves this being: we will have found him, like the pearl hidden in the field.

To come back to Jacob, it is not ultimately the crossing of the Jabbok that is the outcome of his experience, but the blessing on his identity. X. Durand raises this point, breaking free of the historical exegesis that sees in the fording of the torrent the central element of the story: "We are forced to observe that, far from being at the centre of the text, the passage constitutes its periphery and framework. It contributes to the construction of the text around its real centre, the skill of the actors to know what they receive and what they are. The real issue of the struggle can no longer be the fording of a river, but a blessing and a name."[22] The sword must pass: Jacob finds himself "alone" at the beginning of the story (where the "passage" is mentioned three times), differentiated from his family and those around him, and he will be alone when he "passes" Penu'el at the end of the story (the sun shone on him alone), differentiated from those close to him, including from now on his brother, Esau. But what allows us to see the sword of life shining in this story, if not the discovery by Jacob of a divine blessing placed on his "being" [psyche] in Genesis 32:31b?

---

In concrete terms, what is a sword? As P. Claudel writes, "What to do to satisfy this piercing armament that wants my life by means of my death?"[23] There is, first, the need to consent to the slicing of the sword: to admit that others can be my enemy, and that they consider me an enemy. "Love your enemies and pray for those who persecute you, so that you may be children of your Father in heaven; for he makes his sun rise on the evil and on the good, and sends rain on the righteous and on the unrighteous" (Matt. 5:44-45). Spontaneously, we collide with the difficulty of loving our enemies, without even catching a glimpse of how such an invitation can be liberating. Before loving our enemy, we are encouraged to recognize him as an enemy; at that moment a distance is created, especially if the enemy in question is close to us. To admit that he is behaving as an enemy helps us right away to emerge from the confusion, from that exhausting wavering between our bursts of compassion and our blasts of anger towards him, between our guilt and the need to accuse him that he fosters in us.

He is him, with his hostility or his malevolence; I am me, with my thirst for an authentic relationship. For the moment we are incapable of reaching each other; I halt any effort to be friends. I who believe myself to be on good terms with everyone because I always seek to be like "gentle Jacob," I admit, I accept that I have enemies. Here I am alone, provisionally separated; at least things are clear. Now, I notice that my solitude is bearable because the distance created by my decision to name the real as it is (the other is my "enemy" for the time being) immediately puts me in touch with that which is most alive within me: my capacity to pray for him and for me. I turn myself over to Him who takes and will always take my side in the injustices that I experience, and I turn the other over to Him who does not let and will never let the path of the way-truth-life in himself be lost.

It is remarkable that, in the chapter that Matthew devotes to the forgiveness of sins, the only imperative does *not* concern precisely forgiving the offender but distancing ourselves from him. How, in fact, can we love our enemies if we have not begun by accepting that they are enemies? How can we pray for our persecutors if we continue to refuse to see their persecution? Then, in Matthew 18, how to forgive with all one's heart if we have not cut ourselves off from the behaviour experienced as a constant stumbling block? Such is the only imperative mentioned in this key chapter of the gospel: "If your hand or your foot causes you to stumble, *cut it off* and *throw* it away; ... if your eye causes you to stumble, tear it out and throw it away," thus you "will enter life" rather than be consumed in the hell of fusional relationships (vv. 8-9). The decisive moment is not the forgiveness of the offender, but the passing of the sword to the quick of our flesh. Experience confirms it: this is like a mutilation, when we tear off and throw far away from us that destructive behaviour of another that was "sticking to our skin." Violence for a free life, unavoidable violence, without which any attempt at forgiveness is doomed to fail.

This violence may resemble violence we have suffered, for, as the saying goes, you cannot make an omelette without breaking eggs. The advantage is that we leave behind the fantasy of "gentle Jacob." We welcome our counter-violence and we expect to be taken for evil-doers. The sword carried by Christ [machaira] is not, in Greek, initially the warrior's weapon, but the knife of the one offering sacrifice, the surgeon, the butcher, the gardener, the barber. Does this not point to the "violence" that is necessary in everyday life? Because we separate more or less violently from the other, we begin to catch sight of how we participate in some way in the violence around us: our hands are not free of blood. In cutting to the quick to give us back our freedom, the sword revealed to us our identity as "one who confronts." Made powerful, like Jacob, by the passing of the sword, we reintegrate the world of humans, of whom none can claim to live without ever having hurt a fly. Perhaps the time has come to welcome that ambivalence that we had experienced up to now as the malevolence *of the* OTHER (human and divine).

The distance created by the passage of the sword permits us at last to spot the ambivalence, confusion and destruction that others' behaviour keeps alive. But it also sheds light on our behaviours that can be ambivalent, confusing or destructive. It is not a question of knowing if there is more in others than in us, nor of knowing who started it. It is merely a question of seeing more clearly our own involvement, so that we can, so to speak, cease fire. If I do not want to play gentle Jacob anymore, I should expect to be assimilated by the evil-doers and accept that my non-violence will be accused of being violence. By what means can I see that the sword has truly passed? I no longer let myself be carried along by vehement self-justification or by violent accusations: no one will catch me in them again. I can assume that people are treating me as someone who is bad because the sword has set me apart, safe within my difference. I have "disobeyed," as René Girard would say; I can no longer be assimilated by the other, being myself at last delivers me from having to be "nice"; from now on my non-violence no longer requires superhuman efforts. Commenting on the episode of the slap (Matt. 5:39f), Girard writes:

These evil ones desire nothing so much as to exasperate us, so as to drag us with them into a process of ever-increasing violence. They do their best, in the end, to arouse the reprisals that would justify their former outbursts. They hope to use the excuse of a "legitimate defence." *If we treat them as they treat us, they are soon going to mask their injustice in retribution fully justified by our own violence.* We must deprive them of the negative collaboration that they seek from us. One must always disobey violent people.[24]

How far did Jesus of Nazareth, the Son of Man, grappling with the same difficulties as any human being, go in accepting his ambivalence in the eyes of others? He was not afraid to admit that he had enemies; he designated them as such, in the clarity of differentiation, not hesitating to violently drive back one of his disciples whose fusional friendship prevented him from going to the core of himself by "losing his life" (Matt. 16:25). Peter's ambivalence was that he had just clearly perceived the spiritual being of Jesus ("You are the Christ, the son of the living God"), and a few minutes later, he closed himself completely to the I-truth-way-life which was calling Jesus to become himself by the baptism of fire. Jesus "turned" then, confronting Peter: "Get behind me, Satan! You are a stumbling block to me" (Matt. 16:23). According to our criteria, it is not nice to treat a friend this way! Nor is it nice to call the scribes and Pharisees "hypocrites" and "whitened sepulchres," nor to call his coreligionists a "race of vipers," nor to call a pagan woman a "dog" who has no right to the bread of life. It is not nice to overturn by strokes of a whip the money-changers' tables in the Temple.

In contrast, there are the tears of Jesus, his infinite compassion, his distress in the face of others' distress, his thirst for love (come to me, "I am meek and humble of heart"), his desire to be known for his true self ("if you knew me ... if you loved me ..."), his acceptance of the hatred of others ("If the world hates you, be aware that it hated me before it hated you"). The ambivalence of Jesus in the eyes of his contemporaries was that he would never do anything to prove his non-violence, his benevolence, the authenticity of his Beatitudes ("And *you*, who do you say that I am?" It is up to you to decide). This remained his steadfast attitude even during his trial: called to show that he was the self-messiah beyond compare, this perfectly differentiated "king" of all humanity put the ball back in our court: "It is you who say it."

He saw clearly that he provoked diametrically opposed reactions, from nearly blind trust to the most violent rejection. He assumed the role of a stumbling block for others: if he leaves no one indifferent, it is because in his life the sword passed magnificently, making him refuse any fusion and any violence. His person became a mirror for others; before him, each one was thrown back on himself, to his own confusions, to his dysfunctions and his ambivalences. That is what people could not forgive him for. Beyond the pain of not being known for who he was, in the uniqueness of his way, his truth and his life, there was his desire to remain in solidarity with Cain to the end. We recall the enigmatic sign placed on Cain and the ambivalence that has flowed from it in the Jewish tradition; when all is said and done, we decided that Cain himself was a sign, both for murderers and for penitents. Seeing him, murderers saw the endless wandering to which violent action led, and penitents noted the benevolence of God who never gives death the last word.

Descended from Cain, humanity is still confronted by the same ambivalence. Christ assumes that very condition. Like any human he can be a sign of evil — one can see in him an agitator who is doing everything to unleash a violence of which he will be the first victim, one "possessed" or a blasphemer whom society must get rid of if we value social and religious institutions. But he can also be a sign of the inexhaustible divine favour in the human heart: many people saw him blessed, transfigured, "made powerful" in the most unlikely circumstances. At no time did Jesus try to put an end to that ambivalence. The message does not vary: it is up to you to decide, and let your yes be yes! To the end, he will give his enemies the freedom to grasp for themselves the sword that he came to bring to the earth, or to turn it on him in choosing the wrong fight.

The most spectacular renunciation, for Jesus, perhaps concerns sacrifice; there, too, ambivalence was and remains complete. One saw in the sacrifice of his life either a sign of a curse (the victim of divine violence through human violence, he would have undergone an Anger that unfortunately fell on him), or the sign of ascent towards Life, in the prolonging of a life wholly engaged with giving, bearing fruit a hundredfold. However, to the end Jesus relinquishes to his enemies, to his friends and to witnesses the purpose of their conflict: they may project onto him everything they want, but he follows his way alone, towards his truth and his life. What does he suggest to them, that they may escape violence?

René Girard explains,

> Instead of giving back more of the same, we must leave the matter at hand to the potential rival. That is the unique rule of the Kingdom ... To protect themselves from their own violence, humans ended up channelling it towards innocents. Christ does the opposite. He offers no resistance. He does not devote himself to sacrifice in order to play the sacrificial game, but to put an end to sacrifice.[25]

In order to truly consent to the passage of the sword, we need models. Nothing can equal the positive experience of a brother or sister in humanity to lead us to that I-way-truth-life who, in us, desires the All-Living God. We are thereby encouraged to welcome conflict and dissension in our personal and collective histories. Others who are farther along the way tell us again and again: through crisis, it is alongside that God, alongside Job, the blessed rebel of that God, that we are walking. The sword will start there: managing to turn us against God in one way or another. Ending the game that took the place of faith up to then is sometimes the only way to test whether confrontation may be beneficial. Thus, "the extraordinary violence of the cries of Job" signals that the sword is passing between him and those close to him, between him and God, between him and unbelieving believers who fuse with their idea of God to the point of making him have doubts: he whom Job called "the just," of his living relationship with the OTHER of his desire. As R. de Pury notes:

> One cannot stop oneself from thinking that God is more often on the side of those who attack him than on the side of those who defend him and that it is certainly the atheists who are closer to Christian truth than a good number of Christian apologists, that

it is rebels whom God prefers to the submissive people of the Churches, and that it is the unfortunate, crying in their anguish and in their nakedness, who witness to Him more worthily than the lawyers who are too sure of themselves.[26]

Nevertheless, this is slippery ground, for no human model is truly exportable. When friends offer themselves as models (of life and faith) to be imitated slavishly, Job lays claim to being himself, but not in the current way that preserves the illusion of a possible self-restructuring without others. He feels confusedly that he will be able to be himself only in a face-to-face encounter with that OTHER who is totally differentiated yet who nevertheless resembles him. If he no longer has a model along this road, this shows us that the day when we have no more models will be a blessed day for us. The sword has truly passed when, having clearly separated from all those who were models and counter-models, we seek our own path, the path that no one teaches us about.

If our landmarks have already disappeared, perhaps that gives us a hint that we are about to get to know the desire that is forever unequalled that lies within each of us: the desire to resemble Him who alone truly desires resemblance because fusion and confusion never threaten him. For the Christian tradition, not only did Jesus desire this resemblance, but he also lived it right to his last breath, without ever drawing anyone into fusion or confusion. That is why, as René Girard writes, "What Jesus invites us to imitate is his own *desire*; the spirit that directs him towards the goal on which his intention is set: to resemble God the Father as much as possible." He does not claim to "be himself" but "to become the perfect *image* of God." He does not try to prevent violence by forbidding certain behaviours (particularly competitive desire) but by providing humans with "the model that will protect them from mimetic rivalries rather than involving them in these rivalries."[27]

---

For the sword of *life* to pass between two humans, the desire for relationship must be present. This means both wanting the other, even the evildoer, to exist in spite of everything, and wanting to establish at least a minimally viable relationship with this person. If this is the case, a bias will prove to be especially helpful: that of deciding that sooner or later such a relationship will be useful for our growth; our way of bumping up against others, of hurting ourselves in making the contact – even if we hate the experience – may give us insight into *our* fragility, *our* dysfunctionalities, the consequences of forgotten wounds. If God, life, the OTHER allows us to endure what we endure, it is to help us touch that dormant part of us that prevents us from growing. Our enemies will, in the long run, have done us a service by bringing us to ourselves, by pushing us to know ourselves better, by helping us affirm ourselves clearly in our differentiated identity.

According to F. Quéré, it was this way for Jesus himself, whose worst adversaries (among the scribes, the Pharisees and especially the Sadducees) were those with whom he had numerous affinities. Preoccupied by the identity of Jesus, they harassed him, but with "good questions," and "their resistance forced Jesus to explain himself at length"; they thus became "great providers of answers." "When they sneered, the Pharisees posed the essential question: Jesus, who are you? ... Without the context, we would not know if [the questions] came from an enemy lying in wait or from a disciple hungry for instruction." In the light of what we have said, in particular regarding brothers who are enemies of each other, we can say that the more zealous the enemies, the more they resemble each other, and the more they are threatened with confusion. From this comes the violence of their reactions. But by this very fact, the enemies of Jesus drive him to follow to the end the pathway of his desire for sonship, and to give it to us explicitly as the only model of life.

"Jesus' enemies," adds F. Quéré, "collaborate closely in God's designs ... Sketched in broad strokes, they cooperated in the Good News as others did ... What don't we owe to the bad faith of enemies! ... It is they who expose the new faith in the double sense of the word: by hunting it down and making it run a gauntlet of a thousand perils, they help make it known to the people."[28] If our enemy – both adversary and adversity – forces us to say who we are, to appropriate for ourselves what we are fundamentally, to pass on the flame of life that runs through us, it is no longer as certain that the enemy should be eliminated from our relationships.

"If you love those who love you, what reward do you have?" asks Jesus (Matt. 5:46). What does that bring you? You get more from from remaining in relationship with your enemies; they reward you richly by pushing you to "be perfect, therefore, as your heavenly Father is perfect" (v. 48). "Who does the Evangelist consider to be Satan? The Pharisees, Judas, Caiaphas, Pilate? No. The first disciple."[29] Did not Peter, repulsed on that day as a dangerous enemy ("Get behind me, Satan!"), make Jesus more determined to follow his own path, no matter how difficult? In this way an unfortunate word or some fierce opposition can give us all the more comfort in a decision that we have made and strengthen our desire to persevere in what truly belongs to us. There is nothing like an enemy – even an occasional enemy – to make us attentive to what belongs exclusively to us!

The great discovery – usually in hindsight – is that God is at work *even in the enemy*. The New Testament suggests this in having Jesus say the Spirit blows where it wills, even through an act of aggression that knocks us flat. The only question, that we alone can answer, is what we will do with it. The story of Jacob at the Jabbok relates in brief the transformation by Jacob alone of the enemy – adversary and adversity – into a source of blessing. Of course he would have preferred not to have had the experience, and he would not have gone through it again for anything in the world. But it is his reading of it in the light of dawn, when he begins to experience in himself a life that is free in abundance, that becomes and will remain for him a source of blessing. This is like sunlight flooding into a bedroom the morning after a nightmare, when we find ourselves freed of a trauma that had long held captive our life and our feeling of being alive.

Through the biblical story, the people of Israel told something of their emergence from the nightmare of the Babylonian exile. After the event, they saw how much their efforts to be protected and blessed had run up against more and more adversity. Nevertheless, as R.D. Weis writes, "They finally came out of exile, transformed, blessed, saved, wounded – lame." He concluded that "during all that time, they had to deal with God, even if the adversaries who had beaten them were the Babylonians. Looking back, they could see divine grace at work in all the human wiles and deceits, to the point where it was an edict of Cyrus the Persian [and thus a pagan] that freed them."[30] In the meantime, they had not held back from crying out to God their outrage and distress. In expressing to God their thirst for vengeance, they did not enclose themselves within a sterile anger but saw themselves alongside God, fighting a common enemy. The hatred that is freely expressed in the Psalms, for example, says something about this nearness of God when humans ask Him to let the sword pass and to keep them from unjust and destructive behaviours.

Thus the resemblance to the Father, which Jesus desired with his entire being, included resemblance with *His* violence. "There is no other way to heal the violence of hate than the liberation of the violence of love," writes P. Beauchamp. "For there is only one violence and one life, either perverted or converted. Such is ... the basic teaching of the New Testament."[31] This implies precisely that a sword has passed, for we know very well the excesses of the ideology of love, when the "it's for your own good" camouflages the violence of hate in the eyes of the persecuted and the persecutor. Without the sword that differentiates beings, violence is neither perverted nor converted; it remains desperately ambivalent. In return, the sword that Jesus says he brought forces everyone to find themselves. "From the days of John the Baptist until now the kingdom of heaven has suffered violence, and the violent take it by force" (Matt. 11:12).

How can we know for sure that we are entering into the violence *of the kingdom*? How can we escape from the guilt laid on us by others who blame us for a hateful violence, when it already costs us so much to let the sword of differentiation pass? We remember that, to describe the covenant between God and humans, the Hebrew uses the expression "to cut the covenant." The rite is ancient, going back to Abraham: animals are cut in two, and God, symbolized by fire, passes between the divided animals. Thus the pact is concluded, accompanied by oaths and curses. No altar is mentioned;[32] the symbolism is reinforced by a cut that makes a covenant possible. From the time of the patriarchs and more than ever "from the time of John the Baptist until now," of any baptism of fire offered to any human, it is always the divine fire that *sanctifies the cut*. Without it, no relationship lives in truth, and no covenant is really trustworthy. It is impossible for us to leave the domain of belief: from God alone can come the certitude that such a cut with others – which burns and does violence to *us* as well – well and truly resembles *Him*. A hermeneutic of violence is essential: we will have to decode it. In any case, there is no life without violence, but it is our privilege to "translate"[33] it into a language that fosters growth rather than destruction.

# 2   What is holy anger?

Job! Job! ... thou didst not fail men when all was riven assunder
– thou wast an assuagement for all who were rendered dumb
by torments ... a trustworthy advocate who dared to complain
... and to contend with God. Why do people conceal this? ...
woe also to him who would slyly defraud the afflicted of the
momentary consolation of relieving the oppression of his heart
and "contending with God." ... Does one perhaps not dare
to complain before God? Is it now godly fear that has become
greater, or fear and cowardice? ... Speak therefore, O Job of
imperishable memory! Rehearse everything thou didst say, thou
mighty advocate who doest confront the highest tribunal, no
more daunted than a roaring lion! There is pith in thy speech,
in thy heart there is godly fear ... Thee I have need of, a man
who knows how to complain aloud ...

Complain! The Lord is not afraid, He is well able to defend
Himself ... God surely can speak louder, he possesses the
thunder.[34]

Perhaps it is best to discern first of all what holy anger is not. The
experience of Job has already given us a few landmarks. At the
moment of his blackest anger against God, he discovered that he
had never been so bonded to Him: "See, he will kill me; I have

no hope; but I will defend my ways to his face. This will be my
salvation, that the godless shall not come before him" (13:15-16).
It is the godless one who forgets God and breaks the relationship.
Job becomes aware that his anger is holy because it puts him in
closer contact with God than ever before. We can deduce from
this that holy anger rules out the rupture of the relationship with
God. But we must go further. When we break a relationship with
a person for good, this cannot help but affect our relationship with
God. We think we are linked with the Father of every creature,
but we do not wish to be linked with the Father of that creature
whom we have eliminated from our lives. Our perception of God
is diminished, for we are linked with a Father whose paternity we
restrict: if our anger is such that another cannot be our brother or
our sister anymore, we can no longer welcome in God the one
who is his Father in heaven.

But, one could argue, there are cases where the lie is so constant
that a rupture is the only way to defuse a futile and exhausting
anger. Nonetheless, holy anger goes so far as to refuse to break the
relationship. "Putting away falsehood, *let all of us speak the truth to
our neighbours,*" says the Apostle Paul, "for we are members of one
another. *Be angry but do not sin*; do not let the sun go down on
your anger, and do not make room for the devil" (Eph. 4:25-27).
Holy anger, if we are to believe the entire Bible,[35] is anything but
a renunciation of the truth by means of flight, retreat, or a breaking of the relationship. Others need our truth as much as we need
theirs, and it is a simple matter of saying it, without expecting any
particular outcome. The truth seems sufficient unto itself: our only
responsibility is to tell it like it is. And there, we are far from the
plain truths that we throw in the face of someone when we are in
a fit of anger. Holy anger does not speak unpleasant truths; it has
only one truth, which it will never regret having spoken. And if
it resolves to speak it, that is because no one else can. This anger
is not omnipotence: to be "members of one another" presupposes
the acceptance of our limits, but also the certainty that there is no
substitute for each truth.

Anger is essential to avoid the division or "sin" of breaking the relationship. "Be angry but do not sin" could also be interpreted to mean "Be angry so that you do not let yourself be divided." It is a question of not giving the Divider a foothold by abandoning the ground of the relationship to him: once again, holy anger is not a flight into "Everybody is beautiful, everybody is nice, the sun is about to set, so let us forget all about it!" How can we even imagine that in all circumstances we can work through our anger in under twenty-four hours? Do not let "the sun *go down* on your irritation," the Greek text literally says; it could mean, do not allow the night of unconsciousness to engulf for good an anger that was asking to be reinvested in the relationship. For there is always a way to use the energy of anger to reinvest the ground of the relationship with its own truth, which can also push others to do likewise.

Nor is holy anger fed by the illusion of putting an end to violence by means of greater violence. It is the extreme opposite of the revolutionary ideal and of the idea that the end justifies the means, for it knows that the means, ultimately, elude it and that the end belongs to something Greater than it. Because it does not take itself for anything that it is not, it avoids the "hunt for the hunters of the scapegoat," as René Girard says; it has given up the monopoly of victimization. In fact, the heat of anger prevents us from seeing that others are victims, too, that there is a persecutor in us that does not acknowledge itself, and that the more innocent we believe ourselves to be, the more we are indifferent to victims others than ourselves. Our anger becomes sanctified when it lets go of its illusions; from then on, it reveals to us that there are more and more victims, not because this is a new reality, but because our anger had made us short-sighted. We come back to occupy the field of the relationship alongside many others, because we do not want to keep burning up alone in the fortress of the judge who is unaware of his own violence.

"Our society is the most preoccupied with victims of any that ever was," remarks Girard, who believes that "the phenomenon has precedent." He writes, "The most effective power of transformation is not revolutionary violence but the modern concern for victims. What pervades this concern and makes it effective is a true knowledge of oppression and persecution."[36]

Finally, holy anger is above all not that appropriation of God's anger that makes us believe in a divine mission against others. When Christ speaks of "He who sent me," it is never to suggest that he would have been given the vocation of redressing wrongs and keeping humans on the straight path. His insistence on the last judgment, the gnashing of teeth at the end of time, the fear of the Lord to be guarded preciously, the uncertainty about the ultimate value of our behaviours, forbids us from modelling God's anger on ours, and appropriating his to ourselves. On this subject, St. Augustine says:

> Thus even God himself is said in Scripture to be angry, and yet without any perturbation. For this word is used of the effect of His vengeance, not of the disturbing mental affection ... The anger of God is not a disturbing emotion of His mind, but a judgment by which punishment is inflicted upon sin ... He does not, like man, repent of anything He has done ... But if Scripture were not to use such expressions as above, it would not familiarly insinuate itself into the minds of all classes of men, whom it seeks access to for their good.[37]

Holy anger is therefore OTHER than spontaneous human anger; it seeks to be like God's anger, without claiming to achieve it. It thus hints that the "punishment inflicted upon sin [or division]" is that suffering linked to our broken relationships. We say that we are punished where we have sinned: it is because we suffer from having created a permanent division, just where the relationship was asking to evolve and be transformed into something else. God's anger, if we extend what St. Augustine says, would simply be that life energy that hurts us by pressing on the emptiness that is left after the relationship is broken. Why does he speak of "vengeance" on God's part? No doubt by anthropomorphism, as he himself says. There was a time when we used to see leprosy as a curse and any illness as divine vengeance for an unknown fault. Some people even used this argument to judge people with AIDS. Such an approach is an appropriation of divine anger, which we know nothing about, and leaves us at risk of never experiencing holy anger.

Leaving the mystery of God's anger to God is perhaps the first step on the way of holy anger. The Bible returns to this point at least three times, as if to encourage us to put our anger on a sure footing: "Beloved, never avenge yourselves, but leave room for the wrath of God; for it is written, 'Vengeance is mine, I will repay, says the Lord'" (Rom. 12:19). We recall that the Apostle Paul advised, in Ephesians 4:27, "Do not make room [topon] for the devil." Holy anger is anger that has been placed in Him who never stops dispensing justice: "Vengeance is mine, and recompense," we read in Deuteronomy 32:35. This is the best place you can put your anger: your anger is precious to me, it is a thriving plant that I want to prune so that it will bloom and bear fruits of justice and fairness; it is a raw material from which I can and want to make a work of art; it is the most alive part of you, which I want to embrace with my life force. Leaving it to God to be angry at our enemies therefore means believing that God is not going to intervene from the outside, like a bogeyman: by putting our anger on a sure footing, we are putting ourselves at the disposal of the living God who wants justice for all. We will not emerge unscathed, wrapped in our self-justification: "Vengeance is mine, I will repay," he says again, this time in the Letter to the Hebrews. And again: "'The Lord will judge his people.' It is a fearful thing to fall into the hands of the living God" (Heb. 10:30-31).

If holy anger has given up appropriating God's anger, it is because it has agreed to the passage of the sword: it is the Lord who *will judge* [krinei] his people, that is, who will "separate" them, will "distinguish" them, will "sort" them, will "slice" them. If we want justice to be done, we will accept separation, that radical solitude that makes us literally "fall into the hands of the living God" – a breathtaking fall into Him who alone can and wishes to convert the death of pitfall-laden relationships into the birth of men and women who are clearly differentiated, capable of sharing His life. The process causes fear, it is [phoberon], dreadful, for in itself it is like a kind of death. We have said this also about violence: the death that allows something to be born is like the deaths that we endure already but that cause us less fear because we know them. How will we learn that death and violence *shared with God* yield life, if not by one day agreeing to "fall-in into his hands," as the text literally says?

Now let us try to see how anger may be holy. Let us recall that, in the Bible, "holy" means set apart, separated to be made powerful by God. Thus anger is holy when it separates me from the painful chaos that swallows me up, and that separates me from those hostile humans, incompetent and indifferent, to whom I was clinging desperately. That anger is also holy that separates me from stereotypical images of myself as "victim," "guilty," "perfect," "cursed," "nice," etc. Holy also is that anger that separates me from those death-dealing representations of God with which I long nourished my faith and which I at last give myself the right to reject. And that anger is eminently holy that turns against God and implicates him. "This places man in a purely personal relationship of contradiction to God," notes S. Kierkegaard, "in such a relationship that he cannot rest content with any explanation at second hand."[38]

Thus the anger of Job is holy when, in detaching itself from God's pure Providence, at once traditional and anthropomorphic, it finds itself once more in solidarity with the common run of people, prey to social injustice and divine deafness. Chapter 24 is a model of this kind, of an astonishing modernity: that anger is holy that breaks with any philosophical or religious system that contradicts human experience or even the experience of a single human being. If one believes the Book of Job, the holy anger of a single person can defuse an entire religious and socio-political ideology and the fundamentalist behaviours that flow from it! R. de Pury comments:

> In chapter 24, Job, in an impressive manner, extends to the social domain the indictment that he prepared regarding his personal drama. His own unhappiness is not only the occasion of his revolt, but also of all the poor, all the exploited ... Nowhere else does one find so much anti-religious material in the Bible ... The trial to which modern thought subjects God is only a feeble and laughable echo of the proceedings Job institutes against him.[39]

Holy anger does not stop at the simple pleasure of refusing and of separating oneself. The power of freedom with regard to all the evil we have experienced and internalized, it aims in fact at something other than itself: it is the open-sesame for that paradoxical violence that opens to the unforeseeable awareness of the power to forgive. The power to refuse all that one *is* not essentially, it tends to put an end to alienating dysfunctionalities and to help the self to attain peace. In the *Philokalia of the Neptic Fathers*, Isaiah the Anchorite notes that

> without anger a man cannot attain purity;[40] he has to feel angry with all that is sown in him by the enemy. He who wishes to acquire anger that is in accordance with nature must uproot all self-will, until he establishes within himself the state natural to the intellect ... We should expel from our heart the provocation of each evil thought, rebutting it in a spirit of devotion ... turning our desire towards God and His will, and directing our incisive power, or wrath, against the devil [the divider] and sin [the rupture of relationship].[41]

One can thus live a true conversion from covetousness and anger.

"Intelligence" [noûs] is understood as the double faculty of thinking the world and contemplating God; it is therefore at once reason and the breath of the spirit. It would be a question therefore of cleansing the natural intelligence of all the dross that evil has deposited there, to arrive at an anger that is "true to nature." What I call holy anger is for the Anchorite the restoration of a healthy anger given by the Creator to differentiate him from his enemies, from harm suffered and its consequences. We find again the biblical intuition of the sword: "becoming established in the natural state of intelligence" becomes possible when we "cut off" all that is not essentially ourselves, and we abandon to our rival the object of dispute, because we have had the experience of having "another cheek."

In its liberating dynamism, holy anger goes so far as to refuse the paralyzing dogma of an "instinctive violence" in humans. As René Girard correctly remarks,

> Today we know that animals possess individual braking mechanisms to insure that combats between them seldom result in the actual death of the vanquished.[42] Because such mechanisms tend

to assure the perpetuation of the species, it would perhaps be not
inappropriate to term them *instinctive*. To use the same term in
connection with man's lack of such a braking device, however,
would be absurd.

The notion of an instinct (or if one prefers, an impulse) that
propels men towards violence or death – Freud's famous "death
wish – is no more than a last surrender to mythological thinking,
a final manifestation of that ancient belief that human violence
can be attributed to some outside influence – to gods, to Fate, to
some force men can hardly be expected to control.[43]

It seems today that the dogma of the instinct for violence is losing
ground to the benefit of a new dogma, also posited with that im-
personal "one" which gives it the guise of a certain scientificness:
"One never really heals." Woe to the person who claims to be
completely healed of their traumatic history and its consequences!
Woe to he or she who is delivered by holy anger from the fantasy of
an instinct for violence that is stronger than the person. And finally,
woe to anyone who affirms that they do not want to die except
from excessive suffering and from wanting to live a real life!

One single witness is sufficient for the dogma to crumble: if a single
human should evade "one does not really heal [from evil and from
violence]," then the way is open to all. Thus, holy anger opens into
the search for authenticity: we do not delude ourselves into believing that we have been healed the moment we feel and see the anger
of God at work in our own story, at work against our inner chaos
from the time long ago when we were lost, far from any OTHER.
At that time, we were like Cain, incapable of distinguishing the
holy anger of life from the absurd anger of our fantasy God. "How
could Cain, who was not even able to appropriate for himself what
he had made grow, grasp that by not considering his offering, it
was not his existence but rather *his non-existence that the divine was
refusing*?"[44] The holy anger of God is, by our sides and in the very
direction of our deep desire, an age-old struggle against chaos, that
confusion between us and others that keeps us in non-existence.

Holy anger does not need God's guarantee to be considered credible.
No religion or philosophy has a monopoly on it: the OTHER anger

crosses personal destinies and collective histories with the freedom
of the Spirit that blows where it wills. For an atheistic philosopher
such as Camus, it is called "revolt" and deserves its name only insofar
as it has renounced the "all or nothing" sower of death.

> [I]t has never affirmed, in its purest form, anything but the exist-
> ence of a limit ... It is the rejection of one part of existence in
> the name of another part, which it exalts. The more profound
> the exaltation, the more implacable is the rejection. Then, when
> rebellion, in rage or intoxication, adopts the attitude of "all or
> nothing" and the negation of all existence and all human nature,
> it is at this point that it denies itself.[45]

It is then that we might say that it is no longer holy anger.

It is astonishing to find in Camus, as an illustration, the notion
of "anger in keeping with nature" that we encountered in the
*Philokalia*. In this modern philosophy, which makes no reference
to a Creator, the human is the depository of an authentic anger to
which he or she is perfectly capable of remaining faithful: "The
more aware rebellion is of demanding a just limit, the more inflex-
ible it becomes ... Claiming the unity of the human condition, it is
a force of life, not of death."[46] It is thus holy anger, on our terms.
But when it adds the lie to injustice, claiming thereby to put an end
to injustice, it no longer deserves its name. Camus concludes in a
quasi-biblical manner: "He who does not know everything cannot
kill everything ... Rebellion itself only aspires to the relative and
can only promise an assured dignity coupled with relative justice. It
supposes a limit at which the community of man is established."[47]

Holy anger is anger that, without ever denying itself, still does not
claim control over vengeance. Because it does not decide to leave
the human community, it delegates to the OTHER the right to impose
its law. This OTHER is, first, within human societies, any collective
system that tends to put in place a justice OTHER than my counter-
violence. My holy anger seeks that limit that begins by protecting
*me* from an outburst that is ultimately self-destructive. Of course,
even the best judicial system is a stopgap measure, for my holy anger
aspires to perfect justice. But I understand that in taking this stand,
I am not at all compromising myself with injustice if I remain in

solidarity with my holy anger. Holiness – purity, in the sense of non-confusion – is henceforth the place of my anger. Because my anger has a safe place, I can agree to human justice.

> As long as there exists no sovereign and independent body capable of taking the place of the injured party and taking upon itself the responsibility for revenge, the danger of interminable escalation remains ... A judicial system is ultimately irreplaceable, short of a unanimous and entirely voluntary renunciation of all violent actions ... Once violence is installed in a community, it cannot burn itself out.[48]

Because it can do more, holy anger can also do less: if it tolerates humans exercising their justice as they will, provided that it be consensual and applicable to everyone, it can well admit that God is just in his so often incomprehensible fashion. Indeed, we find it more difficult to yield to a justice system that can be criticized and modified than to question God's freedom to practise justice!

Our anger is made holy when we hold our heads high and return from the land of suffering where we were exiled, as under the influence of a divine anger that is impossible to understand. When the fleeing Jacob reached his Uncle Laban's at Haran and asked the shepherds, "Where do you come from?" they replied, "from Haran," or, according to the etymology of the word, "from anger." For A. Abécassis, this probably refers to divine anger, for "the exile had also been considered in the Jewish tradition to be the consequence of a transgression," and Jacob's question resonates with God's question in the garden of Eden: Where are you from? – We come from the place of anger (Gen. 29:4).[49]

We enter into holy anger when we refuse to remain hostages to any suffering that excludes us from the Presence, in the fantasy of his unlimited anger towards us. We come from that place, and our own anger seeks henceforth its ground near the model of any anger of life. No matter what we have done or undergone, we owe to the OTHER of all human justice the freedom to have leaned, to the point of causing pain, on that hardening of heart and spirit that was paralyzing us. On that day, Jacob meets brothers in humanity, at once other and similar, who are on the road to a holy anger.

The exegesis of J. Eisenberg allows us to read the following verse in the same symbolic manner: "'Do you know Laban?' – 'We do.'" Now, [laban] means "white," thus: "Do you know whiteness, that is, purification and absolution? In other words, can one heal from exile and find again his original whiteness? Can one hold onto hope? ... Jacob catches sight of exile. He is worried. Hunted by the divine anger, won't his children despair?"[50] We know from experience, the shepherds seem to say, that one can heal from the chaos that wipes out all differences, that dissolves and confuses people in a common violence: purity exists, the possibility of being oneself without blending. We know it from inside; therefore, for you, also, Jacob, the way of exile is not a dead end.

Holy anger is healthy anger. It is not an end in itself: its function is to restore health in the full sense [shalom]. It allows the subject to attain his own reference points, his own truths, an inner liberty of which he had no idea. Such an anger expresses itself in the most diverse ways, according to our personality. At times, we will take great pleasure in saying "I refuse" in one situation or another, observing that the earth continues to rotate on its axis and that we did not know we were capable of saying no with such confidence in our own consistency. Sometimes, we will not let go of a choice or a plan that raises nothing but skepticism and dissuasion in the people around us. Or we may not grow tired of telling our own truth in a place where it seemed to have no chance of being heard. Or we are determined to be healed when the experts consider the case incurable. Or, finally, we will demand justice, we will hope to meet Christ, we will desire to know unconditional Love ... for as long as it takes, for to renounce it would be to betray ourselves. All this is has to do with holy anger.

In every case, it is essential to remain rooted in the reality of our experience of the moment; no matter how much I struggle in the midst of confusion, one thing is certain: nothing and no one can prevent me from being in solidarity with who I am *in this moment*, even if they want me to believe that I am crazy and even if I fear that I am becoming crazy. Witnesses abound among survivors of the totalitarian regimes and death camps that are some of the educational systems in our countries: humans owe their survival to that particular anger, holy because it is unchanging, which claims "I am" in the face of everyone, even God. At a given moment, Job stops asking to be liberated from his sorrows. When he gets in touch with his will to remain himself at any cost, he has a found a place for his anger, and that place finds itself face to face with God, and thus in the sphere of holiness. Job is no longer threatened by the chaos of indifferentiation at the moment when, moved by holy anger, he gives himself the right to his feelings, the right to the authenticity of what he is living. This is because such an anger grows and strengthens itself in the attachment to his point of view, which is at once fragile and irreplaceable, regarding the world in which lives. He no longer has to work at unseating the ideologies around him. From now on it is enough for him to hold onto the uniqueness of such a standpoint, which is perfectly valid because it is perfectly differentiated.

A major indication that allows us to speak of holy anger is when a subject discovers the force of a decision: he understands that he has given himself the right to be what he is, to feel what is arising in him, to express what is speaking within him *because that is what he is called to*. He unearths his unique and inimitable vocation right in the heart of his holy anger! He begins to see that he was not created to produce or to conform, but above all to tend the divine breath within – which blows in a different way within each person. Made of dust like the others, he becomes uniquely "alive" in his own way only by "the breath of life" breathed into him by God[51] … and no matter what the conditions of existence may be, even exiled far from the safe Presence, he sees that his vocation is "to till the ground from which he was taken" (Gen 3:23). The experience of holy anger brings him back to that dust that is the raw material of his humanity: inert, obstinate, but inspired from above. It is there that his vocation happens: to be at the service of that which he carries within without denying any of it, in order for that sea breeze to blow, that Anger of life that is destined for him.

Cain believed himself to be destined to cultivate the earth. His parents did not teach him to become angry against that programming: they had not understood that God was inviting them to affirm themselves in their unique identity, to put themselves at the service of their [adamah] for it was animated by His breath of life. Thus it may be said that Cain had not yet found his vocation: "[His mother] put him in the position of believing that from her desire she could know *everything*," notes D. Sibony. "In going towards ... God, Cain could only manifest both the complaint about his desire that was at an impasse, and the attempt to get out of it [the maternal sphere], by the unconscious wish to find before him a place from which the desire could be recognized, which presupposes that his request was '*differed*,' marked with difference."[52] Cain did not find the place for his anger. God's anger therefore consisted in opposing him, in rejecting him even if it meant seeming to be Unjust, in differentiating himself from this caricature of a God who is fond of human servility. In indicating His difference, he tried to reveal to Cain the vocation, addressed to every human, to live as different from his neighbour and from God. Only a holy anger would shake him enough to keep him on the path of his living [adamah].

Holy anger is like the experience of a relational power. We are then at the opposite poles of the entry point to anger. Indeed, today's research results make it seem as if anger is gathering energy, even euphoria, and an illusion of power, and even of invulnerability.[53] The sword that the Gospel speaks of begins by breaking the euphoria; brought to our senses, we realize that we are desperately alone, trapped in fear and anger, in anger and fear. Only a face-to-face encounter will give the anger a place; any confrontation that is not destructive of the other opens a space for holiness – a space where each opponent is called to find a place, and therefore to differentiate himself. Jacob's struggle shows that at the moment when we wrench ourselves away from who we are by refusing once and for all to let ourselves be invaded, we become powerful: not to the detriment of the other but *in union with others, in interdependence*. This is what I call relational power.

We are no longer, then, in the fantasy omnipotence of anger: we become powerful *in the field of the encounter*, and nowhere else. This is perhaps also what is said symbolically by Jacob's limping: he has seized the power that was given to him in the limits of his body and his being. The adversary has also marked the place of holiness where an anger of life could be put forth: by limping, Jacob will always be reminded that his own power is made possible each time his body knocks against another body and finds there its limits and its weaknesses. It is as though his power was and should remain marked with the branding iron of differentiation. As C. Vigée writes:

> By nostalgia, perhaps from the feminine side, from the *tsel'a* (the rib, the side, the edge of the body) taken by the Creator from the primordial Adam who is mutilated … Jacob … will climb the other bank of the Jabbok, limping – *tsolé'a* – from the hip. It is as a man dislocated in his most intimate being, *tsolé'a* limping in quest of his feminine part that was lost when Eve was formed, that Jacob will henceforth walk towards the dawn.[54]

The OTHER is the first one who, rushing at Jacob, collides with the limit of his own power: "He can do nothing for him." Holy anger is anger that puts a finger on both the power of the adversary and his limits, also bringing to light his divinity or holiness. Now, if the OTHER agrees to his limits, thus to his differentiation, and if he emerges from it greater, in a relational power such that his blessing becomes a real healing power, then Jacob can do the same and say of the ford of the Jabbok that it was the place where his holy anger emerged.

In crossing the stream, Jacob thereby moves from "deaf and insane" anger to holy anger., The moralist Seneca, a contemporary of Jesus who was attracted by Stoic strictness, proposed banning the madness that is anger: "The best course is to reject at once the first incitement to anger, to resist even its small beginnings, and to take pains to avoid falling into anger," he writes in his treatise *On Anger*, which was widely read in Christian antiquity.[55] What is being observed nowadays about the pumping of blood by the heart during great fits of anger seems to lend weight to Seneca's point: the effects of anger on the heart are now well recognized by science, and they are harmful. But anger that is systematically repressed and transformed into anxiety is also harmful: "There is evidence that trying to completely suppress such feelings in the heat of the moment actually results in magnifying the body's agitation and may raise blood pressure."[56]

But we can leave Seneca behind, for he does not locate spiritual growth where the Bible does. We have seen how God welcomed Cain's anger, asking him only to name it, to talk to him about it, never insisting that it be eradicated. However, the Gospel seems realistic in warning, "If you are angry with a brother or sister, you will be liable to judgment" (Matt. 5:22). Beginning in the second century, copyists tried to soften this radical message by adding "without reason," but Christ's advice is unequivocal: anyone who gives vent to anger is in danger. Many people, pagans and Christians, therefore recommended not taking any risk, "extracting" from the beginning that "mortal poison" that is anger. Thus Cassian the Roman, like most of the Desert Fathers, denounces it as being the passion that "in its boiling, blinds the eyes of the soul"; it is an illusion, he adds, to isolate ourselves from people who are irritating or to close ourselves off in a stubborn silence, because we are responsible for our anger.[57]

The aim of Cassian, among many others, is spiritual perfection, but the means he uses is too extreme. He invokes the New Testament to legitimate hunting down anger not only in acts but also in thought:

> Whoever wants to attain perfection and who desires to undertake spiritual combat according to the rules, should be a stranger to any fault of anger and fury ... One must abstain from exercising anger not only in act but also in thought, for fear that the intelligence, blinded by the mists of bitterness, will lose the light of knowledge and discernment and be deprived of the house of the Holy Spirit ... If, then, we wish to obtain the Lord's blessing, we should ... cut off not only anger in action but also in thought ... and not think evil thoughts against a brother ... The Lord's plan is that we do all we can to cut out the root and the spark of anger ... for fear that in giving rein to anger for a good reason, we may fall into furious and unreasoning anger. Here is the perfect remedy against this malady: let us believe that it is never permitted for us to let ourselves get angry, whether for just or unjust cause ... It will be impossible for our soul to be the

temple of the Holy Spirit if the spirit of anger, having darkened the mind, takes hold of us.[58]

It does not seem to me that the biblical texts ask us to cut off or stifle anything. On the contrary, to act on our anger as belonging to us, to name it in the encounter with an OTHER, thus to welcome it with benevolence instead of banishing it, allow us to let it clarify itself, to cleanse itself of all that was not yet holy anger, in a fair fight for the life of the other and our own life. Having done this,. our anger will be able to take another name:[59] for example, the name of "firmness," as in St. Augustine who saw in the devouring fire descending from heaven in Revelations 20:9 the "firmness of the saints, wherewith they refuse to yield obedience to those who rage against them ... This is the fire which shall devour them, and it is "from God."[60]

Here we find the tongue of fire that we spoke of earlier, a symbol of that holy anger or life anger that does not leave anyone indifferent – not those who welcome it nor those on whom it falls before they are ready to welcome it. These latter could be among those to whom we do good rather than seeking revenge. Paul, after advising us to "leave room for the wrath of God" (Rom. 12:19), adds (citing Proverbs 25:21), "If your enemies are hungry, feed them; if they are thirsty, give them something to drink; for by doing this you will heap burning coals on their heads" (Rom. 12:20). Thus on the day of Pentecost, a "tongue of fire" hovered over each of them. Anger, the formidable energy of life, can make us cross a burning hell, but this is so we could be "made of fire," capable of moving forwards thanks to the fire of God that lives in us and reviving the embers in others.

At the root of any holy anger is the desire not to confine others in their unconsciousness. If I am angry at someone, it is because I believe even minimally in his humanity: that is, in his capacity to continue on the way. This is breathed into me by Him who sanctifies my anger, and it separates me clearly from Seneca, for whom "if other creatures escape your anger for the very reason that they are lacking in understanding, every man who lacks understanding should hold in your eyes a like position."[61] But Christians do not have a monopoly on holy anger. The Spirit blows where it wants the sword to pass, in any culture, religion, or atheism. This is why Camus could say that "rebellion cannot exist without a strange form of love ... it is the very movement of life and ... it cannot be denied without renouncing life. Its purest outburst, on each occasion, gives birth to existence. Thus it is love and fecundity or it is nothing at all."[62]

# 3   A balanced look at those who are "violent"

When we hear someone described as "a monster," or another person is said to have "never done anyone any harm," we are sometimes struck by the symmetry of these fantastical statements. But unless we are God, how do we prove that another is either wholly monstrous or wholly non-violent? That is certainly not how the sword of the Gospel passes, by reinforcing the spontaneous split between good people and evil ones. We will never be able to differentiate ourselves from those who behave monstrously if we imagine that making them out to be monsters protects us from them. Nor will we differentiate ourselves from persons whose behaviour is perfect and who are perfectly controlled if we refuse to see their faults.

The sword does not pass without us putting ourselves to it, without our becoming involved. As long as another's monstrousness does not connect with our own, we are not sizing up the confusion that exists between the two of us, and we remain incapable of differentiating ourselves from the other. As long as we cultivate the fantasy that we can go through life showing only perfectly non-violent behaviour, we denounce the violence of others without having the least idea of our own violence. As a result, we forbid those close to us from giving in to their own violence, but above all – and this is much more serious – we forbid them from giving in to the anger of life that would let them differentiate themselves from us. The sword is far from having passed.

There are multiple strategies for avoiding facing the question of our own violence. The most current one is inspired, more or less, by modern philosophy, which sees the human as a naturally peaceful being, rendered violent by the violence of society. There is nothing false about that; it is rather astonishing that the sum total of injustices and bad treatment that is endured by the majority of humans from birth does not lead to even more violence than it does. But what we forget to add is that the violence that people experience causes not only self-destruction. As long as the victims are alive, they will sooner or later get in touch with the accumulated counter-violence within themselves.

I cannot condemn violence in society and in the world and refuse to see how I take part in it in my own life. The violence that I have experienced is no less serious if I admit that it has led me to dysfunctionality that can wound and do violence to others in turn. If I have been able to let go of the evil that I have undergone, I agree to recognize my counter-violence without wishing to compare it to what I have suffered. The violence I have undergone and that which I have perpetrated upon others are clearly differentiated because I have been able to admit to both of them, each in its own time: the sword has passed.

More recently, we have been able to turn to science to try to avoid the unpleasant examination of personal violence. Biology has made it appear that aggression is the fate of all living beings and that, in animals, it grows between two individuals of the same species, as if their too great resemblance to each other called for a more violent distancing.[63] But among humans, violence assumes proportions unknown in the animal world, which could go as far as destroying the species. We have even reached the point of looking for aggression genes characteristic of humans: it would be reassuring to think that the monster is abnormal, that violence is simply a physical malady that we will eventually eradicate, and that, "normally," humans are not violent.

But no scientific knowledge, no objective reasoning, will deliver us from violence, for the simple reason that it is a question of freedom. In our personal history, is not the first freedom that of once and for all taking account in a personal way of the violence that is destined for us and the counter-violence by which we have survived, for better or for worse? The exit that we will find from the violence that cuts through our lives will be drawn with pencils that we alone choose to use. The fair regard that we will be able to focus on violent people will not depend on a recipe that anyone can follow. It is up to us, in the solitude of differentiation, to name "the violent" of our existence. The term itself is neutral, for it designates all that does violence to us through incidents, words and actions of men and women. Our compass will be the desire to put an end to that "violent one" who triggers the release of our violence, to put an end to it through a means other than physically eliminating the other, or diabolizing him – for to make the other a monster is also a way of eliminating him.

We can consider it lucky that the Bible is full of violence: thus, it is undeniable that it speaks of us and of our societies. The sword had to begin by passing between God and the world of humans: God is OTHER than a projection of *our* understanding of violence. Thus, people long believed that God demanded blood sacrifices and even the sacrifice of children, immersed as they were in great confusion between His will and that of the idols.[64] One of the great intuitions of the Hebrew Bible is that the question of violence and God's violence are intimately intertwined. We are not desperately alone in the face of the insolvable problem of violence: there exists a Third who, from the opening lines of Genesis, says that he is at least as concerned as we are. This is an OTHER in that God knows how to set a limit on his own anger, and it is an OTHER that we resemble, in that he knows anger from the inside. Before reading other texts where God says that he will no longer let himself resort to anger, we are present at a true conversion on his part through the story of Noah.

In Genesis 6:11-13, having noted that violence has reached a peak, he decides to put a stop to it by an even greater act of violence:

> Now the earth was corrupt in God's sight, and the earth was filled with violence. And God saw that the earth was corrupt; for all flesh had corrupted its ways upon the earth. And God said to Noah, "I have determined to make an end of all flesh, for the earth is filled with violence because of them; now I am going to destroy them along with the earth."

Note that it is not a question here of "humans" ['adam], nor of the dust from which they are made ['adamah], but of the country, the earth, the territory ['ereṣ], mentioned five times, compared to four mentions of destruction, in a nearly perfect symmetry.

After the flood, when the sole survivors (Noah and his family) offer the first burnt offering in the Bible, the sacrifice of whole animals, God commits himself to never again destroy the [adamah] because of the [adam]. It is as if he were now remembering what humans are made of – dust animated by His breath – and their resemblance to Him. If He can be dragged into destroying, he can understand their problem, and if He has reached the point of staying his own violence, they can model themselves on Him.

> I will never again curse the ground [the adamah, the clod of earth] because of humankind [adam, the earthly] for the inclination of the human heart is evil from youth; nor will I ever again destroy every living creature as I have done. As long as the earth endures, seedtime and harvest, cold and heat, summer and winter, day and night, shall not cease. (Gen. 8:21-22)

In Hebrew, as in English, we can understand that God will never again curse the original dust *because of the value* he attaches to the human; he will not curse it again, *in view of* humans, according to one of the meanings of ['avur], because he values the human too much not to see in the human a clay pot that was flawed from the beginning. One could say that God has changed his way of seeing those who are "violent": the human is not a monster to be eliminated once and for all. It was enough that God remembered one single human capable of justice, Noah, for him to change his way of seeing the mass of humanity. There will be no more return to the original chaos. God will not cease to do his work of differentiation – between humans, between things and created beings. This means that in no case are any of the experiences of chaos into which humans may fall on account of God. Genesis is very clear on this point. If we refuse to hear it, it is because we prefer to see violence as divine fate, and thus may avoid confronting it for ourselves.

Violence is equally omnipresent in the New Testament. Only an excessive attachment to the "good Lord" who, it is claimed, is allergic to any conflict, and to the pale pink Jesus of pious images can prevent us from seeing this. We can even say that the New Testament never stops speaking of violence, to show us how to get away from it. Thus, the entire Bible orients every human towards an awareness and a decision: victims of violence, we avoid doing counter-violence that cannot be undone by remembering that it is in us, even if it has long been hidden. When we find the memory of our counter-violence, we are in union with Him who remembers everything and who, himself, knows our violence and that of others. He is the OTHER whose flaming sword guarantees an inviolable space between others and ourselves; confusion is no longer possible between the violence we have undergone and that which boils up in us. At the moment when we get in touch with our counter-violence, *we are no longer victims*; we are "made powerful," like Jacob. Henceforth we know that we *can* kill or eliminate the other, and we see the divine sword sheltering us from the violence of others and from our own counter-violence.

As for the decision to which the biblical texts invite us, it involves being in continuous union with that OTHER who stands between others and ourselves, desiring to offer to every human his non-violent omnipotence – the only omnipotence that is accessible to humans. We remain victims, and therefore potentially counter-violent, as long as we fill the space of the OTHER that is between others and ourselves with falsely reassuring signs: "Beware of monster!" It is by choosing to remain always in contact with Him whose non-violent omnipotence tries to communicate itself to us that our counter-violence reveals itself to us, dissolving our fear of the "monstrous" other. Since we are no longer victims, there is no longer a monster but only humans who have violence done to them and humans who are violent, who are not yet conscious of their counter-violence, much less their non-violent omnipotence.

In concrete terms, who is that OTHER who stands between violent people and us who are overwhelmed with counter-violence? According to the gospels, it is the face of Christ, "Son of Man," true human incarnating the true God and continuing to become incarnate *incognito* in "the smallest" of his brothers and sisters. For Christians, that OTHER who intervenes has, therefore, the characteristics of Christ, but as if he came to superimpose himself on the face of others. In this way we see the spiritual being of the other, his christic face. This is what happens between Jacob and Esau, when Jacob says to Esau on the day after the struggle at the Jabbok, "Truly to see your face is like seeing the face of God" (Gen. 33:10) – I saw on your face the face of God.

Nothing is more disarming, and it is also the disarmed face of his father who, according to the Midrash, prevented Abel from becoming a murderer. Where the biblical text says, "When they were in the field, Cain rose up against his brother Abel and killed him" (Gen 4:8), A. Abécassis indicates that according to the Midrash, "They both threw themselves on the ground, rolling in the dust" – like Jacob and his adversary. "Abel was stronger than Cain, for where it is written, 'he got up,' that means that he was on top of Cain. Cain said to Abel, 'We are two in the world, what are you going to tell our father?' Then, Abel was filled with compassion. But Cain got up at once and killed him."[65] It is true that the Midrash concludes with words that are hardly evangelical: "Do not do good to the one who is evil, and nothing bad will come to you!" But the vocation of the "suffering servant" who would rather be killed than to kill is described well in the Hebrew Bible, in Isaiah 52–53.

We will believe in our non-violent omnipotence insofar as we can identify with that human who is like us, Jesus of Nazareth, who experienced violence from his birth and was also pierced with anger even as he came, with God's help, to convert it to holy anger. Born into the difficult circumstances that homeless people know well, he and his parents experienced the tough conditions of refugees, carrying the burden of the massacre of the children of the village where he was born. He was threatened with death all along his way, treated like a crazy person by his relatives and as a blasphemer by his co-religionists. He knew the loss of trust among his best friends – denial by one, betrayal by another that led to an unfair trial and death by torture, and abandonment by all his disciples.

The Christian tradition has seen the "true God" in him not because he would never have given in to anger, but because "true man," familiar with human battles, he opted for the omnipotence of non-violence. It is not for us to judge the degree of his anger in the gospel passages that relate his violent words and gestures: the making of a whip and the scene of overturning the tables of the money-changers in the Temple; the reproaches to the Pharisees and scribes ("whitened sepulchres," "hypocrites," "evil and adulterous generation"); the comparison of the exclusion of the pagan Syrophoenician woman to young dogs, the rejection of Peter by referring to him as "Satan"; the indirect reference to Judas as the "devil." We can only observe that Jesus contented himself with keeping his anger from gaining more and more momentum. In all these examples, we see him facing that which is rising up inside him, discerning the anger of life that comes to him from God, speaking and acting with that energy that passes through him, then holding his peace, refraining, drawing back … letting holy anger act.

One of the ancient texts that could have helped Jesus to move forward on his way is found in the book of Isaiah. It is presented as a prophecy. The first Christians saw in it the whole history of Jesus: his immersion into our world as it is; his attitude towards violence; his understanding of a kingdom where it would be possible for humans to live together, for each one would be well differentiated from the others. In the unfolding of this very prophetic text, we can sense the footsteps of numerous people who could offer a fair-minded look at "the violent" in others, in God, in themselves. There are two conditions for being able to take such a step: one must have renounced the need to establish divine justice here below, and, therefore, never to move out of solidarity with this world to take

God's place in imposing non-violence "from on high." Moreover, one must admit to one's own violence – consequences of that "poor fashioning" due to the hardness of life and noted by God himself on the day after the flood – in order to allow the Spirit or the anger of life to transform its way of seeing "the violent."

We might entitle our text "The Parable of the Wild Animals Affected by Justice":

> 1. *A shoot shall come out from the stock of Jesse,*
> and a branch shall grow out of his roots.
> 2. *The spirit of the Lord shall rest on him,*
> the spirit of wisdom and understanding,
> the spirit of counsel and might,
> the spirit of knowledge and the fear of the Lord.
> 3. [A spirit such that] his delight shall be in the fear of the Lord.
> He shall not judge by what his eyes see,
> or decide by what his ears hear;
> 4. but with righteousness he shall judge the poor,
> and decide with equity for the meek of the earth;
> he shall strike the earth with the rod of his mouth,
> and with the breath of his lips he shall kill the wicked.
> he shall strike the earth with the rod of his mouth,
> and with the breath of his lips he shall kill the wicked.
> 5. *Righteousness [justice] shall be the belt around his waist,*
> and faithfulness the belt around his loins.
> 6. *The wolf shall live with the lamb,*
> the leopard shall lie down with the kid,
> the calf and the lion and the fatling together,
> and a little child shall lead them.
> 7. The cow and the bear shall graze,
> their young shall lie down together,
> and the lion shall eat straw like the ox.
> 8. The nursing child shall play over the hole of the asp,
> *and the weaned child shall put its hand on the adder's den.*
> 9. They will not hurt or destroy
> on all my holy mountain;
> *for the earth will be full of the knowledge of the Lord*
> as the waters cover the sea. (Is. 11:1-9)

When we say that an act or an intention is violent, we are making a value judgment: depending on the time, the culture and even individuals, specific behaviour may be seen as horribly violent or completely normal. We deal with a reality of the spirit that makes it necessary for us to share and listen to each other if we want to come to an agreement within a society, a people or a community – if we want to look fairly on "the violent." It is not surprising that the Hebrew Bible, so unfamiliar with abstractions, evokes a reality of this type symbolically. The basic belief, it seems to me, is that the animals are within us. This is another example of biblical realism: there is something of the wolf and the panther in us, even if, in living our violence through dreams, we resist the idea that it is a question of its being our own violence. It was ever thus, the author seems to suggest by using the word in the perfect tense: "The wolf has lived [and continues to live] with the. lamb" (v. 6).

But the fact is that while there is within us the aggression of the wolf, there is also the lamb's thirst for gentleness. This is neither good nor bad, it just is; and cohabitation is possible. In every human being there coexist a feminine dimension (attention to life, to the inner world, imagination, sensitivity, a desire to welcome), a masculine dimension (combativeness, self-affirmation, the search for coherence and order, the desire to create), and a childish dimension (wonder, trust, the need for relationship, the sense of the beautiful and of the divine). Inside every human being coexist wild animals (the undomesticated elements) and domestic animals (those parts of us that are suited for life in society).

The text puts many "small" creatures in the scene as well: "lamb, kid, calf, lion cub, the young of the cattle and bear." But the small creature that is mentioned most often is the young human: "the offspring, the little one, the suckling, the weaned child." Each such mention is associated with a violent animal, as if to recall that from birth the human is faced with the violence of life and of others, that he has the capacity to be violent: there had to be something of the wolf in him – teeth for biting, for surviving, for defending, more or less, his territory. "A little child shall lead them" (v. 6), all those animals that constitute the child's reality; he or she can do it without fear and without violence.

It is thus a promise, addressed to each human in the course of his or her personal evolution, and at the same time a prophecy that begins to be carried out in an irreversible way with the coming of Christ. We can almost hear Jesus recounting one of the parables that compare the kingdom of heaven to everyday things that are abruptly turned upside down, presented in a new light: the kingdom of heaven, he would say, is like a nursing child playing over the cobra's nest, a weaned child putting its hand on the adder's den ... without fear. Then Jesus would invite his adult listeners, as was his custom, to take up again their spirit of childhood. Isaiah, too, unites the present to the past that endures and to the future that has already begun, by alternating the verbs between the perfect tense and the imperfect tense. The Gospel is apparently in the same vein. Our future finds its roots in visiting the past; a life without destructive violence is impossible without the [re]discovery of our "spirit of childhood" and the [re]adoption of our trust in others regardless of their attitudes.

But trust and unconsciousness are akin to each other, we may object: it is precisely because we trusted that we were bitten by the asp. Nevertheless, in the text as in life, trust comes first, and it is ongoing: "Trust was and remains the belt around the loins," to this offspring. More biblical symbolism: the loins, seat of the emotions, evoke what is uncontrollable. The young human received an invisible belt around his loins, like a safety belt meant to protect him "from the violent" and also from his own violence – a belt that can contain the animals within him. The urgent task is thus to rediscover trust as a form of protection that has been there since the beginning, already given and not to be gained at the cost of superhuman efforts – to believe that nothing could destroy it completely for it is and was *of God*.

If violence is a reality of the spirit, a value attributed to one behaviour or another or to a natural occurrence, the trust that protects us from violence is also a reality of the spirit. It is an invisible belt in which we believe without being able to prove it, as invisible as

the "breath of the Lord that rests" on the little child from the first
words of the text and the first hours of life. An invisible omnipotence without violence is named four times in one verse; that breath
rested and continues to rest on the little child that everyone carries within.[66] Why does God hide in the breath of a nursing child?
Perhaps because the little child is the privileged depository of His
justice. We know that children have a heightened sense of justice,
to the point where injustices that are not recognized by adults may
prevent children from believing in the affection that those same
adults say they feel for them.

Looking closely, v. 5 begins with justice: "Righteousness [justice]
shall be the belt around his loins." The adult who has become violent has experienced so much injustice, in silence, that he has lost
any sense of justice. His belt of justice having come undone, he is
given over to the violence of the animals in him and outside him.
It is possible to translate v. 2 as "The breath of the Lord *leaned over*
him." One might then say that God leans over us, like a child still
thirsting for justice, and tries to make himself heard in this way:
remember that justice was and still is the belt around your loins; it
will help you to avoid becoming unjust in your turn towards others,
but also not to smother your truth by being unjust to yourself.

If a sense of justice is given to us from birth, it is because Justice
precedes us; we have not invented it from whole cloth. Our ideas
of justice are always secondary; they develop *after* we have stored
up a certain number of injustices. But, there again, the verb tense
in Hebrew suggests that there is something of "the Just" in us,
which surrounds us – like a leotard (which in French is called a
"justaucorps," "right against the body") – and keeps us from endlessly reproducing the injustices we have gone through. In the
Bible, the two lines of a poetical verse often express the same idea.
Thus the author orients us to an outcome of violence: that Just One
who surrounds you is part of you, you can trust him, your sense
of justice is to be believed; it is the OTHER who guarantees it, He
who sees in your trust in others and in yourself the greatest justice
that can protect you.

To say, with the gospels, that the sword passes amounts to saying, with Isaiah, that everything is to be taken back to basics: from then on, "A branch shall grow out of his roots" (v. 1). The roots, for a living being, are what is given. It is from this that we will be able to find what will help the wolf and the lamb live together. There is in us, from birth and regardless of whatever violence we have experienced or perpetrated, a "breath of wisdom, of discernment, of counsel and power, of knowledge and fear of the Lord," in short, a "breath to make us feel the fear of the Lord." Our knowledge, our skills, the means that we give ourselves to come to the end of violence remain in vain as long as our efforts are not motivated by the "fear of the Lord" – by that OTHER who was and will always be the ultimate guarantor of justice. To be afraid of that OTHER is to cultivate that humility that makes us always dread being taken advantage of, to have, unlike him, "judged on what our eyes have seen" by trusting in appearances, and to have yielded to violence without full knowledge of the facts.

The human who has kept or rediscovered the spirit of childhood cannot move to action: the context prohibits seeing a physical death in v. 4: "He shall strike the earth with the rod of his mouth, and with the breath of his lips he shall kill the wicked." Such is the human power to stop the violence of the "evil-doer": God suggested this to Cain concerning the violence that was rumbling inside him. Isaiah deepens the understanding of this power that is given at birth: by his word alone, the human can defuse the violence of the other, of life, of the one who is called God, by "striking and killing the evil-doer," by destroying *what there is of violence* in himself and in others. Cain, instead of killing, could "strike" God, life, Abel, his mother "with the rod of his mouth." Having done this, he could fix a just regard – in the double sense of exact and fair – on "the violent" which, in him, was ready to lash out and on "the violent" of which he felt himself to be a victim: he had the power to "kill" them both. The OTHER is that voice which, in our heart of hearts, invites us to view the as yet unnameable violent one and to exercise over him the power of that Word alone that destroys in order to allow life.

Isaiah's text is realistic from one end to the other: the wolves will remain wolves. In the human, the wild animals are not going to disappear; their hunting grounds will simply have limits: "They will not hurt or destroy on all my holy mountain" (v. 9). The earth – both our world of violence and our inner world – is already commandeered as a protected space, set apart, "sanctified" by that OTHER who desires "all [his] holy mountain." We sometimes refer to a place as a little corner of paradise. In this blessed place – which may also be, within us, the secret oasis – "the violent" has no foothold, no power of destruction, for the Holy One has made of it his dwelling place.

The last image of this prophecy may seem absurd: how can "the waters cover the sea"? We must remember that the sea, in the sudden eruption of its violence, overwhelmed the Hebrews, who saw in it a symbol of evil. It is left to us, then, to know the Lord as He who alone has shown himself capable of subduing the sea: "Yes, the earth has been filled with knowledge of the Lord, like the waters covering the sea." The OTHER has always wanted to turn our violent earth into his holy mountain; he has *already* filled – the word is in the perfect tense – it with the means necessary to let Him, in some way, do his work. Only the OTHER, in fact, can "cover" the chaos and confusion of our relationships, the hurly-burly of our beginnings into which violence regularly plunges us. He does this by means of the living water of his Word, given in abundance to whoever wishes to draw from it.

In citing Zechariah 9:9-10, P. Beauchamp indicates that the Septuagint has replaced "I [God]" by "the king," thereby transferring "onto the messiah the capacity to do that which God alone can do for the whole world." "Lo, your king comes ..., humble and riding on a donkey ... I will cut off the chariot from Ephraim ... The battle-bow shall be cut off, and he shall command peace to the nations; his dominion shall be from sea to sea."[67] Following Christ, each human can appropriate for himself that power that is given to us to be a "messiah," that is, a "liberator" each in his own way – that power of destroying "the violent" by the word (the "command of peace") and to have "dominion [over the evil and the violent] from sea to sea." Cain had not heard the OTHER-than-the-violent say to him: "Lord!" In the light of Isaiah's prophecy, we can see the union between the human and the divine take shape: it is in one burst that God "covers the sea" and that the human has dominion over "the violent."

Let us say it again! No justice, even if it were divine, can restore exactly the situation that existed before the violence. From that time, when we portray a God of justice who will punish violence with an equivalent violence, we are fantasizing: in any case, the victim's suffering will always be excessive. Our logic, which is necessarily retributive, finds itself upset by the gospels. There, it is not a question of first seeking divine justice, but of "striving first for the kingdom of God and his righteousness" (Mt 6:33) and thus escaping from the risk of projecting *our* ideas onto divine justice. When Jesus speaks of the kingdom, he seems to be indicating the type of justice that includes both uncontrollable Justice and the human demand for justice – that is, something to implement, as much by God as by us at our level.

It is as though, not wanting to make justice alone, God introduced diversity into his Justice. The human is invited to work so that Justice rules, but exclusively in what I call the "relational of God."[68] One might also hear: "Seek first the relational of God and his justice." It is the relationship that takes precedence: remaining in relationship with God, with the enemy, with oneself, because the relational is always *from God*, however lame it may still be. It is an enormous task: excessive, without limits, as the violence we experience and brewing counter-violence are excessive and without limits. It is a paradoxical power, forever infinite, to implement a justice that we are and will remain incapable of defining on our own, but that we will stubbornly seek together, in the field of the relational, with other subjects of a kingdom whose justice will be defined only by the OTHER alone.

And what if there existed an immediate relationship between the way out of violence and the question of God? Such an immediacy can be seen in the abrupt irruption of the kingdom in many of the parables Jesus told. They use the same type of adverbs – "suddenly, all at once, quickly, as soon as" – and without any transition. All at once, there it is, the unpredictable outcome of the situation that had no way out and that was perpetrating violence on us indefinitely. The "relational of God" has "hit, joined, touched" us, as Jesus said. It happened in the blink of an eye. The experience is lived in immediacy: it puts us in a kind of immediate relationship with God. The outcome was so unthinkable only a few minutes before that we instantly sense behind it the invisible hand of the OTHER. The landscape of faith is changed: and what if the foundational and essential experience of God was the experience of Someone who renders justice to me and rallies me to do justice to another? It would have been necessary to experience the escape from violence as something that was impossible to plan, to have perhaps for the first time the experience of Someone who has control of justice.

Such an immediacy, which others experience as well, prevents us from claiming all responsibility for the victory over violence. The "relational of God" – the kingdom of heaven – is by definition built in diversity and complementarity. It is in the plural that it is "first to be sought," as it is in the plural that the Beatitudes are announced: "Blessed are *those* who hunger and thirst for righteousness, for they will be filled" (Mt 5:6), and "Blessed are *those* who are persecuted for righteousness' [justice's] sake, for theirs is the kingdom of heaven" (Mt 5:10). It is enough to be two for the "relational of the heavens" to increase: a human and one's OTHER form together enough of a plural. That is no doubt why it sufficed for there to be one just person among humans – Noah, seeking divine justice – for the flood not to be the last word on violence. If they were two who wanted it, is it not necessary as well to include God in the Beatitudes? Is not God among those who thirst for justice and those to whom violence has been done because of justice?

On the other hand, as soon as I no longer sense that immediacy of divine justice, I begin to "seek first" and exclusively for it; I lose sight of "the kingdom of God and his justice." By claiming entirely for myself the credit for finding a solution to violence, I sooner or later end up falling back into it. We could say that to do justice alone is only possible when we are engulfed in violence. That is

no doubt why God himself, in Genesis 9, renounced unilateral justice, and therefore also the violence that necessarily flows from it.
It is because there must be an OTHER look if we are not to remain
fascinated only by the evil committed: when I am wounded, I see
only the evil committed by the wounding one. Another person,
less directly involved, can see other things that do not minimize
the violence committed but bring diversity into my single-minded
vision. In the Bible, God lets himself be moved by the prayer of
humans when they plead the cause of their peers: it is because he
desires a plural justice and because he is the first one to seek first
the relational of which he is the inspired inventor, that relational
that is Justice.

In other words, the human will not look fairly at "the violent"
unless God does the same. Job was instructed on divine justice
but that was of no help to him. The only question, for someone
who has undergone the worst kind of violence, is to know if God
is just *for him*. The wanderers and the plunderers hardly matter to
him, although they were largely responsible for his troubles. Being
accused by his community and his friends hardly matters to him,
although they considered him guilty of what had befallen him and
thus cursed by God. His sole quest, from then on, was the relational
with God and his justice. He would not cease to seek justice from
God himself – which rendered him "just" in the eyes of the Jewish
tradition. The secret of his success was to search from both sides
at the same time. He would never give up on Justice – the quest
for God to do justice to him, to look upon him with justice – and
at the same time he will stop doing justice unilaterally himself (by
physical but especially verbal violence, in condemning others).
For Job, fixing a just regard on God meant seeking with Him the
"relational of God and his justice."

In every human, there is a suffering self (a "suffering servant," as
Isaiah said) who longs not to be violent (to others or to himself), nor
to lie (to others or to himself). But in refusing to see my violence,
I lie to myself. In refusing to see the violence that I have experi-
enced, or in underestimating it, I also lie to myself. According to
P. Beauchamp,

*To want to know nothing* of violence is not a side issue nor an addition to human violence, but would rather be the heart of it. All in all, violence lies about itself ... One of the most impressive biblical witnesses of violence – the prophet Jeremiah – is also among those who often use the word "lie" ... There is therefore a need to couple the violence that expresses itself in murder and that which expresses itself against the truth.[69]

That night, the OTHER placed life and death before Jacob: the truth about himself or fratricidal violence. The time was ripe. Jacob now had the means to break the connection between lie and violence. It was the truth about his life that was going to liberate him from the violent impulse. The only issue for Jacob from now on would be to believe in *his* truth, which was made of shadows and light.

Like the Hebrew people from the time of Jeremiah and like many people who had passed through life and not had any particular problems, Jacob had buried his potential for violence, without knowing it, under the glacial peace of his relational life: "They have treated the wound of my people carelessly, saying, 'Peace, peace', when there is no peace" (Jer. 6:14).[70] The OTHER provoked him; Jacob reacted, which left him naked, so to speak, and allowed him for the first time to sense his weak point *in the heart of a relationship* with another. The next day, he would change the way he looked on Esau and on himself, as if he had at last been able to become aware of the victim that had remained silent within him from his youth. This is the awareness Isaiah speaks of in chapters 52 and 53: like Jacob, we remain prisoners of our way of looking at "the violent," as long as our way of looking at the victim does not change. To see in Esau anything other than an intended killer and to see in himself something other than a being forced into counter-violence, Jacob is put in touch with the victim *in himself*: that suffering self that he carried without knowing it, the "suffering servant" which, according to the clear vision of Isaiah, "carried" the evil and the dysfunction of the members of his family.

One could say that for Jacob, the sword had passed in the wrong place: by seeking refuge in a foreign land, he had in fact broken all ties with his own people. But he had also "cut off from the land of the living" (Is 53:8) that suffering self that he had carried into exile: without knowing it, he had removed it from his conscious life, from his living world. All through those years, he had not "taken into consideration" that suffering self, either in himself or in the person of the violent one. His way of looking at Esau, unchanging, made him a killer and nothing else.

In the light of Isaiah's text, we can understand that we interiorize the violence committed by others to the point of practising it ourselves against the suffering self within us, to which we deny the right to speak: "Cut off from the land of the living, stricken for *the transgression* of my people" (v. 8). That was doubtless the situation Jacob found himself in on the eve of his return to his own country: "stricken" by his ancient wound, which continued to "stick to his skin" as long as he "scorned," rejected and "did not take into consideration" the victim he carried within himself.

In the text of Isaiah 11 on wild and domestic animals, it was a question of starting again "from the roots." In a similar way, it is said of the suffering servant that "from the evil of life he will see": a clear vision of himself, others and God is given to him, solely *beginning with his wounds*. To reach our profound truth is the only way, if we believe Isaiah, to become just and to render justice to others. Indeed, the verse unfolds thus: "Out of his anguish he shall see light; he shall find satisfaction through his knowledge. The righteous one, my servant, shall make many righteous ..." (Is. 53:11).

This is to say that the sword will have passed between this human and his fellows: seeing himself in all his truth, he will also be capable of seeing others in all their truth. He will not have emerged from violence by the knowledge of the violence *of others* but by the knowledge of *his violence* and of the violence he has suffered. The heart of justice is this non-lying look. It allows every human, rendered "just," to "treat" others "as just,"[71] to do justice to them by not reducing them to their violence. Only such a look, fixed on them without lying, can encourage them to fix in their turn a just look on themselves, to "take into consideration" their entire being.

# 4   To bring forth blessing

Isaac the meditative wore out the fabric of heaven
by contemplating the stars
without being able to distinguish
the wrath of God from God's munificence ...
Esau is the submission of Isaac bought in exchange for a ram
taken by the horns ... It is to him that Isaac has to transmit the
blessing so he will take over for him in the fear of the Father
...
Jacob is Isaac's challenge, the fire of God against God: provok-
er of lightning, so that it can light up the terrible Face ... It is
Isaac, in his great silence, who weighed heavily on Jacob. The
combat that Isaac refused to engage, Jacob had with God, man
to man! The thick of combat in the night was Isaac's heavy silence. In the silence, God made Jacob see why Jacob had been
able to trick his father. The blessing that God had stolen, with
his own hand God restored to him. I will not let you go, said
Jacob, unless you bless me.[72]

We might think that Jacob carried, without realizing it, the terrible
misgivings about God that the drama of Mount Moriah had instilled
in Isaac when he was a boy: was God really pure benevolence?
Wasn't it necessary to expect the worst from Him, even though *in
extremis* one had been able to escape from Him? We might suppose

that Isaac had remained in the confusion of his past. Under the knife of his father, he had been like the ram that was required for the sacrifice; in the fog of his adult relationships, he had perhaps believed, in blessing the son who was hairy (or dressed in goatskin), that he was exorcising the memory of the ram that had saved his life. But all he had succeeded in doing was to transfer to Jacob the thirst for that blessing that had been forbidden to him from the long-ago time when he had begun to call his God "Terror of Isaac." The trauma is not as great, but history repeats itself: Jacob was not to have the experience of a blessing – one he was entitled to – received from an OTHER and savoured without a second thought.

It was not a question of material or social success. Even with his two wives, his twelve children, his flocks and his entourage, Jacob did not feel blessed. He had blessed himself since, not recognized as being Jacob, he had always had to give to himself what an OTHER – beginning with those close to him – did not give him. In conferring on himself a blessing that his father would never have given him, he tried to silence the voice of his distress and of his anger. This was a painless way of saying "I can manage without you" – and to spare himself the experience of want. But it was the wave of violence, on that night when so many unexpected things happened, that set him the challenge of appropriating for himself not what he conquered through combat, but what had been given to him from all eternity. He is going to ask, equal to equal, and he is going to receive what he had never received because he had taken it by force and thereby reduced it to crumbs. He was not able to appropriate what had been given to him, to make it his own so the blessing would spread around him, until the sword had passed, stripping him of what was not his, what was not him.

What prevents us from feeling blessed? No doubt a long and sad habit: we have always had to fight our own battles. "It's time he took control!" or "That is her problem!" people are fond of saying nowadays. God is truly shown to be powerless to prevent evil and the chaos of violence. Doubt is ingrained in us: why wouldn't he let these things happen again? At worst, he is not pure benevolence. At best, he always arrives after the battle, when the harm has been done. Like many humans, perhaps Jacob had to build his life with an inner conviction that things would always end badly, that to let himself be blessed was the equivalent of deluding himself. It would be better to stay constantly on his guard. Now, on that strange night when everything went against the plan, Jacob let down his guard: he gave in to solitude and even to sleep, according to our hypothesis.

From the distant days of the Hebrew patriarchs, the blessing was both something that one did not deserve and something that no one could quite catch sight of when it came from God. Humans could only observe its fruits, like the way we look back at the past and see how blessed we have been. One knows the tree by its fruits, says Jesus. "Blessing is not in its essence a verbal phenomenon," says A. de Pury. "It is the hidden action of God in humanity and in nature. When God blesses, he can only do it by 'realizing' the blessing."[73] In the Semitic West and the Hebrew Bible, [berakah], blessing, designates the *life force*, the *fullness of life*, the *power of fertility*, *prosperity* — in short, the action of God on behalf of life in the sphere of humans, animals, plants.

At the end of his exile, Jacob was able to observe that he had been blessed but that he had not believed it. Whatever happened that night so that by dawn, in a situation that looked on the outside identical to that of the night before, he almost instantaneously believed he was blessed by God? He came unhinged, emerging from the mould into which he had been poured without the least reaction on his part, as if for the first time in his life he had cried out to God: "Too much! It's too much! Now I will not let go of you, you, my forbidden blessing; you are the one I always wanted, even if I had written you off for twenty years!" Doubtless the OTHER was waiting for that moment: "And *there* [in that place] he blessed him" (Gen 32:29). That is the basic meaning of [shām], an adverb that is rarely used, apparently because it is superfluous.

A very interesting detail, nevertheless, when we remember that the OTHER had touched in Jacob the only place that could make him doubt whether he had been blessed: the hip socket, the symbolic site of his evil and his evil-mindedness. This was the place of his past and thus of his identity, which had an urgent need of blessing. The OTHER came to assure him that he had been made powerful, that he could at last trust himself, for he had what he needed to protect himself from humans and from God. He could observe for himself that he was able to confront his adversary all night long. But a doubt remained: beneath that story of the new name is hidden the name of Jacob-heel-usurper, which functions somewhat like a land mine; Jacob fears that at any moment his former name will catch up with him and blow up in his face.

But everything had been said. To argue would be futile from now on: the OTHER cuts short any "explanations" and "questions" (mentioned three times in one verse). Under [shēm], the new name, is hidden [shām], the place of the wound or lie. There is reason to believe that the worst is beginning again, but that is where Jacob's struggle stops. The OTHER blesses him there. The new name will not do away with the place of the wound, the scars from past violence, but this place will be eternally blessed: in the literal sense of benediction, the OTHER *speaks well* of this place, and as we have seen, to speak well is to do well; Jacob's lameness will no longer be cursed to the point of keeping him in exile from God and his own people; his whole being beaten, he was entirely set beside himself, and now it is entirely with the consequences of his history that he finds himself blessed.

Blessing becomes flesh at inaccessible depths. This is the reason that the Bible places so much importance on dreams, that playing field that the Spirit of life favours, where He can elude our conscious control. It is there, in the most intimate place of our hidden wounds, that our baptismal name glows – any name given by an OTHER, without opposition, in the pure recognition of the fact that we exist. The adversary – or adversity – freed Jacob's combativeness. As long as he was fighting himself, it was night; he did not understand the rhyme or reason. It was only with the dawn that he saw his anger become holy anger: he gave up all notions of God as evil or unjust, of Jacob-heel or usurper; he no longer knows who the OTHER is, or who he himself is. It is at the moment when he stops wondering about his identity and that of the OTHER[74] that he feels blessed.

Here the biblical text is akin to experience. We experience especially blessed encounters when, abandoning all questioning about the worth of the person we are speaking to and our own worth – Am I being hypocritical? Can I really trust him? Do I live up to the image he has of me? etc. – we turn to him to let ourselves be completely invested in the encounter of the moment, without second-guessing ourselves. For Jacob also, blessing becomes flesh when, giving up trying to reassure himself of what Paul Ricoeur calls his "value-identity," he *turns towards the* OTHER. That is, as we have seen, the meaning of Peny'el. As soon as he felt blessed "there," he "called the place 'Peny'el, turn to God!'" This means asking himself whether the place where he had been blessed was the same as the place where he had been wounded: his capacity to face the OTHER.[75] As he cries out the name, in the Hebrew way that gives existence to something that one names, Jacob would recognize the existence of both his woundedness and his power to face it.

We experience blessing when, having given up exploring our name and that of the other – for they conceal an inexhaustible reality – we at last name our unnamed place, beyond the reach of any blessing. It does us good for people to speak well of us. And it suits the OTHER when *we* are finally able to speak well of ourselves, acting with full knowledge, with our wounded part and our capacity to wound turned towards Him. The dawn thus dispelled Jacob's final doubts about God's benevolence. He will never know to what extent God is impotent to prevent injustice, nor to what extent God deliberately allows injustice to happen. It is the blessing itself that invalidates his need to know the OTHER so as to stop doubting him. By analogy, we may come to receive a sign of friendship from someone that instantly demolishes the endless questions in which we had lost ourselves, regarding the value and authenticity of the relationship.

Holy anger hopes for blessing: "I will not let you go unless you bless me," unless I am sure that you will take me as I was and as I am, and unless I can go on my way without having to be on the lookout all the time, without having to hide (from myself) a big part of who I am. We have seen how obstinate Job remained in this regard, stubbornly claiming that God should restore what Job thought was only just. Jacob had been successful enough in his adopted country that the flame of his combativeness was dangerously low. The Adversary – in the guise of Jacob's adversary, Laban – was nevertheless watching for Jacob never to overshadow that demand for justice-for-himself that he experienced as a divine blessing. As Calvin wrote:

> If Laban had treated him kindly and pleasantly, his mind would have been lulled to sleep ... So the Lord often better secures the salvation of his people, by subjecting them to the hatred, the envy, and the malevolence of the wicked, than by suffering them to be soothed with bland address. It was far more useful to holy Jacob to have his father-in-law and his sons opposed ... because their favour might have deprived him of the blessing of God ... This passage [v. 27] teaches us always to expect the blessing of God, although we may have experienced his presence to be harsh and grievous, even to the disjointing of our members. For it is far better for the sons of God to be blessed, though mutilated and half destroyed, than to desire that peace in which they shall fall asleep.[76]

Rereading the whole story of Jacob, we have the impression that even before his birth[77] he benefited from that particular combativeness that allows many people who got off to a bad start in life to stay alive, to take their place in the sun, and finally to see themselves as being blessed, for they have been formed to take hold of their destiny. That sheds new light on the notion of election: we do not become one of the elect as opposed to others who are not of that number. If every human being is of the elect, by their vocation to "serve *adamah*" – the fragile dust of his origins, yet animated by the breath of God – each has, however, to fight to make this election their own.

It is as if Jacob, after so many years of spiritual lethargy, was no longer content with the "collective" promises he inherited from his ancestors: so long as you have not blessed me, *me* with my whole history and personality – me and not a link in the chain that transmits religious beliefs from one generation to the next – your blessing will go unheeded as it remained unheeded in the life of my father, Isaac. "Judaism considers that it is not enough for God to have said something for it to be done," notes A. Abécassis. "The human must have the *memory* and the *consciousness* of it. The human *also* must take on the promise; he has harvested the prediction; he must also be at the rendezvous, with the same level of conscious- ness, to harvest its realization."[78]

The Jewish and Christian commentators agree in recognizing that the blessing extorted from Isaac was indeed of God, which goes to prove once again the truth of the proverb "God writes straight with crooked lines." But what robbed Jacob of the feeling of being truly blessed was his chronic injunction to count on no one but himself. Paradoxically, he could not take for himself the blessing that God had destined for him since all eternity, *because he, Jacob, had believed he could obtain it through his own efforts.* During the combat, he is freed of the compulsion to bless himself: an OTHER "seeks" him, in an unstoppable encounter that bares all his areas of inauthenticity. It happens as well that the adversary breaks up the borrowed blessing that takes the place of identity in us. The Adversary has better things to offer us. It is a question for us of being liberated once and for all of the feeling of usurping the place that we occupy in society and the good reputation we enjoy. For W. Dietrich, we must read the whole cycle of Jacob as a struggle for blessing. For a Jewish legend explains it thus, turning the assailant into the archangel Michael:

> Now, tell me if you recognize the father's blessing as my own, or will this usurped blessing always remain among my faults? Michael responds: "I recognize it as yours and as righteous; by deceit and trickery you failed to receive it; I and the heavenly powers recognize it as worthy, for you revealed yourself as the master of the heavenly powers just as you revealed yourself as the master of the power of Esau and his legions."[79]

The sign that the blessing belongs solely to us is the reflex that it instantly causes us to turn towards the OTHER, human and divine. We stop using that OTHER to strengthen our borrowed blessing. Others may oppose us and give us nothing but disappointment, but our feeling of having the blessing of God in order to live as we are remains intact. Confrontations with others become occasions for verifying the solidity of our experience of blessing. Our combativeness confronts our insatiable will to be blessed in that which we profoundly are ... and it is thus that our blessing becomes flesh over the long term. That is why we can say that the human experience of blessing takes root in the anger that progressively makes us reject all that is not strictly our name, a name given to call upon, and be called upon by, a clearly differentiated OTHER.

There is the blossoming of an experience of blessing and there is the period of integrating it. It takes time to own the idea that we are completely blessed in our deepest being, in all that we still carry of the painful and the dysfunctional, and that being blessed *even "there,"* we can legitimately persist in wanting such a blessing at every moment. No human has ever come closer to the secret of blessing. Jacob immediately communicated to his people the way to access an experience that by definition cannot remain esoteric. Right away, *Peny'el* is changed to *Penu'el*: turn [yourself] towards the OTHER becomes turn [yourselves] towards the OTHER. But the new order will continue to be valid for Jacob: confronted the next day with Esau, he will avoid speaking of his nocturnal experience of blessing, perhaps so as not to reawaken an old resentment in Esau,[80] but also because he needs time to appropriate what has happened to him.

In the same sense, one can note the etymology given by S.R. Driver[81] for "Israel": if the verbal root [sarah] is the Hebrew equivalent of the Arab [sariya], it should mean "persist" or "persevere." The rest of the story shows Jacob still anxious about his brother's good faith, as if he were being asked to persist in believing, regardless of what happens, that the blessing will forever remain on him. G. von Rad suggests, in a similar vein, that the biblical authors themselves needed time to integrate the name of the blessing of Jacob:

"It is true that the change of name itself remains curiously isolated; the stories that follow seem to ignore it."[82] Elie Wiesel notes as well that it will be difficult for Israel to remain Israel: "What if all this was only a dream? He seems melancholy but determined. He may have to fight. And kill. And die. But he is no longer alone."[83]

---

A blessing is a birth, and makes it possible to give birth to blessing. It is not insignificant that the Hebrew Bible speaks of it in terms of genealogy. Like a child, a blessing is at once that which is given and that which one makes wholly one's own: it is greater than oneself, indefinitely, as infinite as the sands of the sea. The modern expression "to make a baby" says much about a society that believes that by and large we can count only on ourselves. If we do not experience the child as one hundred per cent *given*, that it comes from Elsewhere and returns thereto, like the messenger of a Love that is pure blessing, we do not receive the child as a blessing meant for us, and run the risk of being unable to welcome the child fully as he or she is. The child is thus only a blessing for the person who receives the child as a blessing. It is more than a question of physically giving birth; the human gives birth to the blessing that comes from Elsewhere. But we can say that God is the alpha and omega of the whole experience: in retrospect, we see clearly that everything is gift and that there is more, infinitely.

When it comes to blessing, God has the first word: he and he alone has given us that astonishing law of Life that permits an opposing force, even actual violence, to be turned into blessing. The more the alchemy of such a transformation escapes us, the more it is of God. But it is up to us to own and allow to ripen that anger of life that destabilizes us and that we don't know what to do with: He knows. In the second place, God and God alone has initiated that non-violent violence of the gospels that will always remain as unpredictable in its outpouring as in its effects. Spontaneously, we have no other model of eradicating violence than to seek out and eliminate someone who is guilty ... and nothing more. It is here that the gospels show, according to René Girard, the necessity, linked to what we are by our nature, of suppressing violence by means of violence. But the gospels speak of a God who treats violence another way, because, being OTHER, he *begins by blessing.*

> The violence of the cultural order is revealed in the Gospels … and the cultural order cannot survive such a revelation. Once the basic mechanism is revealed, the scapegoat mechanism, that expulsion of violence by violence, is rendered useless by the revelation … The good news is that scapegoats can no longer save men, the persecutors' accounts of their persecutions are no longer valid, and truth shines into dark places. Got is not violent, the true God has nothing to do with violence … Those who do not see it remain in Satan's universe, on the level of the immediate reading, believing that there exists a divine violence, the rival of Satan's violence, and remaining prisoners of the persecution mentality.[84]

It is God, in the end, who initiates, from one end of the Bible to the other, this "breakthrough economy" or this "overflowing of the kingdom" that no one can plan. According to J. Eisenberg and A. Abécassis, there are two types of economy in the Bible: natural progression and the breaking through of limits that is the economy of blessing. It is said of Isaac that "he harvested a hundred times more than he sowed … It is the abundance and the good distribution of the rain from heaven – in both the literal and figurative senses – that transforms a planned economy into a breakthrough economy." The authors see in Jacob's refusal to receive a salary from Laban (Gen 30:31) his desire to "situate himself in a breakthrough economy in which he wants to participate in blessing." They then cite this luminous affirmation from the Talmud: "There is no blessing for that which is weighed, counted, measured."[85]

At a time when everyone is encouraged to "manage" everything – including their emotions and even their spontaneity! – there is food for thought there. It is up to us to know if we want to set a limit on the fantasy of control that we exercise in our lives, with the violence that it entails. The OTHER waits for the signal to pronounce the first word of a blessing that right away puts us in the realm of abundance, of "all things given in surplus," which is that of the gospels, which flows directly from the ancestral blessing.

When it comes to blessing, God also has the last word. Whatever crooked lines we follow along the path of our life, God's blessing ends up writing straight, as long as we go to the end of our angers, our rebellions, our questions. If the last word does not belong to us, it is because we do not know how much our wandering and our division deprive us of tasting blessing. Jacob's journey has much to teach us about this. A. de Pury notes that, for the early tradition, Jacob had been astute enough to trick his father and seize the blessing with God's help. The listeners, however, feared that his fraud would imperil the blessing – the danger coming from outside, from the hostility of Esau, of Laban, of the assailant at the Jabbok. The Yahwist narrator (to whom we owe the present text) explains the story a bit differently: it is the frauds of Jacob – let us say, his roundabout ways, his dysfunctionalities, his inauthenticity – that cause him to wander far from that blessing that God intends for him. His division with the God of truth (his sin) destroys in him the effect of the blessing. But the *credo* of the narrator is that the divine will to bless has the last word.

Indeed, at the Jabbok, we see God himself calling the blessing into question: "The problem that the Yahwist poses is thus no longer that of knowing how Jacob will succeed in preserving the blessing in the face of Esau's vengeance and Laban's covetousness, but to know if [the LORD] will decide, in his sovereignty, to make a blessing that is tainted from the start."[86] In the course of his flight and his exile, Jacob saw himself by turns confirmed in his blessing and threatened with annihilation. It is finally in the assault at Penu'el that the blessing is given and received without further objections. A. de Pury highlights once again the link between conflict and blessing:

> When Jacob is in conflict with his next of kin, the realization of the blessing is suspended, and it is only when he reconciles with his adversary that the blessing unfolds again ... If Israel watches for the establishment of that peace and intercedes for the nations, then the blessing that it received from [the LORD] will be realized not only for Israel but also for all the nations of the earth.[87]

Thus the blessing comes to crown the human process of unification. There is no blessing for anyone who remains divided from the OTHER, human and divine; at the same time, there is no blessing – or inferior version thereof – for anyone who has not found inner unity. We understand that Jacob has been blessed when, at Genesis 33:18, he is seen arriving at Shechem "whole" and "at peace"; such is the double sense of [shālēm][88] that the Midrash comments on, giving preference to the "wholeness" of Jacob. This commentary is summarized by Rashi as follows: "Unimpaired in body (health) because he was cured of his lameness;[89] whole as regards his possessions for he was not short of anything even though he had given that gift; and perfect in his knowledge of the Torah for while he was in Laban's house he had not forgotten what he had learned."[90] Once and for all, in spite of losses, consequences and disabilities incurred, we can feel deliciously "whole" because we are enveloped in benevolence, blessed in even the darkest corners of our being. That regard perfects in us, beyond our wildest dreams, the feeling of our election. An OTHER has chosen to give us life; he can give it to us in abundance from the moment when, ceasing to live as spare parts, we become real partners for him, whole and full members. Commenting on the conflict between Jacob and Esau from their mother's womb, Origen believed he could "say also of us as individuals, that 'two nations and two peoples are within you.'"[91] To say that our entire being is elect amounts to saying that our shadow side is also blessed. Knowing this encourages us to follow the path of our unification. As C. Vigée writes,

> To hold onto our hope, let us recall that Esau, walking towards death, is the twin of Jacob on whom rests the divine election. In Jacob is outlined the shadow of Esau; but in the soul of Esau sprouts the redemptive seed of Jacob his brother … That these twins, for so long enemies, should at last reconcile with each other, that they become once again one spirit, like Abraham, their ancestor, was one before the Eternal.[92]

Where we still question the unconditional Benevolence, we can be sure that we have not yet finished with anger. When we have exhausted anger, we observe that we have exhausted the fear aroused by the OTHER, both human and divine. We see well, then, that we have been "rendered powerful," like Jacob. Inner sabotage comes from the doubt that lurks in us regarding our capacity to face up to things anew: we still have to appropriate for ourselves what is given to us – that blessing on *our* power. God thereby effects the healing of our usual pattern – evil equals divine anger; divine anger equals the risk of death – from which our own anger has been banished. With a sure hand, the OTHER will continue to provoke our anger of life in order to make us get out of the pattern, even if it means being taken for Someone who curses. "The curse," says M.-D. Molinié, "is the same face as the blessing for anyone who refuses it … God's love [we would say, God's blessing] never gives up – and that same obstinacy, according to *our* manner of welcoming it, takes the face of anger or of mercy."[93]

The time of blessing is that time of great clarity when it is clear to us that there has never been the least curse from God, even if, in the violence of our combats, we were convinced that there was. In an ordinary way of speaking, misfortune hounded us; others could always "get out of it," but not us; "it" always caught us; we had to make it on our own, etc. Even if the Yahwist narrator presents Jacob in the situation of someone who has been cursed, A. de Pury recognizes that no curse has been retained, and that is in line with the rest of Genesis, which replaces the curse of nomadism (a form of excommunication away from the clan, with the sterilization of the women and the fields) by such a divine concern for the exiled humans that the curse virtually disappears.[94] From there to thinking that *we* project onto the events of our history a divine curse that hides our own anger is only one step away from freeing ourselves without delay from the moment we experience the blessing.

In the end, God has the last word in that he perfects in us the capacity to give what we no longer doubt ourselves to have fully received. The humans who give their lives are those who know that they have received life in abundance. We let go of our children, our dear ones, our friends when, having no further accounts to pay, we were able to receive them from God as gifts that nothing can ever take away from us: neither separation nor even death. Our blessing – the one that we taste – communicates itself to them as if we had been chosen to offer, in the midst of so many who are in search of blessing, living proof that the outcome of violence and conflict is to be found in relationships with the human and divine OTHER. Thus, "for the first time in Genesis 31, God's blessing to Jacob is spoken in the light of day, to everyone." Each person submits to another without losing face, and therefore, in fact, each submits to God. "The solution for the conflict becomes realistic, attainable, like another aspect of the blessing."[95]

---

When it comes to blessing, humans do not receive passively what is given to them: it is through a bitter struggle that Jacob makes his own what God had always wanted to give him. "What God wanted, was for Jacob to claim his blessing," notes J.-M. Tézé. "And that desire could not encounter any resistance before him."[96] It was the same for Job, who sought only in the heart of his relationship with this All-OTHER, whom he no longer understands, the outcome of an anger of life that he ended up realizing was also his own. Job also is "made powerful," to the point of hearing God answer him – a non-violent omnipotence that God offers untiringly to each human. "When heaven loves a sinner [a being cut off from God] more than 99 righteous ones, the sinner does not know it at first; on the contrary, he only feels the anger of Heaven, until at last he forces It, as it were, to talk."[97]

The child is given but childbirth is to be lived. That is why we can speak, beginning with the account of the night at the Jabbok, of the human way of giving birth to blessing. The Targum sets us on the path. It includes a very interesting variant at v. 30: "And *Jacob* blessed him there."[98] The Hebrew text does not forbid this, for the "he" is no more precise than in the preceding verses. It is written in a note that the addition of "Jacob" is perhaps a commentary that was left in the text, but that the tradition of a blessing of the angel by Jacob seems to be otherwise known. It is therefore not unthinkable to maintain an ambivalent meaning. In the same moment that the OTHER blesses Jacob, in the same breath Jacob blesses that OTHER who no longer provokes neither fear nor anger in him! Having exhausted all fear and all anger, he benefits from

unconditional Benevolence and, at the same time, from his own
capacity to welcome the OTHER unconditionally. Let us note that
according to the second meaning of [shām], one can translate this
as "he *therefore* blessed him." The richness of the Hebrew language
means we do not have to choose between this kind of interpretation and the one we developed above: there is no incompatibility,
no more than there is in our experience.

"Accept my gift," Jacob will later say to Esau (Gen. 33:11). The
word used for "gift" is [berakah], blessing, which may mean both.
In the five preceding occurrences, another word, [mine*h*ah], had
been used. It is as though Jacob was saying to his brother: "Accept
my blessing!" The sign that Jacob now feels blessed is visible in his
capacity to bless others, and not only the OTHER – including those
with whom he had been in conflict that could not be resolved. We
could say that the formerly usurped blessing now comes back to
Esau. It is completed by these words: "May your mother's sons bow
down to you! Cursed be everyone who curses you, and blessed be
everyone who blesses you!" (Gen. 27:29). It is Jacob who will bow
down before Esau (33:3), and it is Jacob who blesses his brother
because he knows himself to be blessed. We cannot express the
biblical outcome for every conflict any better: a blessing on everyone, inexhaustible ...

Does there exist anywhere else in the Bible such an explicit story
where blessing, lived as a truly mystical experience – "I have seen
God face to face," exclaims Jacob – follows immediately after anger, violence, desperate struggle? I don't think so. We see that holy
violence does exist and that God desires it for us: it prepares us to
receive blessing and to live the contemplative experience. If that
were better known, we would perhaps see mystical experience being
available to many more humans than just a few privileged ones. In
any case, anger would be welcomed with greater benevolence, as
that which God wants it to be: an extraordinary path of life.

# Conclusion

The fruits of the union between human anger and divine anger are endless. That is because it is a question of a shared struggle for holiness. We have seen that holy anger gives human beings access to their "tough core," the indestructible seed of Life within. There is something deep inside that resists, and that something is related to holy God – to the Differentiated One, the One who forever remains above all confusion. Any reflection on holiness can only be renewed by considering the theme of anger. The Bible keeps repeating it: the initiative is God's. Anger is first, even for God. It is of a piece with the reality of differentiation. It is the "Holy One of Israel" – because he claims to be wholly OTHER than poor humans, lost in their miseries – who first renounces anger and offers himself in a real encounter, towards and against all. His anger highlights his "stability" towards humans: constancy and friendship, the same word in Hebrew, as we have called to mind from the beginning of this book.

> "The Holy One of Israel is your Redeemer [= Liberator] ... In overflowing wrath for a moment I hid my face from you, but with everlasting love (friendship, constancy) I will have compassion on you, says the Lord, your Redeemer [= Liberator] ... I have sworn that I will not be angry with you and will not rebuke

you … My steadfast love (friendship, constancy) shall not depart from you, says the Lord who has compassion on you." (Is. 54:5b, 8, 9B, 10b NRSV)

We humans have great difficulty in believing that anger can produce anything good. The idea that it can point the way to our sanctification is frankly "against nature." To be able to believe this, it must be revealed to us: that is, we must experience it. There again, the writings of the prophets help us move forward: the prophet Hosea tells us explicitly why God renounces his anger; it is because he is *holy*, apart, differentiated … but not just anywhere:

> "My heart recoils within me;[99] my compassion grows warm and tender. I will not execute my fierce anger; I will not again destroy Ephraim; for I am God and no mortal, *the Holy One in your midst*, and I will not come in wrath." (Hos. 11:8b, 9)

This is fascinating: God declares himself to be holy, and is recognized as holy, only when his holiness is liberated from his terrifying aspect, and is able to be perceived in the most intimate of human spiritual experience – at a gut level.

Many are the passages, especially in the Hebrew Bible, where the manifestations of divine holiness plunge humans into great dread.[100] On the other hand, the witness of Hosea lets us discover the presence of the Differentiated One (forever above all confusion) at the very site of the symbol that most powerfully speaks of union – the breast, the womb, the guts! This means that God can stay in the most intimate closeness without threatening to swamp us in the violence of His power of life and differentiation. Such an experience gives us a guarantee that he will not destroy us: since he has chosen to dwell there, it means destroying himself. If humans renounced anger, they would end up leaving Him to choose to reside in that place of great confusion. It is never a question of renouncing our anger, but of going through it without attributing it to the Differentiated One who has already come back from his anger.

We are invited to go to that point, to the point of that genuine con-version: as long as we cling to suspicion, still slightly dreading the anger of the wrathful God, we are not quite ready to have the

experience of Hosea. The Holy God is either total and unconditional benevolence or he is not: if he is not, then to our eyes he
is still angry, in the process of differentiation. The day when he
is "holy within our guts" – when he is "God and not a human,"
for we have accepted to be only humans, limited, lacking holiness
and life – on that day we see that we have stopped projecting on
him the violence of our attempts at differentiation. The time has
come to know the holy "I am" that gives birth in us to nothing
but blessing.

Job went to that point: according to J. Lévêque, "Job could have
opted for approval or for permanent rebellion ... He could have
converted from the aggressive god that he made in his own image, to the God who is, who was, and who came for him in the
storm."[101] But it is striking that Job does not disown the violence
of his intention, nor does God reproach him for it. In fact, Job
begins by declaring, "I reject/I refuse [with no direct object] and
I am consoled in dust and ashes" (42:6). That has the ring of the
ultimate self-affirmation: I reject all that is not strictly of my living
self, based *on my life in dust*, so I also reject anger, to receive my
consolation – the passive voice implying, in biblical language, God:
I am consoled by God ...[102]

In the next verse God's response runs into the words spoken to
Eliphaz, one of Job's friends: "My wrath is kindled against you and
against your two friends; for you have not spoken of me what is
right, as my servant Job has" (42:7). The friends, having appropriated
God, have not spoken of him as the Differentiated One. Having
merged with Him, they have left their own counter-violence intact.
As always, it is God who is going to make a sword pass between
them and him, whereas Israel is going to see in Job a "servant of
God" and the early Church will see him as the Christ!

---

The suspicion remains in the biblical texts, nevertheless, that divine
anger will eventually return: the New Testament actually ends with
an Apocalypse shot through with violence. What we call Anger,
largely by anthropomorphism, is the unceasing work of differentia-

tion by which God locates and holds back the living being from what kills the living being. The greatest divine resistance has to train against the worst of confusions, that which makes us take the place of God. The Holy One who resides within our depths has to wage a daily battle, more or less violent, against our descent into confusion with Him. For Y. Ledure, this stems from our resemblance to God, which is affirmed all the way from Genesis to the Gospels:

> Similarity does not reduce differences; on the contrary, it creates the irreducible gap between God and humans … In a reversal of Genesis, which affirms a similarity, a resemblance, the evangelical discourse offers a similarity of difference … A burst-open image, an ef-faced copy, man no longer knows who he is … Only a similarity of difference will let him find his own ground once again: there he will be able to celebrate his God. For God is the difference of man; he affirms the difference in man.[103]

… in his guts, according to Hosea.

But "Who warned you to flee from the wrath to come?" shouts John the Baptist (Matt. 3:7) in a gospel that does not hesitate to evoke the tears and gnashing of teeth that are inseparable from the coming of the Kingdom in the last days. And Luke in vain reports the first preaching of Jesus, in Nazareth, by having him find fault with his quotation from Isaiah – the proclamation of a divine welcome and a total liberation, without the "day of vengeance" that accompanies it (Lk. 4:7ff.). However much we learn from E. Jacob that if the "Day of the Lord" that is expected in the Hebrew Bible was a day of anger simply because divine anger was a way of expressing the formidable power of holiness, it remains that the fear of his anger can easily overtake us. In other words, how can we be through with the threatening God? Hasn't the life of Christ put an end to "the anger to come"? Didn't he himself declare that John the Baptist, the "greatest" of humans born of a woman, had nevertheless been surpassed by "the least in the Kingdom of heaven" (Matt. 11:11)? And did he not indicate the reason for this, in the following verse? "From the days of John the Baptist until now the kingdom of heaven has suffered violence, and the violent take it by force" – as if divine anger was henceforth at the disposition of humans: "great" is the human who resists, who faces the OTHER, who affirms himself in the manner of God and not by exorcising his fear by calling upon vengeance. Once again, it is Nietzsche the rebel who puts us on the right track:

> Obviously, the little community had not understood what was precisely the most important thing of all: the example offered by this way of dying, the freedom from and superiority to every feeling of *ressentiment* ... On the contrary, it was precisely the most unevangelical of feelings, *revenge,* that now possessed them. It seemed impossible that the cause should perish with his death: "recompense" and "judgment" became necessary (– yet what could be less evangelical than "recompense," "punishment," and "sitting in judgment"!).[104]

Perhaps we shall have finished with the threatening God when, following Christ, we will have gone to the end of our own counter-anger ... and no longer let ourselves be deformed and forced to conform by the malevolence of others. When we stop wishing others ill, and indirectly wishing God ill, as he lets others get away with it, we perceive that, really, God does not wish us any harm at all. But to have worked through our personal anger presupposes the awareness of having unjustly "carried," like Isaiah's suffering servant to whom Job is often compared, burdens that do not belong to us. And this goes through belief in the free anger of God: "I was at ease, and he *broke* me in two" (Job 16:12). Job will understand later that in *breaking* him, God was persisting in *breaking* all the consequences of the violent acts he had undergone and that were like a prison for him. Indeed, in the only two other biblical passages where this verb is used, we see God *break* the powers of evil.[105] It is a question of one, and only one, divine "anger" at work to save the living from destructive confusion.

The fear of the wrathful God is transformed into that "fear of the Lord" that seems to be the prerogative of the "little ones." Our text of Isaiah 11 evoked this fruitful path whose starting point is "from the roots." The "Spirit of the Lord" that rests on us from childhood and that we find again when we start afresh from our roots is a "Spirit of wisdom and understanding, ... of counsel and might, ... of knowledge and fear of the Lord" (vv. 2, 3). We see clearly from this that all fear has disappeared, to the advantage of an experience, of a *knowledge*, by the encounter with the OTHER: we *discern* what is of him and of us, we receive *wisdom* and *might* from him, we take *counsel* from him ... and we respect him as that perfectly differentiated OTHER that we refuse to incorporate into ourselves. The Hebrew word [ir'at] means both fear and respect: it is the breath of God, and therefore an intimate experience recalling the expression "in your depths I am holy," which according to Isaiah makes us "feel the fear or respect of the Lord" – of the Holy One, the perfectly differentiated. According to Mark the Ascete, no power, no force is to be dreaded any longer: he is saved from the anger to come. "He who has come to know the truth does not oppose the afflictions that befall him, for he knows that they lead him to the fear of God."[106] If the "fear of the Lord" continues to evoke for us something of a threat of the unknown that is his Difference, this can be beneficial: it is yet another reason to opt resolutely, at all times, for an unconditionally Benevolent God.

---

In the first letter of John we find the following affirmation: "There is no fear in love, but perfect (fully realized) love casts out fear; for fear has to do with punishment, and whoever fears has not reached perfection in love" (4:18). The perfection or accomplishment of love in us does not happen without violence: "to cast out fear" refers to the anger of life, to holy violence and to the violent ones who are tearing down the Kingdom. Perfect love in us, and only that, casts out the fear that prevents us from living perfect love. However, the first sense of [kolasis] is not punishment, but, very concretely, pruning or trimming. As long as we are afraid, we experience a pruning. We still have something to lose. We will be more fully ourselves if we allow ourselves to be relieved of it.

We usually say that "fear presupposes or implies punishment": it carries punishment within itself, and for this reason is a kind of pruning that we see as a punishment. We behave as if we were guilty when we face the person we fear, not daring to be ourselves. But it is not a question of being pruned of who we *are*. It is a matter of getting rid of what prevents us from "fulfilling ourselves in love." It is not a step towards impassivity nor towards self-sufficiency. To be "perfected in love" is to have nothing left to cut away, to be constantly ready to "cast out fear" anew, if necessary without imagining that we can do it alone. It is perfect Love that does this in our "guts" to render us perfect (fully realized) in Love.

To call to mind this link between anger and love, we can look at what Elie Wiesel relates of Rabbi Baroukh de Medzebozh, the grandson of Besht, who "introduced anger into Hasidism." Gifted with an intense inner life, "perhaps too enflamed," he preferred challenge and continual calling into question to a quiet and respectable existence. "He rebelled, rising up without knowing what he rebelled against." One day, "He indicated a passage in the Book of the Zohar that mentions a remarkable anger, blessed from on high and from below, and which is called: Baroukh.[107] And, strange to say, at his bedside, when he died, was found the Zohar open to this very passage." If his grandfather was approaching God by means of love, he wanted perhaps to "go farther and clear an almost unknown path: that of rage. It is possible that he suddenly understand that love alone – in a world without love, shaken by violence, invaded by enemies – would not be enough to ensure the survival of his people … Whence his sadness and his despondency: how not to despair of a world where anger is necessary for its redemption?"

Rabbi Baroukh died in 1811, possibly leaving us as a key to his enigma his passion for the Song of Songs, the song of sublime and tragic love between God and Israel, that couple that was definitely separated, torn but criss-crossed by an ever-present love, from one uprooting or stripping to another. Rabbi Baroukh teaches, according to Wiesel, that

> … anger and love are compatible, provided that they are mo-
> tivated by friendship for Israel and humanity … He was angry
> because something touched him, personally, directly; because
> the destiny of others engaged his, and because he stayed close to
> those who suffered, who were in agony, who were begging for
> certainty, an answer, a crumb of consolation, of faith … "I know
> that it is possible to find the injustice in Creation," he said. I also

know that we have only too many reasons to allow our anger to burst forth. And yes, I know why you are angry. What do I have to say to you? Let's go ahead; let's be angry. Together."[108]

For Christians, the commandment to love that is at the heart of the New Testament and that comes to us straight from the Jewish Scriptures presupposes a passage through violence.[109] The *One* Lord to whom we are invited to attach ourselves had to eliminate all that was not of Him, to uproot his people from that Egypt that was alienating them, to have them emerge from the confusion of the desert and its mirages. The people – and each of us – will love this other ONE which gives them the means to become ONE, body, psyche, spirit and mind, wholly as one before Him. And what Jesus calls the second commandment, which is like the first, "to love one's neighbour as oneself," is the outcome of Leviticus 19:17, which asks us to *first* "reproach" the other so that we "do not hold anger" towards him and do not "hate" him. However, to reproach someone does not occur without a passage through the pain of the wound, keeping our distance, opposition, resistance, differentiation. That is why an even deeper reflection on Love – and on the human process of sanctification that leads towards perfect Love – could not, in my opinion, happen without the passage through anger.

When I see Jacob, on the far bank of the Jabbok, limping beside Esau, he seems to me to be hearing the words of Jesus: "It is better for you to enter life maimed or lame than to have two hands or two feet and to be thrown into the eternal fire" (Mt 18:8). The quest of the "relational of God and his justice," the quest for perfect Love, can only be undertaken haltingly, carrying the marks of violence and counter-violence, but walking towards perfection, the fulfillment of perfect Love at the most intimate level of body and spirit. In C. Vigée's words,

> The hesitant limping of Jacob, apparently a sign of a lack, of an imperfection ... an endless quest ... of unattainable fullness, the mad conquest of the perfection to come. The limping of Jacob, arising freely from the struggle with the angel at the ford of judgment, is like the dance of pain linked to the unprecedented

begetting of the "son of man," which completes the imperfect creation of the first Adam by bringing it to a close.[110]

According to John the Evangelist, Jesus promised humans "perfect joy in this world." But he did not promise perfect love in this world. He thought it possible that his joy was "in us and that it would be completed in us" without urging us to it. But he did not say this about love, to which he invites us. It is up to us to come ever closer to perfect Love as we travel the rocky road of human life – the road where love lives, of necessity, through the wounding and anger of differentiation. This is perhaps the deepest paradox of the Gospel: we do not progress towards perfect Love without limping.

# Appendix

## Genesis 4:1-16*

1.  And the man of the earth knew Eve, his wife, and she became pregnant and she gave birth to Cain.

    And she said, "I have produced/gained a man with the Lord."

2.  And she gave birth again [literally, she added to give birth] his brother Abel.

    And here was Abel, a herder of small livestock. Cain was a servant of the earth.

3.  And, in time, Cain brought fruit from the earth as an offering to the Lord.

4.  And Abel brought, he too, newborns from his small livestock and their fat.

    The Lord turned his eyes towards Abel and towards his offering.

5.  Towards Cain and towards his offering he did not turn his eyes.

    It burned Cain badly, and his countenance fell.

6.  The Lord said to Cain:
    "Why did this burn you and why has your countenance fallen?"

7.  Is it not [true] that if you do well [it is] to raise it,
    and if you do not do well,
    at your door sin lurks and its impulse towards you, and you must master it!"

8.  And Cain said to Abel, his brother ...

    and then, when they were in the field,
    Cain rose up against Abel his brother and killed him.

9.  The Lord said to Cain,
    "Where [is] Abel your brother?"

    And he said: "I do not know. Am I my brother's keeper?"

10. He said: "What have you done?  The voice of blood [literally: of bloods] of your brother  [is] crying out to me from the earth ...

11. And now you are cursed more than the earth that has opened its mouth to receive from your hand your brother's blood.

12. Yes, you serve the earth: it does not give its strength for you, you are unsettled and without a home on the earth."

13. Cain said to the Lord: "My fault/punishment is too heavy to bear.

14. Here, today you have chased me from the [sur]face of the earth and from your face I am/will be hidden, unsettled and without a home on the earth. Whoever meets me will kill me."

15. The Lord said to him: "Then whoever kills Cain will fall seven times under vengeance."

    And the Lord put a mark on Cain, so that whoever met him would not strike him.

16. Cain left the face of the Lord and lived in the land of Nod to the east of Eden.

\* *translated by Lytta Basset*

268

# Notes

## Introduction

(Where English versions of quoted material were not available, quotations were translated by the translators of this book.)

1 Cf. S. Terrien, *Job: Poet of Existence* (Indianapolis/New York: The Bobbs-Merrill Company, 1957), 29, 128.

2 L. Beirnaert, *Aux frontières de l'acte analytique: la Bible, saint Ignace, Freud et Lacan* (Paris: Seuil, 1987), 30.

3 St. Augustine, *Confessions*, VII, 3, trans. R.S. Pine-Coffin (Penguin, 1961), 136–137.

4 P. Ricoeur, *Finitude et culpabilité* (Paris: Aubier/Montaigne, 1960), 302ff. Translated into English in two parts, as *Fallible Man*, trans. Charles L, Kelbley (New York: Fordham University Press, 1986) and *The Symbolism of Evil*, trans. Emerson Buchanan (Boston: Beacon Press, 1969).

5 Translator's note: Unless otherwise indicated, citations from the Bible use the New Revised Standard Version. Occasionally the author cites a specific French translation (e.g. the Traduction œcuménique de la Bible [TOB], André Chouraqui, etc.) or translates a passage herself in order to make a point about the wording of the original; in those cases and where the citation differs from the NRSV in significant ways, I have translated from the version used in the French edition.

6 The root of the verb is not the same as in 1:40. Here it is [sullupeô], which contains the suffix [sun], "with," and which means "being afflicted with" or "having compassion for."

7 Plutarch, *De cohibenda ira* in *Moralia* VII, pt. I, trans. as *On the control of anger*, trans. Harold Frederik Cherniss, 2 vols. (Cambridge, MA: Harvard University Press, 1976).

8 Ibid., 38–39.

9 C. Vigée, *Dans le silence de l'Aleph. Écriture et Révélation* (Paris: Albin Michel, 1992), 25.

## Part I

1   E. Wiesel, *Messengers of God: Biblical Portraits and Legends* (New York: Random House, 1976), 60, 63.

2   The author's translation of Genesis 4:1-16 may be found in the appendix. This is one of the most ancient texts in the Bible, possibly from the kingly period (8th or 7th century BCE).

3   Other expressions are: blowing violently, heat/being hot, bursting, overflowing.

4   Heat [*hemah*] is said 90 times of God and 25 times of human beings; fury ['evrah] 24 times of God and six times of humans; rage [qesef] 26 times of God and only twice of humans. Cf. E. Jacob, *Théologie de l'Ancien Testament* (Neuchâtel: Delachaux et Niestlé, 1968), 91.

5   "And his countenance fell," says the Targum *Jonathan* with reference to Cain in v. 5 ("It burned Cain badly, and his countenance fell"). A Jewish "translation" that clearly evokes the broken image of himself that Cain could not bear, for it all too closely resembled Abel the inconsistent, the "vaporous," according to the etymology of his name.

6   After having eaten of the fruit of the dangerous tree, Adam and Eve "hid themselves from the face of God."

7   E. Wiesel, *Messengers of God*, 51.

8   R. Girard, *Celui par qui le scandale arrive* (Paris: Desclée de Brouwer, 2001), 113ff.

9   Cf. note m in the French Traduction œcuménique de la Bible (TOB) with reference to Job 2.7. In psychosomatic medicine, inflammations and infections are said to have a link to repressed anger.

10   For a more detailed approach to the book of Job, see L. Basset, *Guérir du malheur* (Paris and Geneva: Albin Michel/Labor et Fides, 1999).

11   R. Girard, *Celui par qui le scandale arrive*, 59ff. The italics are mine.

12   Ibid., 169. Cf. also by the same author, *The Scapegoat*, trans. Yvonne Freccero (Baltimore: Johns Hopkins University Press, 1986), 18.

13   L. Beirnaert, *Aux frontières de l'acte analytique: la Bible, saint Ignace, Freud et Lacan* (Paris: Seuil, 1987), 193.

14   The same wrath is attributed to God, but this time directed against the inhabitants of Jerusalem, in Jer. 13:14: "I am about to fill ... all the inhabitants of Jerusalem with drunkenness. And I will dash them one against another, parents and children together, says the Lord. I will not pity or spare or have compassion when I destroy them."

15  J. Lévêque, *Job et son Dieu*, v. 2 (Paris: Gabalda, 1970), 375. This practice was common during the pillaging that followed the capture of a town (Ps. 137:9, note g in the TOB).

16  A. Vergote, *Dette et désir* (Paris: Seuil, 1978), 295ff.

17  Up till this point based on the TOB translation in French, the NRSV in English.

18  Following the French translation by J. Lévêque, *Job et son Dieu*, 380ff. In the active voice (at [qal]) the verb translated by "demolish" is used to refer to a man only here and in Ps. 52:7. Elsewhere, it always means a material demolition: it is as if to say that Job no longer saw himself as a human being!

19  Or to use a common expression, Why me? What did I do to God, who exists only to be angry with me, or rather, that I bring into existence only so that he may be angry instead of me?

20  M. Perrin, "L'exemple de Lactance," in M. Perrin, ed., *Le pardon* (Paris: Beauchesne, 1987), 75ff.

21  According to R. Girard, a misunderstanding of our own violence lies behind the theology of sacrifice. "It is the god who supposedly demands the victims … It is to appease his anger that the killing goes on." In *Violence and the Sacred*, trans. Patrick Gregory (Baltimore: Johns Hopkins University Press, 1977, 7).

22  M.-D. Molinié, *Le combat de Jacob* (Paris: Cerf, 1967), 31 and 39.

23  As for the translations (from Hebrew to Syrian, Coptic, Latin, NRSV, etc.), they have chosen the passive voice, leaving the mystery untouched: "I was pushed."

24  There are analyses in the Midrash based on the details of the text that stress Eve's possessiveness, the inner necessity for Cain to prove himself, his jealousy linked to his fear of death, etc.; J. Eisenberg and A. Abécassis, *Moi, le gardien de mon frère?* (À Bible ouverte vol. 3, Paris: Albin Michel, 1981); M. Balmary, *Abel ou la traversée de l'Éden* (Paris: Grasset, 1999); L. Beirnaert, *Aux frontières de l'acte analytique*; L. Basset, "Où est ton frère 'souffle'?" *Études théologiques et religieuses* 73/3 (1998).

25  St. Augustine, *The City of God*, XV, 7, trans. Marcus Dods (New York: Random House, 2000), 484–486.

26  When leaving the garden of Eden, Eve heard a realistic description of the condition of women: "In pain you shall bring forth children, yet your desire shall be for your husband, and he shall rule over you."

27  E. Wiesel, *Messengers of God*, 63–64.

28  St. Augustine, *The City of God*, I, xi, 11.

29   Cf. Gen. 22:1-19: the unexpected only son of the aged Abraham and Sarah,
     Isaac as a young boy was to be ritually slaughtered ("as a holocaust," NAB)
     by his father who heard "the god" demand this of him; at the last minute,
     the angel *of the Lord* stopped him and a ram, appearing at the requisite mo-
     ment out of a thicket, was sacrificed in his stead.

30   E. Wiesel, *Messengers of God*, 96–97.

31   Ibid., 97.

32   Ibid., 97.

33   Augustine, *The City of God* XVI, 37, 560.

34   Chouraqui translates this passage as: "Isaac trembled with a great shaking,
     very violently"; and the anger of Esau is all the more eloquent, by contrast, in
     the following verse: "He shouted a great and bitter shout, very violently."

35   P. Emmanuel, *Jacob* (Paris: Seuil, 1970), 44ff.

36   The root ['anah], from which flow these three meanings, is related to an
     Akkadian verb that means "to change" and an Egyptian verb that means
     "to return." All the verbs are in the imperfective, which indicates both the
     present and the future tense. It is as if to say that Jacob is in the process of
     changing for good!

37   Note k in the TOB concerning Gen. 43:23 indicates that the "god of the
     father" was invoked in contracts and treaties, and refers precisely to verse
     46:54: the meal could also signal the conclusion of a treaty. Nevertheless,
     there is nothing to say that through cultural practices and religious customs,
     some essential elements may not come into play and unfold in the lives of
     the biblical figures and in their relationships with their entourage.

38   Cf. previous note.

39   See R.D. Weis, who does not hesitate to put these two spiritual events
     on the same level as the politico-diplomatic strategies adopted by Jacob:
     dividing his camp (men and beasts) in two in order not to risk everything
     at once, sending considerable gifts to Esau as one would wave a white flag,
     in "Lessons on Wrestling with the Unseen: Jacob at the Jabbok," *Reformed
     Review* 42 (1989): 100 and 106.

40   M. Balmary, *Abel ou la traversée de l'Éden*, 226.

41   A frequent answer evoked here is that of the possessiveness of Eve: "In
     Hebrew, *qanah* [the origin of the name Cain] means "to purchase" an object
     and thus designates a commercial relationship," writes A. Abécassis in J.
     Eisenberg and A. Abécassis, *Moi le gardien de ma frère?*, 43. Eve does indeed
     say in Gen. 4:1: "I have produced a man with the help of the Lord."

42   Similarly, does Adam hiding in his tree feel the presence of the OTHER as a threat? And why can Cain not tolerate the very existence of an OTHER by his side (a weak, submissive one in this case)?

43   L. Basset, *La joie imprenable* (Geneva: Labor et Fides, 1999²), 239; Cf. also the whole section entitled "Le combat [the struggle]," 232–41.

44   L. Beirnaert, *Aux frontières de l'acte analytique*, 187, 190.

45   Cf. M. Garat, "La violence dans la Bible," *Cahiers de l'Atelier* no. 409 (oct.–déc. 2000), 14.

46   Following the French translation of J. Lévêque in *Job et son Dieu* (Paris: Gabalda, 1970), except in the last verse, which is taken from the NRSV.

47   Job 13:3 in Ibid. The verb [iakar] means to reproach, blame, plead, argue, debate.

48   R. Girard, *Job: The Victim of His People*, trans. Yvonne Freccero (Stanford, CA: Stanford University Press, 1987), 26.

49   Ibid., 27.

50   E. Wiesel, *Messengers of God*, 57.

51   Where it took several men to roll the stone from the top of the well, the young Jacob was able to perform the feat alone.

52   Cf. *Midrash Rabbah. Genesis.* (London–Jersualem–New York: Soncino Press, 1977), 702. The same interpretation is given by Rashi, in *Rashi on the Pentateuch: Genesis*, trans. and annotated by James H. Lowe (London: Hebrew Compendium Publishing Co., 1928), 155.

53   Cf. J. Eisenberg and A. Abécassis, *Jacob, Rachel, Léa et les autres* (À Bible ouverte IV, Paris: Albin Michel, 1981), 352ff.

54   M. Balmary, *Abel ou la traversée de l'Éden*, 113.

55   L. Beirnaert, *Aux frontières de l'acte analytique*, 195.

56   John Chrysostom, *Homilies on Genesis* no. 53, trans. Robert C. Hill (Fathers of the Church vol. 87, Washington, D.C.: Catholic University of America, 1992), 80–81.

57   For details on this interpretation, which relies upon the Zohar, see J. Eisenberg and A. Abécassis, *Moi le gardien de mon frère?*, 82–89.

58   According to Jewish tradition, Jacob represents all Israel. We can therefore stress the communal value of such an individual prayer of complaint that takes the place of violence in actions. With regard to the whole passage, see L. Basset, "Guérir en Église: un temps liturgique pour la plainte," *Perspectives missionnaires* 41/1 (2001): 27–36.

59   Daniel Goleman, *Emotional Intelligence* (New York: Bantam Books, 1995), 47–48.

60  Ibid., 6.

61  Ibid., 11, 12, 17, 24–25. My italics.

62  Given a slap by a guard, Jesus replied: "If I have spoken wrongly, bear witness to the wrong [I have said]: but if I have spoken rightly, why do you strike me ?" (Jn. 18:23)

63  We can also read it as "Offer him *the other* [cheek ] *also.*"

64  Eisenberg and Abécassis, *Moi, le gardien de mon frère?*, 226.

65  Ibid., 95.

66  Augustine, *The City of God*, IX, 5, 284–285.

67  According to Eisenberg, the richness of the Bible may never appear as clearly as in this verse, which is incapable of being translated. *Moi, le gardien de mon frère?*, 96.

68  Ibid., 106.

69  Cf. Letter 11 by Evagrius, cited by I. Hausherr, *Les leçons d'un contemplatif. Le Traité d'Oraison d'Évagre le Pontique* (Paris: Beauchesne, 1960), 108.

70  *Targum Pseudo-Jonathan: Genesis*, trans. Michael Maher (Edinburgh: T&T Clark, 1992), 32.

71  P. Beauchamp and D. Vasse, "La violence dans la Bible," *Cahiers Évangile* 76 (Paris: Éditions du Cerf, 1991), 8. Cf. also A. Wénin, "De la violence à l'alliance. Un chemin éthique inspiré des Écritures," *Revue d'éthique et de théologie morale*, Supplement, 213 (June 2000), 109. A. Wénin sees in this word an invitation to humanity to "master their inner animality," to "learn to allow their own animality to emerge without eliminating or crushing it, but by orienting these inner forces in such a way as to permit life to flourish."

72  Imagine the shock that would result if such a proposition became common practice – to abstain from all "religious" activity as long as we had not changed our attitude towards another who is angry and hurting!

73  It is also from the "field" that the most deceitful of animals came, namely the serpent in Genesis. The word refers to that which is untamed, in a wild state, beyond the bounds of the protected garden.

74  *Targum Pseudo-Jonathan: Genesis*, 32–33.

75  Evagrius Ponticus, *Treatise on Prayer* ch. 12, in *The Philokalia: the Complete Text Compiled by St. Nikodimos of the Holy Mountain and St. Makarios of Corinth*, vol. 1, trans. G.E.H. Palmer, Philip Sherrard and Kallistos Ware (London/Boston: Faber & Faber, 1979), 58.

76  B. Bro, *Le pouvoir du mal* (Paris: Editions du Cerf, 1976), 46.

77  Ibid., 55ff.

78  Anselm Grün, *Petit traité de spiritualité au quotidien* (Paris: Albin Michel, 1998), 51ff., 113, 132.

79  E. Wiesel, *Night*, trans. Stella Rodway (New York: Hill and Wang, 1960), 64.

80  S. Kierkegaard, *Repetition: An Essay in Experimental Psychology*, trans. Walter Lowrie (Princeton: Princeton University Press, 1946), 115–116.

81  Ibid., 112–113.

82  According to the meaning given it by S.A. Geller in "The Struggle at the Jabbok: The Uses of Enigma in a Biblical Narrative," *JANESCU* [Journal of the Association of Near Eastern Studies of Columbia University] 14 (1982): 37–60, here 44.

83  P. Claudel, *Emmaüs* (Paris, 1949), 71.

84  Thus, according to R. de Pury, "Job, whom God treated as an enemy, appealed not to some higher authority, not to the god of his friends, but to the very God who was afflicting him. Job seeks refuge with the God whom he accuses. Job entrusts himself to the God who has disappointed him and made him despair. Job sees his friend in the God who is his enemy. Not another God, but the same one," in *Job ou l'homme révolté* (Geneva: Labor et Fides, 1982), 29.

85  Samuel Terrien, *Job: Poet of Existence* (Indianapolis/New York: The Bobbs-Merrill Company, 1957), 49.

86  The French original follows the translation of J. Lévêque. The English is slightly adapted from the NRSV.

87  Cited by G. Hammann ("Luther," *WA* 44, 101.6f.), who also speaks, but in reference to Jacob's struggle, of "a paradoxical [Christian] life" in "Le songe de Jacob et sa lutte avec l'ange (Genèse 28 et 32): Repères historiques d'une lecture et de ses variations," *Revue d'Histoire et de Philosophie Religieuse* 6 (1986), 38.

88  E. Wiesel, *Messengers of God*, 126, 128–129.

89  J.-C. Sagne, *Conflit, changement, conversion* (Paris: Éditions du Cerf/Desclée, 1974), 61, 63.

90  *Targum Neofiti: Genesis*, trans. Martin McNamara (The Aramaic Bible vol. 1A), I, 67.

91  *Targum Pseudo-Jonathan: Genesis*, trans. Michael Maher (Edinburgh: T.&T. Clark, 1992), 34.

92  The Targum further specifies, concerning Cain's life "in the land of Nod [= wandering] east of Eden" (4:16): "Now before he killed Abel, the earth used to produce before him like the fruits of the garden of Eden; after he had sinned, however, and killed Abel it changed to produce before him

thorns and thistles," as was the case for Adam in Gen. 3:18 (*Targum Neofiti: Genesis* 1, 68).

93   Paul Claudel, *Emmaüs*, 39.

94   J. Rachower, "Testament dans la fournaise," *Bible et vie chrétienne*, no. 64 (July–August 1965), 71.

95   The Hebrew text permits a reading either as "my eyes and not those of a stranger behold my living defender" or "my eyes behold my defender living and not another [God]": the ambivalence of the expression is a good reflection of this experience of a Presence at work in the most intimate part of one's being.

96   According to Elie Wiesel, "the beauty of the Jewish tradition is that it is based on a strong man. God does not want a slave.... God replies to Job: 'Be a man!' – 'Gird up your loins like a man' (38:3)." Cf. J. Eisenberg and E. Wiesel, *Job ou Dieu dans la tempête* (Paris: Fayard/Verdier, 1986), 336, 380.

97   Based on Chouraqui's French translation where it departs from the NRSV.

98   NRSV.

99   J. Rachower, "Testament dans la fournaise," 73ff.

## Part II

1   The three *hapax* of the text (words that occur only once in the Bible) are in italics.

2   The only three verbs in the perfect tense are in capital letters.

3   Another possible translation is "For you are prince-with-God and with-men."

4   E. Wiesel, *Messengers of God*, 106.

5   Cf. H. Cazelles, "Patriarches," *DBS*, vol. VII, col. 81–156 (Supplement to the *Dictionnaire de la Bible*), 82ff, 120.

6   A name that was known at Chagar Bazar (Syria) before 1650 and on the Hyckos scarabs as well as on the topographical lists of Touthmès III (late 16th–early 15th century).

7   H. Cazelles, "Patriarches," 140ff.

8   Cf. F.C. Holmgren, "Holding Your Own Against God! Gen 32:22-32 (in the context of Gen 31–33)," *Interpretation* 44, 1990, 6.

9   H.A. McKay, "Jacob Makes It Across the Jabbok: An Attempt to Solve the Success/Failure Ambivalence in Israel's Self-Consciousness," *JSOT* 38 (1987).

10   According to J. Skinner, "The writers appear to have strung together a number of Transjordanian legends connected with the name of Jacob, but without much regard to topographical consistency or consecutiveness." *A Critical and Exegetical Commentary on Genesis* (Edinburgh: Clark, 1930), 403 footnote.

11   A. de Pury, *Promesse divine et légende cultuelle dans le cycle de Jacob*, vol. 1 and 2 (Paris: Gabalda, 1975), 614.

12   Cf. H. Cazelles, "Patriarches," 120.

13   A. de Pury, *Promesse divine et légende cultuelle dans le cycle de Jacob*, 525ff, 570.

14   H. Cazelles, "Patriarches," 91, 94.

15   Ibid., 95.

16   R. Martin-Achard, "Un exégète devant Genèse 32, 23–33," in R. Barthes et al., *Analyse structurale et exégèse biblique* (Neuchâtel: Delachaux et Niestlé), 1971, 49, 53.

17   Ibid., 45, 60.

18   In agreement with H. Gunkel, G. von Rad, E. A. Speiser and K. Elliger.

19   Or "brought me luck" (TOB) or "made him appear before me" (Chouraqui). In either case, the divine blessing forges a path right through a deception.

20   L. Hicks, "Jacob," *The Interpreters' Dictionary of the Bible* (New York/ Nashville: Abingdon Press, 1962), vol. 2, 786.

21   Cf. *Midrash Rabbah*, 718: "For thou art a prince (*saritha*, from *sar*, a prince) together with God, thy features being engraved on high."

22   S.A. Geller considers that taken in this sense, the verb is practically a *hapax*. Several versions derive it from the Aramean "to be solid," while others from a different root, "to reign" ("The Struggle at the Jabbok: The Uses of Enigma in a Biblical Narrative," 53). A rather rare word to describe a rare experience.

23   R. Couffignal, *La lutte avec l'Ange. Le récit de la Genèse et sa fortune littéraire* (Publications de l'Université de Toulouse-Le Mirail, 1977), 14.

24   P. Emmanuel, *Jacob*, 128, 143, 155ff.

25   Y. Eliach, *Hasidic Tales of the Holocaust* (New York: Oxford University Press, 1982), 170–171.

26   A. Vergote, "Visions et apparitions: Approche psychologique," *RThL* 22 (1991): 211.

27   Cf. J. Eisenberg and A. Abécassis, *Jacob, Rachel, Léa et les autres*, 63.

28  E. Fleg, *Écoute, Israël* (Paris: Cahiers de la Quinzaine, 15th series, no. 1, 1913), 37ff.

29  Ibid.

30  Both pagans and Christians, but with the exception of Hippocrates and his disciples (cf. A. Vergote, "Visions et apparitions: Approche psychologique," 208).

31  According to A. de Pury, *Promesse divine et légende cultuelle dans le cycle de Jacob*, 370–397.

32  Ibid., 373, 397.

33  *Midrash Rabbah*, 713, n. 5.

34  Ibid., 714 and n. 1.

35  According to F.C. Holmgren, "Whether or not that is the case, the story has taken on the colour and character of a dream" ("Holding Your Own Against God!" 7).

36  W.G. Niederland, "Jacobskampf am Jabbok," in *Psychoanalytische Interpretationen biblischer Texte*, ed. Y. Spiegel (Munich: Kaiser Verlag, 1972), 128ff.

37  A. Vergote, "Visions et apparitions: Approche psychologique," 213.

38  For A. Vergote, the same processes are at work in both visions and dreams, with the same "characteristic of a lived reality that is actually present." Ibid., 214.

39  In Hebrew the imperfect tense can be translated by a present and a future.

40  "To take a large flock across the Jabbok – the present-day Nahr ez-zerka – which runs through the bottom of a deeply entrenched gorge, was a major undertaking." G. von Rad, *La Genèse* (Geneva: Labor et Fides, 1968), 326.

41  E. Wiesel, *Messengers of God*, 125.

42  J. Skinner, *A Critical and Exegetical Commentary on Genesis*, 408. For more details about the geography of the place and the absurdity of the venture, see B. Vawter, *On Genesis: A New Reading* (Garden City, NY: Doubleday, 1977), 348ff.: "Why cross the Jabbok at all, either north to south or south to north?"

43  His daughter Dinah, who is not counted, will be raped the next day – it is still, after all, a patriarchal society.

44  Cf. R.D. Weis, "Lessons on Wrestling with the Unseen: Jacob at the Jabbok," 102ff.

45　Gen. 27:38: "Esau replied to his father: 'Do you have only one blessing, my father? Bless me too!' Esau raised his voice and cried." Isaac then spoke to him of his future, but did not bless him.

46　The Midrash prefers the term "touch" rather than "injure," which it puts in parentheses (*Midrash Rabbah,* 713).

47　Rashi, *Rashi on the Pentateuch: Genesis*, 59.

48　R. Couffignal, *La lutte avec l'Ange. Le récit de la Genèse et sa fortune littéraire*, 19.

49　E. Fleg, *Le Livre du commencement* (Paris: Éditions de Minuit, 1959), 130.

50　"These thoughts and fears [linked to memories] are, as it were, materialized in his dream," notes S.R. Driver, *The Book of Genesis* (London: Methuen and Co., 1904), 297.

51　*Targum Neofiti: Genesis*, I, 159.

52　*Targum Pseudo-Jonathan: Genesis*, trans. Michael Maher (Edinburgh: T&T Clark, 1992), 115.

53　Ibid., 115.

54　John Calvin, *Commentary on Old Testament*, edited and translated by John King (Calvin Translation Society, 1847), vol. 2, pt. 11 (commentary on Gen. 32:24, 26), repr. 1975 by the Banner of Truth Trust.

55　The root used here, [nagad], means "make visible or evident."

56　G. von Rad, *La Genèse*, 330.

57　R. Couffignol gives an account of this reading in the chapter entitled "Jacob, l'Oedipe biblique," *La lutte avec l'Ange. Le récit de la Genèse et sa fortune littéraire*, 23ff.

58　Ibid., 62. Likewise, Georges Bernanos, in *The Star of Satan*, trans. Pamela Morris (New York: Macmillan, 1940), 220, has Abbé Menou-Segrais say regarding Fr Donissan, "How can I tell you whether or not you really saw him face to face, whom we meet every day – alas, not at the turn of the road, but within ourselves! How do I know whether you saw him in a dream or in reality?".

59　In the words of G. Hammann, "Luther," 36.

60　G. von Rad, *La Genèse*, 330.

61　J. Skinner, *A Critical and Exegetical Commentary on Genesis*, 410.

62　B. Cyrulnik, *Les vilains petits canards* (Paris: Odile Jacob, 2001), 224ff. Cf. S. Freud, who writes in *Essays on Psychoanalysis*, "One sees in the insistence on reflecting even in the sleep of a patient, proof of the force of the impression which [the situation of his accident] produced." For Jacob, it is a question of the threat of death that made him flee Esau.

63   E.H. Maly, "Genesis," *Jerome Biblical Commentary* vol. 1, 1968, 34.

64   Cf. The Mishnaic treatise of *Hullin* §7, mentioned by R. Martin-Achard, "Un exégète devant Genèse 32, 23-33," in R. Barthes et al., *Analyse structurale et exégèse biblique*, 52.

65   Thus, for W.G. Niederland, the symbolism of the watercourse, of the sister, of the mother, of birth, refer to the œdipal conflict and to castration anxiety. At the end of the combat, Jacob was delivered of the anxiety of the vengeful river and of rivalry with his father, accepting symbolic castration.

66   St. Augustine, *The City of God* XVI, 39, 562. Cf. C. Westermann, for whom "The most likely explanation is that this part of the body was subject to taboo because it was regarded as belonging to the reproductive area." *Genesis 12–36 : A Commentary* (Minneapolis, Augsburg Publishing House, 1981) 520.

67   R. Martin-Achard, "Un exégète devant Genèse 32, 23-33," in R. Barthes et al., *Analyse structurale et exégèse biblique*, 52.

68   It is a question, explains a note, of the generation that suffered huge losses in the Hadrianic Wars (132–135 CE) and the subsequent persecutions (*Midrash Rabbah*, 713).

69   According to an old Jewish tradition, cf. N.M. Sarna, *The JPS Torah Commentary: Genesis* (Philadelphia: The Jewish Publication Society Torah Commentary, 1989), 228.

70   S.A. Geller, "The Struggle at the Jabbok: The Uses of Enigma in a Biblical Narrative," 52ff.

71   B. Cyrulnik, *Les vilains petits canards*, 228ff.

72   Regarding parental favouritism (there can be the favourite of the father and that of the mother), F. Smyth notes that "The father identifies the son as his eldest, and makes him his only child, as if the son was the only child of his own father." Abraham had heard God say to him, "Take your son, your only son, Isaac whom you love," as if Ishmael did not exist, in J.-D. Macchi and T. Römer, eds. *Jacob. Commentaire à plusieurs voix*, 2001, (Geneva: Labor et Fides, 2001), 61, 64.

73   Cf. Gen. 24:2: "Put your hand under my thigh … and I will make you swear by the Lord," Abraham said to his oldest servant; and Gen. 47:29: At the end of his life, Jacob asked his son Joseph not to bury him in Egypt ("If I have found favour with you, put your hand under my thigh …").

74   Cf. the commentary of Rashi, *Rashi on the Pentateuch: Genesis*, 227: "Admit my right to the blessings which my father gave me and to which Esau lays claim … It shall no longer be said that the blessings came to you

through supplanting and subtlety but through noble conduct and in an open manner."

75 A. de Pury, *Promesse divine et légende cultuelle dans le cycle de Jacob*, 102.

76 Rashi, *Rashi on the Pentateuch: Genesis*, 159.

77 B. Cyrulnik, *Les vilains petits canards*, 230ff.

78 S.A. Geller, "The Struggle at the Jabbok: The Uses of Enigma in a Biblical Narrative," 50.

79 P. Beauchamp, *Cinquante portraits bibliques* (Paris: Seuil, 2000), 51.

80 G. von Rad, *La Genèse*, 327.

81 E. Wiesel, *Messengers of God*, 129–130.

82 Cf. A. Abécassis, in J. Eisenberg and A. Abécassis, *Jacob, Rachel,Léa et les autres*, 327ff. For these authors, Esau represents the Nations to which Israel, in exile, was forced to submit, and a certain tradition of submission was thus able to remain current through the twenty-five centuries of Israelite exile.

83 A. de Pury, *Promesse divine et légende cultuelle dans le cycle de Jacob*, 92.

84 J.G. Janzen, *Abraham and All the Families of the Earth: Genesis 12–50* (Grand Rapids: Eerdmans, 1993), 131.

85 R. Martin-Achard, "Un exégète devant Genèse 32, 23-33," in R. Barthes et al., *Analyse structurale et exégèse biblique*, 55.

86 Cf. L. Hicks, "Jacob," 783. The ancient form would Ya'aqov-el, or Ya'aquv-el, and it is known that there was a Palestinian place called Yaqob-el in 1490–1436 BCE.

87 J. Eisenberg and A. Abécassis, *Jacob, Rachel, Léa et les autres*, 101.

88 J.L. Ska, in J.-D. Macchi and T. Römer, eds. *Jacob*, 18ff.

89 For example, N.M. Sarna, for whom the new name Israel, because of its root that means "to be upright, straight," is forms a perfect antonym of Jacob, which is understood to be connected with "craftiness, deceit," *Genesis*, 405.

90 J.L. McKenzie, "Jacob at Peniel: Gn 32:24-32," *Catholic Biblical Quarterly* 25 (1963), 75.

91 P. von Gemünden, in J.-D. Macchi and T. Römer, eds. *Jacob*, 358ff.

92 J. Eisenberg and A. Abécassis, *Jacob, Rachel, Léa et les autres*, 301.

93 R. Michaud, *Les Patriarches: Histoire et théologie* (Paris: Éditions du Cerf, 1975) 116, 128.

94 Augustine, *The City of God*, XVI, 37, 559.

95   F.C. Holmgren, "Holding Your Own Against God! Gen 32:22-32 (in the context of Gen 31–33)," 9–14.

96   *De trinitate* VIII, 5, cited in *Bible chretienne* 1, 156.

97   H.A. McKay, "Jacob Makes It Across the Jabbok: An Attempt to Solve the Success/Failure Ambivalence in Israel's Self-Consciousness," 7.

98   E. Wiesel, *Messengers of God,* 122, 124.

99   The issue seems the same for Jacob and Cain; in touching the hollow of the thigh or in inciting Cain to lift his face, God is trying to provoke the human into facing himself by a confrontation with the OTHER that He is.

100  E. Wiesel, *Messengers of God,* 125.

101  W. Brueggemann, *Genesis: Interpretation Commentary* (Atlanta: John Knox Press, 1982), 268–69.

102  The traditional appellation "Eternal One of armies" (or Eternal Sabaoth) and the French translation of Chouraqui ("Elohim des milices" / "Elohim of hosts") have all too well inserted into the history of Christianity a militaristic image of God and forgetfulness of a power that he had shared with humans in the framework of their confrontations with *Him.*

103  J. Eisenberg and A. Abécassis, *Jacob, Rachel, Léa et les autres,* 78.

104  Rashi, *Rashi on the Pentateuch: Genesis,* 162.

105  P. Emmanuel, *Jacob,* 157, 159.

106  W. Brueggemann, *Genesis,* 267.

107  R. Couffignal notes that A. Spire wrote his book *Samaël* several years later and that for C. Vigée as well, the adversary is Samaël. "By that means the benevolent character of the Elohim is preserved, distanced from the scandal of a divine aggressor." C. Vigée, *Dans le silence de l'Aleph,* 48ff.

108  E. Fleg, *Écoute Israël,* 38ff. The Targum suggests an interesting parallel between this Samael and Cain: "Adam knew his wife Eve who had conceived from Sammael the angel of the Lord. Then, from Adam her husband she bore his twin sister and Abel" (*Targum Pseudo-Jonathan* IV, trans. Michael Maher, Edinburgh: T&T Clark, 1992, 31). Human violence would have something to do with God from the beginning.

109  E. Wiesel, *Messengers of God,* 124.

110  R.D. Weis, "Lessons on Wrestling with the Unseen: Jacob at the Jabbok," 112, n. 24.

111  G. Bernanos, *The Star of Satan,* 156, 160, 161.

112  Cited by J.M. Tézé, "La Lutte de Jacob avec l'Ange," *Christus* 33 (1962), 72.

113 Cf. J. Eisenberg and A. Abécassis, *Moi, le gardien de mon frère?*, 185.

114 R. Girard, *I See Satan Fall Like Lightning*, trans. James G. Williams (Ottawa: Novalis, 2001), 119.

115 We find this interpretation in S.L. Shearman and J.B. Curtis, "Divine-Human Conflicts in the Old Testament," *JNES* 28 (1969), 232ff. I add that Beth-el (= the house of God) makes one think of a community of life, a God with whom one feels at home, as opposed to a god who kills interpersonal relationships by the ideology of sacrifice.

116 In familiar terms, "uncleanable," which recalls the dust and the mud at the edge of the Jabbok.

117 For more detail on this subject, refer to my work *Le pardon original* (Geneva: Labor et Fides, 2000), 362–71.

118 R. Girard, *Celui par qui le scandale arrive*, 99, 103.

119 R. Barthes et al., *Analyse structurale et exégèse biblique*, Neuchâtel 34ff. One could add, he acts counter-culturally and even counter-educationally.

120 Cf. J. Skinner, *A Critical and Exegetical Commentary on Genesis*, 398.

121 V.K. Elliger, "Der Jakobskampf am Jabbok," *Zeitschrift für Theologie und Kirche* 48, 1951, 30.

122 M.-D. Molinié, *Le combat de Jacob*, 164, 166.

123 Ibid., 32.

124 Cited by Sister Isabelle de la Source, *Lire la Bible avec les Pères*, t. 1, *La Genèse* (Paris and Montreal: Médiaspaul et Éditions Paulines, 1988) 110.

125 What astonishes me is the astonishment of R. Martin-Achard, although it is true that he began by admitting with G. von Rad that the desperate eagerness of Jacob was less piety than an "almost primitive reaction of the man who wants to acquire divine power" ("Un exégète devant Genèse 32, 23-33," in R. Barthes et al., *Analyse structurale et exégèse biblique*, 59). It all comes clear to me when it is a question for Jacob of a confrontation that is necessary to live, and for God of a combat that is indispensable for the partnership that he has desired from the beginning.

126 From the verb [bara'] used at the beginning of Genesis to speak of divine creation, and the word [ra'] which occurs in the well-known "tree of the knowledge of good and *evil*."

127 F.C. Holmgren, "Holding Your Own Against God! Gen 32:22-32 (in the context of Gen 31–33)," 16.

128 R. Girard, *Celui par qui le scandale arrive*, 80.

129 A. de Pury, *Promesse divine et légende cultuelle dans le cycle de Jacob*, 601.

130 A. Abécassis, in J. Eisenberg and A. Abécassis, *Jacob, Rachel, Léa et les autres*, 391.

131 A. de Pury, *Promesse divine et légende cultuelle dans le cycle de Jacob*, 94.

132 H.A. McKay, "Jacob Makes it across the Jabbok: An Attempt to Solve the Success/Failure Ambivalence in Israel's Self-Consciousness," 9.

133 N.M. Sarna, *Genesis*, 228.

134 D. Goleman, *Emotional Intelligence*, 115.

135 A. de Pury, *Promesse divine et légende cultuelle dans le cycle de Jacob*, 570, n. 380.

136 J. Skinner, *A Critical and Exegetical Commentary on Genesis*, 405.

137 *Targum Neofiti: Genesis* 1, 156–57.

138 Several writers and artists have seen it as an amorous embrace.

139 Ambrose, *On Jacob and the Blessed Life [De Iacob et vita beata]* 7/30, trans. Michael P. McHugh, in *Fathers of the Church* v. 65 (Washington, D.C.: Catholic University of America, 1972), 163–64.

140 R. Michaud, *Les Patriarches*, 111.

141 C. Westermann, *Genesis 12–36*, 518.

142 To bless [barak] has as the derivative meaning of "transfer of strength," according to C. Westermann (ibid.).

## Part III

1 St. Augustine, *The City of God* XIX, 5, 681 and 8, 684.

2 J. Eisenberg et A. Abécassis, *Moi, le gardien de mon frère?*, 279f.

3 A. Abécassis recalls that "to communicate by signs, is to create an obstacle to the violence and aggressiveness of the other" (ibid., 288).

4 Ibid., 292.

5 According to the literal tradition of Gen. 4:2: "Next she bore his brother Abel."

6 M. Balmary, *Abel ou la traversée de l'Éden*, 306, 331.

7 Cf. W.G. Niederland, "Jacobskampf am Jabbok."

8 R. Girard, *The Scapegoat* (Baltimore: Johns Hopkins University Press, 1986), 130–131, 132. See also *I See Satan Fall Like Lightning*, 9–10: "To maintain peace between human beings, it is essential to define prohibitions in light of this extremely significant fact: our neighbour is the model for our desires. This is what I call mimetic desire."

9 R. Girard, *I See Satan Fall Like Lightning*, 8, 10f.

10  R. Girard, *The Scapegoat*, 165. See also *Celui par qui le scandale arrive*, 24:
    "The real secret of conflict, and of violence, is desirous imitation, mimetic
    desire and the fierce rivalries that it engenders."

11  R. Girard, *The Scapegoat*, 30.

12  R. Girard, *Celui par qui le scandale arrive*, 30 and 34. When there is perse-
    cution, says the author, it is because a too-great difference (of the disabled,
    the stranger, the marginalized) terrifies society which dreads falling back
    into indifferentiation, confusion, chaos – the matrix of all violence – which
    always threaten every member (*The Scapegoat*, ch. 2). Thus everyone fears
    becoming disabled, estranged, marginalized …

13  R. Girard, *Celui par qui le scandale arrive*, 30.

14  The citation of Mic. 7:6 (in Italics) does not appear in exactly this form in
    either the Hebrew text or the Greek translation (Septuagint).

15  R. Girard, *Celui par qui le scandale arrive*, 70f.

16  Cf. the verse which precedes the words regarding the sword: "Whoever
    denies me before others, I also will deny before my Father in heaven," for
    you cannot deny *your truth* without denying me also, and I have no grasp
    on it.

17  The word [paraginomai] means first *to be close to*, then, *to come to help, assist,
    rescue* and finally, *to come to join oneself to*: the Christ unites himself to humans
    to help them accomplish their differentiation.

18  It is once again a question of the same Greek root [diamerizomenai] which
    contains the word [meri], "part."

19  The expression, already known in Judaism, appears five times in the syn-
    optic tradition (in Matthew, Mark and Luke): see P. Bonnard, *L'Évangile
    selon saint Matthieu* (Geneva: Labor et Fides, 2002), 157f. To me, one does
    not have to oppose the context of everyday relationships with the context
    of persecutions; to follow the way that Christ shows can provoke violence
    and scorn among one's companions in either case.

20  P. Bonnard, *L'Évangile selon saint Matthieu*, 157.

21  This step is proposed to humans from Genesis, when the first man meets the
    first woman: "Therefore a man leaves his father and his mother and clings to
    his wife, and they *become* one flesh." (Gen 2:24) Some think that "one flesh"
    designates the child to come: the man and the woman, differentiated from
    their parents, unite *with the intention* of the birth of a new being, essentially
    OTHER.

22  X. Durand, "Le Combat de Jacob (Gn 32,23-33): pour un bon usage des
    modèles narratifs," *Le Point théologique* 24 (1977), 111.

23  P. Claudel, *Le Livre de Job*, Paris, Plon, 1946, 13.

24  R. Girard, *Celui par qui scandale arrive,* 42. I emphasize here the mechanism of perversion, in which one lets oneself be taken all the more than persons who behave extremely perversely and who are often those who apply themselves today to denouncing the "perverse effects" of this or that.

25  Ibid., 76.

26  R. de Pury, *Job ou l'homme révolté* (Genève: Labor et Fides), 1982, 48.

27  R. Girard, *I See Satan Fall Like Lightning,* 13, 14.

28  F. Quéré, *Les Ennemis de Jésus,* Paris, Seuil, 1985, 101, 103, 105, 113.

29  Ibid., 117.

30  R.D. Weis, "Lessons on Wrestling with the Unseen: Jacob at the Jabbok," 108.

31  P. Beauchamp, in P. Beauchamp and D. Vasse, "La Violence dans la Bible," 52. "The Spirit does violence to violence," according to D. Vasse (ibid., 31).

32  Cf. H. Cazelles, "Patriarches," 149f. This rite, mentioned in Gen. 15:10, 17f., and explained by Jeremiah (34:18) is not found in the Levite ritual and "is not a prototype" – which highlights even more strongly its symbolic meaning.

33  In *Violence and the Sacred,* 288, R. Girard remarks that "the 'translation' of this violent process into terms of expulsion, evacuation, and surgical operations is made in the most diverse cultures."

34  S. Kierkegaard, *Repetition,* 110–112.

35  The first phrase in italics is a quotation from Zechariah 8:16. The second is the Greek translation of Psalm 4:4.

36  R. Girard, *I See Satan Fall Like Lightning,* 161, 168.

37  St. Augustine, *The City of God,* IX, v, 285; and XV, xxv, 515.

38  S. Kierkegaard, *Repetition,* 130. The author is speaking here of the "category of the trial of probation," of which he specifies that it is "absolutely transcendent": to make the experience a category of thought (a candidate for dogmatics), it is necessary to have traversed it. To my eyes, it appears then like that unique occasion in life of facing God in that *distressing* solitude in which the human is plunged.

39  R. de Pury, *Job ou l'homme révolté,* 37f.

40  Beyond moral purity, one must think of the chemical notion of "unmixed": something is pure which is not intermingled with anything else; pure or holy is anyone who remains alone before God, in their difference and their own responsibility.

41  *Philokalia of the Neptic Fathers,* vol. 1, 22, 27, 28.

42  When he witnessed a combat of two male wolves, biologist Konrad Lorenz observed that at the moment when the older one, in the position of power, was about to throw himself at the younger, the latter "holds away his head, offering unprotected to his enemy the bend of his neck, the most vulnerable part of his whole body ... to which a bite must assuredly prove fatal ... As soon as he abandons his rigid attitude of submmission, the other again falls upon him like a thunderbolt and the victim must again freeze into his former posture ... Thus an animal that senses that he is beaten can evoke an inhibition in an aggressor in offering himself defenselessly to his attacker." Recalling the story of the other cheek, K. Lorenz concludes: "A wolf has enlightened me: not so that your enemy may strike you again do you turn the other cheek towards him, but to make him unable to do it." (K. Lorenz, *King Solomon's Ring,* London: Methuen, 1970, 186, 188, 197.)

43  R. Girard, *Violence and the Sacred* (Baltimore: Johns Hopkins University Press, 1977), 145.

44  M. Balmary, *Abel ou la traversée de l'Éden*, 118. Trans. B. Henry, Indeed, Abel alone seems to have appropriated what belonged to him, "Abel for his part brought of the firstlings of his flock, their fat portions"; Cain "brought to the Lord an offering of the fruit of the ground." (Gen. 3:3, 4)

45  A. Camus, *The Rebel: An Essay on Man in Revolt* (New York: Alfred A. Knopf, 1978), 251.

46  Ibid., 285.

47  Ibid., 289–290.

48  R. Girard, *Violence and the Sacred,* 17, 18, 81.

49  Cf. J. Eisenberg and A. Abécassis, *Jacob, Rachel, Léa et les autres,* 65.

50  Ibid., 66.

51  Cf. Gen 2:7: "The Lord God formed man from the dust of the ground, and breathed into his nostrils the breath of life; and the man [dust] became a living being."

52  D. Sibony, "Premier meurtre," *Tel Quel* no. 64, 1975, 46f.

53  Cf. D. Goleman, *Emotional Intelligence,* 82, 85.

54  C. Vigée, *Dans le silence de l'Aleph,* 59.

55  Seneca, *Dialogues: On Anger,* Book III, xlii, 1. http://www.stoics.com/ seneca_essays_book_1.html#ANGER1. Accessed April 2, 2007. "Let us not try to regulate our anger, but be rid of it altogether – for what regulation can there be of any evil thing? Moreover, we can do it, if only we shall make the effort." Book III, xlii, 1, Ibid.

56  Cf. D. Goleman, *Emotional Intelligence,* 171.

57 Cf. John Cassian, *Cenobitic Institutions* (Books 5–12) in *The Philokalia of the Neptic Fathers*, 8.1, 86.

58 Ibid., 8.5, 86; 8.7, 89 ; 8.7–8.18, 8.20, 90ff. On malice 8.6, 87.

59 "If, therefore," commented Seneca, "anger suffers any limitation to be imposed upon it, it must be called by some other name – it has ceased to be anger; for I understand this to be unbridled and ungovernable. If it suffers no limitation, it is a baneful thing and is not to be counted as a helpful agent. Thus either anger is not anger or it is useless" (*Dialogues: On Anger*, Book I, ix, 3, 12; http://www.stoics.com/seneca_essays_book_1.html#ANGER1. Accessed April 2, 2007). Holy anger is to my eyes in the same family as anger; it uses anger that is at first "unchecked" as a life energy to be channelled, without which it would never be able to incarnate itself.

60 St. Augustine, *The City of God*, XX, xii, 730.

61 Seneca, *Dialogues: On Anger,* Book III, xxvii, 2. http://www.stoics.com/seneca_essays_book_1.html#ANGER1. Accessed April 2, 2007.

62 A. Camus, *The Rebel*, 304.

63 K. Lorenz, for example, has articulated the rule according to which "fish are much more aggressive towards their own congeners than towards any other species of fish." *Il parlait avec les mammifères, les oiseaux et les poissons* (Paris: Flammarion, 1968), 26. Darwin's struggle, "that struggle which keeps evolution in progress, is in the first place a *competition* between close relatives" (ibid., 30).

64 Cf. P. Beauchamp, in P. Beauchamp and D. Vasse, "La Violence dans la Bible," 12f.: "God appears and can only appear to humans through that which humans in reality are."

65 J. Eisenberg et A. Abécassis, *Moi, le gardien de mon frère?*, 179.

66 Even if the words are different, one recalls the breath of God coming to rest on Mary to sanctify her unborn child. One thinks also of the prophet Elijah, taking refuge in the grotto after the series of murders in which he was implicated, who received in response to his fear of being killed, the vision of a God as invisible as a held breath: God was not in the thunder or lightning, nor any all-powerful violence.

67 P. Beauchamp, in P. Beauchamp and D. Vasse, "La Violence dans la Bible," 47.

68 For a detailed analysis of the expression "kingdom of heaven," that highlights the eminently relational dimension of the "good news," see L. Basset, *Le Pouvoir de pardonner*, Paris/Geneva, Albin Michel/Labor et Fides, 1999, especially 175–179.

69 P. Beauchamp, "La Violence dans la Bible," 26f.

70   The TOB translates it thus: "Ils vont bien vite fait de remédier au désastre
     de mon peuple, en disant: 'Tout va bien! Tout va bien!' Et rien ne va."
     ["They rush to remedy the disaster of my people, saying, 'Everything is fine!
     Everything is fine!' And nothing is fine."]

71   For Isaiah, the summum of the omnipotence of non-violence consists in
     remaining in solidarity with the violent, even "unto death" (53:9): how
     would that be possible if one had not fixed a just regard on him, and seen
     his unhappiness behind his dysfunctionality?

72   P. Emmanuel, Jacob, 61, 66f., 75.

73   A. de Pury, Promesse divine et légende cultuelle dans le cycle de Jacob, 339f. (trans.
     B. Henry), refers to the study done by G. Wehmeier on the root brk in the
     Hebrew Bible, the source, via Arabic of the French expression "avoir la
     baraka," to have blessing or good luck.

74   It is well known that unconsciousness is egocentred. If it really is a dream,
     behind the interest in the name of the assailant, one might think that the
     dreamer is upset about his own name: "Explain [the story of] your name!"
     The other responds, "Why are you asking me about [the story of] my
     name?"

75   A. Chouraqui translates Peny'el as "face of El."

76   J. Calvin, 451, 474.

77   Cf. Gen. 25:22f.

78   A. Abécassis, in J. Eisenberg and A. Abécassis, Jacob, Rachel, Léa et les autres,
     368.

79   Treatise Tanchuma B, 1:127, cited by W. Dietrich, "Jacokskampf am Jabbok
     (Gen 32:23-33)," in J.-D. Macchi and T. Römer, eds., Jacob, 206.

80   Cf. Gen. 33:5: "(Here are) the children whom God has graciously given your
     servant," instead of "here are the children God blessed me with," according
     to the root that is much more commonly employed (88 times in Genesis).

81   S.R. Driver, The Book of Genesis, 295.

82   G. von Rad, La Genèse, 332.

83   E. Wiesel, Messengers of God, 135.

84   R. Girard, The Scapegoat, 189, 192.

85   Treatise Taanith 8b, in J. Eisenberg and A. Abécassis, Jacob, Rachel, Léa et les
     autres, 276f. In familiar terms, the blessing is for him or her who expects to
     receive their bread and butter, or the money for it, from God.

86   A. de Pury, Promesse divine et légende cultuelle dans le cycle de Jacob, 106.

87   Ibid., 107.

88  Cf. J. Kodell, "Jacob Wrestles with Esau (Gen 32:3-32)," *Biblical Theology Bulletin*, 10/2, 1980, 69.

89  "There is no indication he was permanently lamed." (C. Westermann, *Genesis 12–36*, 520).

90  Rashi, *Rashi on the Pentateuch*, 164.

91  Origen, Homily XII, 3 in *Homilies on Genesis and Exodus* (Washington: Catholic University of America Press, 1982).

92  C. Vigée, *Dans le Silence de l'Aleph*, 146.

93  M.-D. Molinié, *Le combat de Jacob*, 144f.

94  A. de Pury, *Promesse divine et légende cultuelle dans le cycle de Jacob*, 112.

95  D. Clerc et al., *Jacob. Les aléas d'une bénédiction* (Geneva: Labor et Fides, 1992), 110.

96  J.-M. Tézé, "La Lutte de Jacob avec l'Ange," 75.

97  Ibid., 93.

98  *Targum Pseudo-Jonathan, op. cit.*, Gen 32:30, 309.

99  Note q of the TOB reflects once again the ambivalence of anger – destructive violence or force of life and even love: "The *upheaval* of the heart of the Lord is expressed with the help of the term used precisely for the destruction of the guilty cities in Gn 19:25; Dt 29:22; it stresses the radical change that is at work in God himself."

100 Cf., for example, Is. 6:1-8, the call of Isaiah.

101 J. Lévêque, *Job et son Dieu,* 532.

102 The verb [naham] signifies either "to be sorry, to repent," or "to be comforted, to console." With Chouraqui, who translates it as "I comfort myself," and because of the entire passage, especially the verse that follows it, the second sense seems to me to be indicated.

103 Y. Ledure, *Si Dieu s'efface. La corporéité comme lieu d'une affirmation de Dieu*, (Paris: Desclée), 1976, 93 and 96.

104 F. Nietzsche, *The Antichrist*, section 40, translated by H. L. Mencken, http://www.fns.org.uk/ac.htm. Accessed March 28, 2007.

105 Cf. J. Lévêque, *Job et son Dieu,* 374.

106 Mark the Ascetic, no. 50, in *The Philokalia*, vol. 1, 138.

107 This noun, like [berakah] is from the root [barak], to bless.

108 E. Wiesel, *Célébrations. Portraits et légendes* (Paris: Éditions du Seuil, 1994), 803, 814, 821f.

109 Micah 12:30; Mt 22:34; Lk 10:27, closely linked with Dt 6:4 and Lv 19:17.

110 C. Vigée, *Dans le silence de l'Aleph*, 59.

# Bibliography

Ambrose. *On Jacob and the Blessed Life [De Iacob et vita beata].* Michael P. McHugh, trans. In *Fathers of the Church,* vol. 65. Washington, DC: Catholic University of America, 1972.

Augustine. *The City of God.* Marcus Dods, trans. New York: Random House, 2000.

_____. *Confessions.* R.S. Pine-Coffin, trans. New York: Penguin, 1961.

Balmary, M. *Abel ou la traversée de l'Éden.* Paris: Grasset, 1999.

Barthes, R. et al. *Analyse structurale et exégèse biblique.* Neuchâtel: Delachaux et Niestlé, 1971.

Basset, L. "Où est ton frère 'souffle'?" *Études théologiques et religieuses* 73/3 (1998).

_____. *Guérir du malheur* Paris and Geneva: Albin Michel/Labor et Fides, 1999.

_____. *La joie imprenable.* Geneva: Labor et Fides, 1999.

_____. *Le Pardon original.* Geneva: Labor et Fides, 2000.

_____. "Guérir en Église: un temps liturgique pour la plainte." *Perspectives missionnaires* 41/1 (2001).

Beauchamp, P. *Cinquante portraits bibliques.* Paris: Seuil, 2000.

Beauchamp, P. and D. Vasse. "La violence dans la Bible." In *Cahiers Évangile* 76. Paris: Éditions du Cerf, 1991.

Beirnaert, L. *Aux frontières de l'acte analytique: la Bible, saint Ignace, Freud et Lacan.* Paris: Seuil, 1987.

Bernanos, Georges. *The Star of Satan [Sous le soleil de Satan].* Pamela Morris, trans. New York: Macmillan, 1940.

*Bible chrétienne* 1 [Le Pentateuque]. *Commentaires.* Quebec: Éditions Anne Sigier, 1982.

Bonnard, P. *L'Évangile selon saint Matthieu.* Geneva: Labor et Fides, 2002.

Bro, B. *Le pouvoir du mal.* Paris: Editions du Cerf, 1976.

Brueggemann, W. *Genesis: Interpretation Commentary.* Atlanta: John Knox Press, 1982.

Calvin, John. *Commentary on Old Testament.* John King, ed. and trans. Calvin Translation Society, 1847. Vol. 2, pt. 11 (commentary on Gen. 32:24, 26). Reprinted 1975 by the Banner of Truth Trust.

Camus, A. *The Rebel: An Essay on Man in Revolt*. Anthony Bower, trans. New York: Alfred A. Knopf, 1978.

Cazelles, H. "Patriarches." *DBS*, vol. VII, col. 81–156. Supplement to the *Dictionnaire de la Bible*.

Claudel, P. *Le Livre de Job*. Paris: Plon, 1946.

_____. *Emmaüs*. Paris: Gallimard, 1949.

Clerc, D. et al. *Jacob. Les aléas d'une bénédiction*. Geneva: Labor et Fides, 1992.

Couffignal, R. *La lutte avec l'Ange. Le récit de la Genèse et sa fortune littéraire*. Publications de l'Université de Toulouse-Le Mirail, 1977.

Cyrulnik, B. *Les vilains petits canards*. Paris: Odile Jacob, 2001.

de Pury, A. *Promesse divine et légende cultuelle dans le cycle de Jacob*. Vol. 1 and 2. Paris: Gabalda, 1975.

de Pury, R. *Job ou l'homme révolté*. Geneva: Labor et Fides, 1982.

Driver, S.R. *The Book of Genesis*. London: Methuen, 1904.

Durand, X. "Le Combat de Jacob (Gn 32,23-33): pour un bon usage des modèles narratifs." *Le Point théologique* 24 (1977).

Eisenberg, J. and A. Abécassis. *Moi, le gardien de mon frère?* À Bible ouverte III. Paris: Albin Michel, 1981.

_____. *Jacob, Rachel, Léa et les autres*. À Bible ouverte IV. Paris: Albin Michel, 1981.

Eisenberg, J. and E. Wiesel. *Job ou Dieu dans la tempête*. Paris: Fayard/Verdier, 1986.

Eliach, Y. *Hasidic Tales of the Holocaust*. New York: Oxford University Press, 1982.

Elliger, V.K. "Der Jakobkampf am Jabbok." *Zeitschrift für Theologie und Kirche* 48, 1951.

Emmanuel, P. *Jacob*. Paris: Seuil, 1970.

Evagrius Ponticus. *Treatise on Prayer,* chapter 12. In *The Philokalia: The Complete Text Compiled by St. Nikodimos of the Holy Mountain and St. Makarios of Corinth*. Vol. 1. G.E.H. Palmer, Philip Sherrard and Kallistos Ware, trans. London/Boston: Faber & Faber, 1979.

Fleg, E. *Le Livre du commencement*. Paris: Éditions de Minuit, 1959.

_____. *Écoute, Israël*. Paris: Cahiers de la Quinzaine (15th series, no. 1), 1913.

Garat, M. "La violence dans la Bible." *Cahiers de l'Atelier* 409 (Oct–Dec 2000).

Geller, S.A. "The Struggle at the Jabbok: The Uses of Enigma in a Biblical Narrative." *JANESCU* 14 (1982).

Girard, R. *The Scapegoat*. Yvonne Freccero, trans. Baltimore: Johns Hopkins University Press, 1986.

_____. *Job: The Victim of His People*. Yvonne Freccero, trans. Stanford, CA: Stanford University Press, 1987.

_____. *Violence and the Sacred*. Gregory Patrick, trans. London: Athlone, 1995.

_____. *Celui par qui le scandale arrive*. Paris: Desclée de Brouwer, 2001.

_____. *I See Satan Fall Like Lightning*. James G. Williams. trans. Ottawa: Novalis, 2001.

Goleman, D. *Emotional Intelligence*. New York: Bantam Books, 1995.

Grün, A. *Petit traité de spiritualité au quotidien*. Paris: Albin Michel, 1998.

Hammann, G. "Le songe de Jacob et sa lutte avec l'ange (Genèse 28 et 32): Répères historiques d'une lecture et de ses variations." *Revue d'Histoire et de Philosophie Religieuse* 6 (1986).

Hausherr, I. *Les leçons d'un contemplatif. Le Traité d'Oraison d'Évagre le Pontique*. Paris: Beauchesne, 1960.

Hicks, L. "Jacob." In *The Interpreters' Dictionary of the Bible*, vol. 2. New York/Nashville: Abingdon Press, 1962.

Holmgren, F.C. "Holding Your Own Against God! Gen 32:22-32 (in the context of Gen 31–33)." *Interpretation* 44, 1990.

Sister Isabelle de la Source. *Lire la Bible avec les Pères*, t. 1. *La Genèse*. Paris and Montreal: Médiaspaul et Éditions Paulines, 1988.

Jacob, E. *Théologie de l'Ancien Testament*. Neuchâtel: Delachaux et Niestlé, 1968.

Janzen, J.G. *Abraham and All the Families of the Earth: Genesis 12–50*. Grand Rapids: Eerdmans, 1993.

John Chrysostom. *Homilies on Genesis,* no. 53. Robert C. Hill, trans. In *Fathers of the Church*, vol. 87. Washington, DC: Catholic University of America, 1992.

Kierkegaard, S. *Repetition: An Essay in Experimental Psychology*. Walter Lowrie, trans. New York/London: Harper Torchbooks, 1941.

Kodell, J. "Jacob Wrestles with Esau (Gen 32:3-32)." *Biblical Theology Bulletin*, 10/2, 1980.

Ledure, Y. *Si Dieu s'efface. La corporéité comme lieu d'une affirmation de Dieu*. Paris: Desclée, 1976.

Lévêque, J. *Job et son Dieu*. Paris: Gabalda, 1970.

Macchi, J.-D. and T. Römer, eds. *Jacob. Commentaire à plusieurs voix*. Geneva: Labor et Fides, 2001.

Maly, E.H. "Genesis." In *Jerome Biblical Commentary*, vol. 1. Englewood Cliffs, NJ: Prentice-Hall, 1968.

Marc l'Ascète. *De ceux qui pensent être justifiés par les œuvres*. In *The Philokalia: The Complete Text Compiled by St. Nikodimos of the Holy Mountain and St. Makarios of Corinth*. Vol. 1. G.E.H. Palmer, Philip Sherrard and Kallistos Ware, trans. London/Boston: Faber & Faber, 1979.

Martin-Achard, R. "Un exégète devant Genèse 32, 23-33." In R. Barthes et al. *Analyse structurale et exégèse biblique*. Neuchâtel: Delachaux et Niestlé, 1971.

McKay, H.A. "Jacob Makes It across the Jabbok: An Attempt to Solve the Success/Failure Ambivalence in Israel's Self-Consciousness." *JSOT* 38 (1987).

McKenzie, J.L. "Jacob at Peniel: Gn 32:24-32." *Catholic Biblical Quarterly* 25 (1963).

Michaud, R. *Les Patriarches: Histoire et théologie*. Paris: Éditions du Cerf, 1975.

*Midrash Rabbah. Genesis*. London/Jerusalem/New York: Soncino Press, 1977.

Molinié, M.-D. *Le combat de Jacob*. Paris: Cerf, 1967.

Niederland, W.G. "Jacobskampf am Jabbok." In *Psychoanalytische Interpretationen biblischer Texte*. Y. Spiegel, ed. Munich: Kaiser Verlag, 1972.

Nietzsche, F. *The Antichrist*. H. L. Mencken, trans. (http://www.fns.org.uk/ac.htm. Accessed March 28, 2007.)

Origen. *Homilies on Genesis and Exodus*. Washington: Catholic University of America Press, 1982.

Perrin, M. "L'exemple de Lactance." In *Le pardon,* M. Perrin, ed. Paris: Beauchesne, 1987.

*The Philokalia: The Complete Text Compiled by St. Nikodimos of the Holy Mountain and St. Makarios of Corinth*. Vol. 1. G.E.H. Palmer, Philip Sherrard and Kallistos Ware, trans. London/Boston: Faber & Faber, 1979.

Plutarch. *De cohibenda ira* in *Moralia* VII, pt. I. (*On the control of anger)*. Harold Frederik Cherniss, trans. Cambridge, MA: Harvard University Press, 1976.

Quéré, F. *Les Ennemis de Jésus*. Paris: Seuil, 1985,

Rachower, J. "Testament dans la fournaise." *Bible et vie chrétienne*, no. 64 (July–August 1965).

Rashi. *Rashi on the Pentateuch: Genesis*. James H. Lowe, trans. London: Hebrew Compendium, 1928.

Ricoeur, P. *Finitude et culpabilité*. Paris: Aubier/Montaigne, 1960. Translated into English in two parts, as *Fallible Man*, Charles L, Kelbley, trans. (New York: Fordham University Press, 1986) and *The Symbolism of Evil*, Emerson Buchanan, trans. (Boston: Beacon Press, 1969).

Sagne, J.-C. *Conflit, changement, conversion*. Paris: Éditions du Cerf/Desclée, 1974.

Sarna, N.M. *The JPS Torah Commentary: Genesis*. The Jewish Publication Society: Philadelphia: 1989.

Seneca. *Dialogues: On Anger*. Book III, xlii, 1. (http://www.stoics.com/seneca_essays_book_1.html#ANGER1. Accessed April 2, 2007.)

Shearman, S.L. and J.B. Curtis. "Divine-Human Conflicts in the Old Testament." *JNES* 28 (1969).

Sibony, D. "Premier meurtre." *Tel Quel* no. 64, 1975.

Skinner, J. *A Critical and Exegetical Commentary on Genesis*. Edinburgh: Clark, 1930.

*Targum Neofiti: Genesis*. In *The Aramaic Bible*, vol. 1A, I. Martin McNamara, trans. Edinburgh: T&T Clark, 1992.

*Targum Pseudo-Jonathan: Genesis*. In *The Aramaic Bible*, vol. 1A, I. Michael Maher, trans. Edinburgh: T&T Clark, 1992.

Terrien, S. *Job: Poet of Existence*. Indianapolis/New York: The Bobbs-Merrill Company, 1957.

Tézé, J.M. "La Lutte de Jacob avec l'Ange." *Christus* 33 (1962).

Treatise *Tanchuma* B, 1:127, cited by W. Dietrich, "Jacokskampf am Jabbok (Gen 32:23-33)," in J.-D. Macchi and T. Römer, eds., *Jacob. Commentaire à plusieurs voix*. Geneva: Labor et Fides, 2001.

Vawter, B. *On Genesis: A New Reading*. Garden City, NY: Doubleday, 1977.

Vergote, A. *Dette et désir*. Paris: Seuil, 1978.

_____. "Visions et apparitions: Approche psychologique." *RThL* 22 (1991).

Vigée, C. *Dans le silence de l'Aleph. Écriture et Révélation*. Paris: Albin Michel, 1992.

von Rad, G. *La Genèse*. Geneva: Labor et Fides, 1968.

Weis, R.D. "Lessons on Wrestling with the Unseen: Jacob at the Jabbok." *Reformed Review* 42 (1989).

Wenham, G.J. "Genesis 16–50." In *World Biblical Commentary*, vol. 2. World Books: Dallas, 1994.

Wénin, A. "De la violence à l'alliance. Un chemin éthique inspiré des Écritures." *Revue d'éthique et de théologie morale*, Supplement, 213 (June 2000).

Westermann, C. *Genesis 12–36. A Commentary.* Minneapolis: Augsburg, 1981.

Wiesel, E. *Célébrations. Portraits et légendes.* Paris: Éditions du Seuil, 1994.

_____. *Messengers of God: Biblical Portraits and Legends.* New York: Random House, 1976.

_____. *Night.* Stella Rodway, trans. New York: Hill and Wang, 1960.

100%

This document has been printed on 100% post consumer
waste paper, certified Eco-logo and processed chlorine free.